WOMEN IN PRE & POST INDEPENDENT INDIA

75 VICTORIES VISIONARIES VOICES

MONICA LAKHMANA

ISBN 979-8-88749-866-9

To my beloved parents…Until we meet again.

Arwiend and Sunaina…For believing that it is possible.

Dedicated to the Memory of countless Indians who secured us our freedom, to them all future generations remain indebted.

Contents

Preface											9

Section One: Victories							13

  1. Veeramangai-the Brave Woman.............21

  2. Veerathai-the Commander in Chief.............24

  3. The Defiant Queen of Kittur.............26

  4. The Daring Queen.............28

  5. The Fearless Maharani.............31

  6. The Begum in Charge.............39

  7. The Gutsy.............42

  8. The Rebellion in Uniform.............44

  9. The Trusted Warrior.............49

Section Two: Visionaries							51

 10. The Reformer Educationist.............65

 11. The Radical Victorian.............69

 12. The Nightingale of India 'Bulbul-I-Hind'.............74

 13. The Pandita.............82

 14. Mother of Indian Revolution.............85

 15. The Traveller.............89

 16. Gandhi Buri.............92

 17. BA.............94

 18. The Mehri.............98

 19. The Catalyst.............102

20. The Author 108

21. The Banyan Tree 111

22. The Empowered Writer 113

23. The Flag Bearer 117

24. Sister 119

25. First Ever 122

26. The Visionary Princess 126

27. The Conscience Keeper 132

28. The Lioness of Punjab 137

29. The Motaben to Everyone 140

30. The Benevolent 143

31. Maiji 145

32. Mother of the Year 148

33. Author and Nationalistic Poet......................................151

34. The Social Activist 155

35. Maa of Orissa 158

36. The Fearless Nehru 163

37. The Khadi Activist 167

38. The Visible Diplomat...170

39. For the Better 176

40. The Champion 180

41. The Devi of the Hills 184

42. The Loyalist 186

43. The Creative Freedom Fighter......................................189

44. Tofani 196

45. The Women's Rights Activist 199

46. The Social Reformer 202

47. The Purposeful Justice 207

48. The Accountant 209

49. Durga Bhabi 211

50. The Dutiful 215

51. I Too Am a Riddle 218

52. The Limitless 222

53. The Gallant Tara 225

54. The Jhansi Rani of Travancore 226

55. The Grand Old Lady 231

56. The Defiant Short Storyteller 236

57. The Daring Durgabai 242

58. The Young Revolutionary 248

59. The Gandhian 256

60. The Determined 259

61. The Revolutionist 266

62. The Captain of the Ship 271

63. The Rani of the Nagas 275

64. Lady Maa 278

65. The Respected Mataji 281

66. The Supporting Tai 284

Section Three: Voices **287**

67. The Stylish Calligrapher 289

68. The Versatile Dancer 293

69. The Educationist 300

70. The Multi-Faceted Personality 307

71. The Creative Think Tank 310

72. The Independent Director 312

73. The Sustainable Entrepreneur.......................................322

74. The Production Designer 327

75. The Candle...334

Preface

I wrote this book for three reasons. The first was to trace the women lost in pages of history, less acknowledged but equally dynamic. The second was to understand for myself how a generation of these remarkable women navigated their lives at the peak of British imperialism and undertook to mobilize India's journey toward self-governance and freedom. The third reason was to share 75 narratives, to coincide with 75 years of India's independence.

The book is divided into three sections. The first section, 'Victories,' looks at the moral strength of the majestic Ranis to resist opposition and their unwillingness to admit defeat during the British rule of 'interference' in their states owing to the introduction of the Doctrine of Lapse.

The second section, 'Visionaries,' puts a spot on the women activists of the nineteenth century and early twentieth century, the nationalists, freedom fighters, educators, writers, poets, and women's rights activists. Their narratives are impressive and you begin to wonder how they accomplished the extraordinary at a very young age. During an era when India was an orthodox patriarchal country. Child marriages were common and customary, caste order prevalent, low female literacy, and when women were confined within the four walls of their homes. These nationalist women were not mute spectators to what was happening in Colonial India but actively participated in the freedom struggle. They were unified in their approach, gave strength to new perspectives, and championed the emergence of a free India.

The third section, 'Voices,' brings forward my conversations with modern independent present-day women in the twenty-first-century world.

The narratives weave between the eighteenth century and the twenty-first century and the stories tie back to the title of the book. Indian nationalist women are part of our history and during the freedom struggle, they lived and advanced a credible existence for the wider good of the nation. The Women's movement gained prominence with the emergence of the Women's Indian Association (WIA) founded in Madras, the National Council of Women in India (NCWI,) and the All India Women's Conference (AIWC) in Delhi. Formed during a period when the struggle against colonial rule escalated and nationalism became the foremost call. Non-Cooperation and Civil Disobedience Movements further motivated the women to take a lead. More recent studies attempt to point to gender equality and educational efforts for women during that period and it is in the backdrop of my book to provide significant insights into this transition.

Selecting 75 inspirational women for my book was comprehensive. I was looking to share narratives of women from diverse backgrounds, both in terms of social class and circumstances. Women who influence with resilience. I reflect on the contributions of these hyper-intelligent women and share their outstanding stories. It's most necessary to inform future generations about past events and the 'telling' of the history of India's courageous women. Only then can present-day independent India be truly inclusive. The past also offers a pattern of how people addressed differences and inequality.

Dedicated to the brave Indian women who played an integral role in the freedom struggle. For a majority who lived to see a free India. For the multitudes who carry on to work earnestly in the economic growth of India. Finally, I write to not only publish this book on India's 75th Independence Year, but as I write, I learn of the 'victories' of the daring women of pre-Independent India. I get a deep sense of the 'visionaries' the nationalists, the social activists, and educators who advocated reforms for the women of India. I also hear the 'voices' of the present-day enterprising women.

I have relied on archives and memoirs to express the magnificence and intricacies of numerous lived experiences. My book counts on historical data that is accessible in the public domain and I have endeavoured to make the best use of these sources. I hope I got their story right. My attempt is to build narratives around what the women were against, and their moments of crisis. There were many! Had there been technology in eras gone by, we would be inundated with stories of these brave women!

The narratives are arranged in chronological order, for readers to context the era and for clarity of the intended message. I have deliberately kept a set format. Firstly, each account begins with the date of birth of the woman profiled and the events inform the overall atmosphere of the generation as well as the tone of society in that period. Second, the intent is to create a relationship between the story and the readers: the background and circumstances of why something happened. Third, personality insights of women featured in the book, and the context of how people behaved during that period in history.

Quotes from memoirs for authenticity and facts that the event took place. I have tried to adopt the most commonly used spellings for individuals. Have referred to the women by their given names and have retained the colonial spellings for Indian cities, Kolkata remains Calcutta, Mumbai remains Bombay, Bengaluru remains Bangalore, Bangladesh remains Bengal, etc. Further, my focus is only on the subject matter, the women, hence I have not written about families and so on.

My book will be of interest to readers curious to learn about women in Indian history. If, after reading this book, readers get to know a little more about the many contributions of the women in history, and the challenges they dealt with, Women in Pre and Post Independent India, 75 Victories Visionaries Voices would have served its objectives.

Monica Lakhmana

Mumbai

August 2022

SECTION ONE

VICTORIES

THE MAJESTIC RANIS AND THEIR CONFIDANTS

India was the centre of Europe's trade circuit for many centuries. Thus, the British merchants landed in India as traders in spices, tea, silk, opium, and cotton. Similar to the Portuguese, French, and Dutch. These merchants whose headquarters were in a small office in London petitioned Queen Elizabeth for a charter granting them control of trade with the East. She went ahead and accorded them a broad assumed authority. Under this charter, the British East India Company soon established trading posts on the Indian coasts at Surat, Bombay, Madras, and Calcutta in the 1600s. This was, however, formed without the controlling authority of the government.

The charter now permitted the British East India Company dominance in all trade with India. Of course, within Queen Elizabeth's sphere, and a brazen syndicate for an overall trade between India and Europe.

No other trading group in England could compete with the East India Company and this charter allowed the company to venture across the oceans, looking for new lands, to buy cheap and carry back the goods and sell high.

On the one hand, the rationale was to trade with India. They soon looked at acquiring the country.

The British at first concentrated on the Spice Islands in Indonesia, where they discovered that there was a market for Indian calicoes. Hence, they could barter calicoes (cotton) in the Indonesian Islands for spices. The Portuguese objected to this. However, the British merchants then took permission from the Mughal Emperor Jahangir to set up a trading post in Surat.

The first trading post of the East India Company was set up in Surat. Shortly, the British established trading posts in Calcutta, Madras, and Bombay. The company set up a factory on the banks of the river Hugli, Calcutta in 1651, which was their base and warehouse. By 1696 they constructed a fort around the settlement.

The East India Company soon realized that India was a group of provincial states. They took advantage of this, manipulated, and interfered with the states. With unanticipated hostility, the East India Company entered into treaties with Indian Maharajas which often secured their ruling rights.

Rapidly, the East India Company transitioned from a trading company to a ruling one in 1757. Initially infiltrating the princely states and later assuming sovereignty.

They first conquered Bengal in the Battle of Plassey on 23 June 1757, in the most treacherous manner and betrayal. Robert Clive's East India Company defeated the Nawab of Bengal, Siraj-ud-Daulah's army. The battle began at dawn and by the end of the day, their first big victory established the British Empire! (The town of Plassey, is between Calcutta, the East India Company's headquarters, and Murshidabad, the capital of Bengal.) This was followed up with the battle of Buxar on 22 October 1764. The Company now consolidated its power and authority in Bengal. They began appointing Residents in Indian states, who were assigned only to further the interests of the Company. And through these Residents, the Company officials began meddling in the internal affairs of Indian states. Deciding on successors or heirs to the throne and administration. They even dictated to Indian rulers their requirement for independent armed forces and that they would henceforth be protected by the Company.

Many battles followed, the second Anglo- Maratha War which lasted from 1803-1805, and the third Anglo-Maratha War of 1817-1818, which gave the British East India Company control of almost all of India. Next was the annexation of Sind in 1843. Two long wars with the Sikhs, the Anglo Sikh Wars, and in 1849, the Sikh Empire fell, and Punjab was annexed.

Further, to deal with the succession of the princely states, the cleverly worded and controversial Doctrine of Lapse came into effect. This Doctrine gave the British the right to approve or reject an heir to the state. The policy was created and enforced under James Broun-Ramsey Dalhousie. He was the Governor-General of India from 1848 to 1856. The doctrine read that if an Indian ruler died without a male heir, his kingdom would "lapse" and become part of Company territory. 'If the king did not have a natural-born heir, then the non-British state would lapse to the British or be administered and occupied by the British.' Because of this policy, several Indian heirs were dethroned and many suspiciously died. The annexations consolidated the East India Company, strengthened its military, and added economic resources to the Company.

The Company continued to increase its power or should we say misuse its power. State after state was annexed citing the doctrine. In 1848 the company annexed Satara, then Sambalpur in 1850, Udaipur in 1852, Nagpur in 1853, followed by Jhansi and finally Awadh.

The doctrine of lapse further contributed to increasing uneasiness and the collective grievances against the East India Company and its regime. Considered by the Indian rulers illegal and authoritarian, it created anger among the dynasts. Denying the Maharanis equal rights, unlike their male counterparts added to the tension among the monarchs.

The Rebellion of 1857 followed. The sepoys of the Bengal Artillery initially precipitated this rebellion based on the outskirts of Calcutta. They heard rumours that the Government was manufacturing cartridges greased with the fat of cows or pigs, and the sepoys would have to bite the forbidden substance before loading. The sepoys were in any case disgruntled by the mistreatment they were meted by the British and now they were convinced that the British had devised a plan to destroy their caste, honour, and social position. When threatened by the British

Colonel, that they have to use the cartridge, the sepoys showed their anger. On 29 March 1857 a sepoy Mangal Pandey, posted at the garrison in Barrackpore charged at a British officer, and when outnumbered he shot at himself. He was wounded, tried, sentenced, and executed two days later.

The distrust between the British and the sepoys of the Bengal army eventually led to an open revolt in the Barrackpore cantonment and the inevitable happened, the Indian Revolt or Sepoy Mutiny of 1857, (sepoy from the Indian word sipahi, meaning soldier.)

This news spread like wildfire from Barrackpore to Meerut, the headquarters of the Bengal Artillery. (After taking over Punjab, Sindh, and Awadh, the company transferred its military interest to the North and the headquarters of the Bengal Artillery were shifted from Calcutta to Meerut.) And a few days later, sepoys in the Meerut regiment in defiance refused to use the new cartridges in the army drills. They were dismissed as well as sentenced to ten years in jail on 9 May 1857. The next day the sepoys marched to the jail in Meerut and released the imprisoned sepoys. They attacked and killed British officers. Capturing guns, ammunition, and ransacking the cantonment bungalows. They set fire to the buildings and declared war.

The sepoys then rode all night of 10 May 1857 and reached Delhi in the early hours. As the news of their arrival spread, the regiments in Delhi also joined the uprising and Delhi became the launch pad of the insurgency activity. Regiment after regiment mutinied and joined other contingents. The people of the towns also rose in dissent along with local zamindars and chiefs.

The mutiny propagated quickly across cantonments of north India and by the end of May 1857, the most important region of the country was boiling with anger, while the British scampered for reinforcements. As smaller cantonments came to know of the mutiny, they followed.

On 30 May 1857, the sepoy regiments revolted in Lucknow, after which a series of mutinies took place in Sitapur, Faizabad, Gonda-Bahraich, Sultanpur, Salon, Bareilly, and Kanpur. Jhansi took the lead, followed by mutinies in four other towns of Bundelkhand. Thought to be insignificant by the British, it escalated into many serious altercations. By 6 June 1857, entire cantonments were against the British.

The Bengal sepoys dictated the beginning of the 1857 rebellion. After the success of the revolt in the cantonments, the mutiny metamorphosed into an extensive event engaging a broader civil uprising. The revolt was a significant threat to the British and the likelihood of them ceasing to control India. However, contained with the rebels' defeat in Gwalior on 20 June 1858.

Following the Rebellion of 1857, a bill was passed in the British parliament, to end the rule of the East India Company and transfer the powers of the East India Company to the British Crown. On 2 August 1858, the British parliament passed the Government of India Act, transferring British power, a member of the British Cabinet was appointed Secretary of State for India to oversee the governance of India. He had a council, called the India Council to advise him on all matters. The Governor-General of India was re-designated as Viceroy, a direct representative of the Crown.

The British government now took direct control and that was the beginning of British rule. It ended when India got its independence from their administration on 15th August 1947.

The Indian Ranis and their women commander-in-chief played a crucial role in ruling their states after the Rajas were either treacherously killed or exiled. They won and lost fierce battles and were an inspiration to many women who followed and rose against British rule. One of the well-known women rebellions of 1857 was the fearless Rani Lakshmi Bai. The first name that comes to most of our minds when we discuss women freedom fighters. She was a feminist way before the suffragette movement and holds a significant place in the history of India.

We have grown up listening to the lines from Subhadra Kumari Chauhan's famous composition and one of the most recited poems in Hindi literature, 'Khoob Ladi Mardani Woh Toh Jhansi Wali Rani Thi.' The poem describes the life of the brave Rani of Jhansi in the

1857 rebellion. Often taught in Indian schools and mentioned in history books, the poem celebrates Jhansi Ki Rani as the leading example of female valour.

Women's participation in India's freedom struggle against British rule began as early as the 1700s and 1800s. We are aware of the men who took part in India's independence movement. However, in an inherently patriarchal society, the unsung women freedom fighters are unremembered. Their selflessness, courage, and achievements are invisible in Indian memories. Historical accounts of their participation in fighting the British administration remain either unacknowledged or brief passages or even lost. You would believe that these women played a tiny part in our fight for freedom when their strategic acumen needs much more attention and credit than what is documented. One reason behind this could be our illusion of patriarchy, that men have all or most of the power to influence! Furthermore, colonial historians wrote historical events from a colonists' standpoint and a colonized perspective, thus biased.

There are limited details of the lives of the women; the queens and their confidants. Their stories are at times vague, contradictory facts to support and interpret the documentation. In the first section of the book, I explore the victories of the women who played critical roles in the early nationalist movement and their fight for freedom against Colonial rule. The Magnificent Ranis were strategists and astonishingly skilled to rule. They fought relentlessly to save their states and continue as symbols of their contribution to the struggle for freedom from the British colonists.

Rani Velu Nachiyar

Kuyili

Rani Chennamma

Rani Avanti Bai Lodhi

Maharani Jind Kaur

Begum Hazrat Mahal

Uda Devi

Rani Lakshmi Bai

Jhalkari Bai

CHAPTER ONE

VEERAMANGAI-THE BRAVE WOMAN

Rani Velu Nachiyar can be considered the first woman ruler to fight the British, over seven decades before the Rani of Jhansi.

Born on 3 January 1730, in Ramnad estate, Tamil Nadu. Velu's parents Vijaya Ragunatha Sethupathi and Sakandhi Muthal ruled the Ramnad state. Trained in horse-riding, archery, and martial arts, Velu was a linguist with a command over languages like English, French, Tamil, and Urdu.

She was married at sixteen, to Muthu Vaduganatha Thevar, of Sivaganga. His father was one of the 72 Poligars granted political control on the condition they pay tribute. After his father Sasivarna Peria Oodayan died in 1750 Muthu Vaduganatha became the ruler of Sivaganga.

The Nawab of Arcot wrote to Madras Council that the Sivaganga Ruler had ascended the throne without his approval. Over time the Nawab managed to make Hindu zamindars acknowledge his power, either voluntarily or by force. Those who accepted his authority paid tribute and fulfilled their military obligations and were allowed to keep their states and dynastic titles. On 25 June 1772, the British under Colonel Joseph Smith and the Nawab of Arcot attacked Kalaiyar Kovil. Muthu Vaduganatha Thevar was caught unawares and treacherously killed while the temple was ransacked. All the jewels of the historic Kalaiyar Kovil temple and the palace were looted by the army. British records mention that Kalaiyar Kovil became a scene of 'lamentable slaughter.' To make certain the Rani safely escapes, her brave bodyguard Udaiyaal stayed behind, she was captured during the battle and it is believed her head was cut off.

The British had just started their conquest of India through the East India Company. They plundered the tall 155 feet temple and looted jewellery worth 50,000 pagodas (gold coins minted by Indian dynasties.) Rani Nachiyar escape with her daughter Vellachi to a neighbouring state Virupatchi in Dindigul, where she took refuge and lived for eight long years while she planned to take back her estate with the support of the Marudu brothers and Hyder Ali, who was already at war with the British.

She formed an all-women army and trained the woman herself. Called the regiment 'Udaiyaal' in honour of her bodyguard who was killed ensuring a safe passage for her. Though her army was well-trained, the British had very advanced armoury. To counter this, Rani Nachiyar sent her spies to check where the British forces kept their ammunition at the Sivaganga Fort. Along with Kuyili, her Commander-in-Chief she devised a strategy to attack the British.

During the Vijayadasimi festival, the British permitted women from across the state to visit the temple of Rajarajeshwari. This was the family deity of the royal family and located within the Sivaganga Fort. Unnoticed by the British forces, Kuyili led her army of women and entered the fort. They had hidden weapons inside fruit and flower baskets. On Kuyili's cue, they attacked, taking the British forces by surprise. Kuyili then doused herself in ghee, kept for burning the lamps at the temple, set herself on fire, and plunged into the armoury.

With the brilliance and selflessness of Kuyili, combined with Hyder Ali's troops Rani Nachiyar reclaimed her state in 1780. An agreement was signed with the Marudu brothers that Rani Nachiyar would govern the state, one of the Marudu brothers became the principal minister, and the other the army chief. Rani Nachiyar governed the state till her death on 25 December 1796. Remembered as a valiant queen, Rani Nachiyar is called 'Veeramangai' or the 'brave woman.' She is one of the few monarchs to have recaptured her state. In 2008, the government released a stamp honouring Rani Velu Nachiyar. A six-foot bronze statue of the Rani stands tall in Sivaganga. As part of his album Tamilmatic,' the Tamil American hip hop artist Professor A.L.I. dedicated a song in her remembrance titled 'Our Queen.' The Brave Woman played a critical role in the history of India's fight against the British colonial power.

CHAPTER TWO
VEERATHAI-THE COMMANDER IN CHIEF

Her date of birth is unavailable, her name was Kuyili, in Tamil it means 'sweat voice' and she was the fearless Commander-in-Chief in Rani Velu Nachiyar's army. A daring soldier, Kuyili belonged to the scheduled caste, Arunthathiyar community. Her parents, Periya Muthan and Raku, were farmers. Sources mention that her brave mother Raku died saving the fields from being destroyed by a wild bull. After her mother's death, her father would share stories of the heroics of her mother, which inspired Kuyili, and she wanted to carry the legacy forward.

Rani Nachiyar was in hiding in Dindugal, after the British and Nawab of Arcot invaded Sivaganga and killed her husband. She employed Kuyili's father as a spy and Kuyili as a companion. Later Kuyili was made her bodyguard. Some stories mention that the brave Kuyili saved the Rani's life several times. At one time when an intruder tried to murder Rani Nachiyar and once when Kuyili sensed that the martial art teacher was a spy working against the Rani.

In 1780, when Rani Nachiyar was forming an army to reclaim her state, she made Kuyili the head of the women's army, Udaiyaal. While Rani Nachiyar and Kuyili were planning their attack, they came to know of the British armoury storehouse in the Sivaganga Fort and devised a plan. Along with her regiment, Kuyili reached the Sivaganga Fort, hiding weapons in fruits and flower baskets meant for the temple. Kuyili took the British troops by surprise and forced them into an unprepared battle. She then made her way into the arsenal and poured the oil which was kept to light the temple lamps on herself. She set herself on fire, leading to the destruction of the weapons stored in the area.

The unsuspecting British could not make sense of this attack and Kuyili's courage secured Rani Velu Nachiyar her estate. The Tamil Nadu government built a memorial of the daring Kuyili in Soorakulam village in Sivaganga for her fearless sacrifice.

CHAPTER THREE
THE DEFIANT QUEEN OF KITTUR

Rani Chennamma led one of the first armed revolts against Colonial rule in India. She resisted the doctrine of lapse to keep Indian control over Kittur. She fought for her right to rule her State and questioned the British , 'why should my state lapse!'

Chennamma was born on 23 October 1778, in Kakati, a small village in Belagavi, a princely state of Karnataka. Her father Desai Dhulappa Goudru encouraged the young Chennamma to learn horse riding, sword fighting, and archery. In 1793, at fifteen, Chennamma was married to Raja Mallasarja Desai, of the princely state of Kittur, Belgaum, Karnataka. Her husband died in 1816 followed by their only son who died in 1824. Leaving no choice for Kittur Chennamma but to adopt a boy, Shivalingappa, as an heir to the Kittur state.

However, the East India Company did not accept this and ordered Shivalingappa's expulsion stating the Doctrine of Lapse which meant refusing to acknowledge the long-established rights of Indian rulers without an heir or the next in line. In a plea that her adopted son inherits the throne, Rani Chennamma wrote a letter to Mountstuart Elphinstone, Lieutenant Governor of Bombay Presidency. Instead of hearing out the problem, he staged a war against Kittur. The purpose was to make her financially vulnerable and then overthrow her.

In 1824 the British attacked Kittur. In the first assault, they came with a large force of 20,797 soldiers. However, they met with fierce resistance from Rani Chennamma, who not only won the Battle but imprisoned two British officials later released in an exchange for the promise of non-interference and an understanding that the war would end.

The British of course broke the promise and resumed the battle with more reinforcements. The forces robbed everything in the Bailhongal Fort, destroying the rich heritage of an important fort in Kittur. Outnumbered in the second assault, they imprisoned Rani Chennmma at the Bailhongal Fort where she remained till she died five years later on 21 February 1829. Her lieutenant Sangoli Rayanna continued to fight on her behalf with the hope they would declare her son Shivalingappa the ruler of Kittur, but the British arrested and hung the lieutenant. They arrested the young Shivalingappa and annexed the state of Kittur.

Kittur is a place of historical importance because of the armed rebellion of Kittur Chennamma and she is a celebrated freedom fighter in the state of Karnataka.

To celebrate the heroics of Rani Kittur Chennamma and her legacy, the annual Kittur Utsava is held between 22 and 24 October. On 23 October 1977, the Government of India released a postage stamp of the courageous Rani, and in 1983, a Coast guard ship was commissioned and named Kittur Chennamma. On 11 September 2007, a statue of Rani Chennamma was unveiled at the Indian Parliament Complex. And a daily train named Rani Chennamma Express runs between Bangalore and Kolhapur.

The Bailhongal Fort stands as confirmation of a very rich history associated with it. There is a palace within the fort, known as Rani Chennamma's palace, however, all that remains today of the great legacy are the walls of Bailhongal Fort, in ruins.

CHAPTER FOUR
THE DARING QUEEN

Trained in archery, horse riding, and wielding a sword, the young Avanti Bai Lodhi learned military strategy while she was growing up. Avanti Bai was born on 16 August 1831 in a zamindar family of Mankehadi, Seoni, Madhya Pradesh. Her combat skills and astute political knowledge intrigued the royal family of Ramgarh, Raja Laxaman Singh. The family reached out to her father, Jujhar Singh with a marriage proposal for their son Vikramaditya Singh Lodhi and they were married in 1849.

After a year of their marriage, Vikramaditya Singh fell ill and was incapable of attending to the daily affairs of his state. Rani Avanti Bai took over the reins of Ramgarh's internal administration and after the death of her husband in 1851, ruled the Ramgarh state. The kingdom prospered under her, which worried the British. They disapproved of her as a female ruler and rejected Rani Avanti Bai's son as a legitimate heir to the throne since he was a minor.

Soon enough, on 13 September 1851, the British East India Company declared Ramgarh as the 'Court of Wards,' a legal body created by the East India Company to protect heirs and their estates when the heir was minor and therefore incapable of acting independently. This allowed the British East India Company to place their administrator and take away Rani Avanti Bai's right to appoint an heir apparent. Angry, the courageous Rani sacked the administrator and declared war against the British!

During the sepoy mutiny the British executed Raja Shankar Shah a heroic ruler of the Gondwana Empire and his son on 18 September 1857. The region was angry with the Raja's execution and determined to revolt. Ramgarh citizens counted on Rani Avanti Bai to lead the rebellion. She sent messages to the rulers of neighbouring states for their support and to join her in the rebellion.

Along with a handwritten letter she sent a set of bangles to the rulers challenging them to fight the British. She wrote, "If you think you have a duty towards our enslaved motherland, raise your swords and jump into the war against the British. Otherwise, wear these bangles and hide in houses." This urgent appeal provoked the rulers of the central provinces to unite and join the 1857 revolt. The feisty Rani mobilized and commanded an army of 4000.

The first battle with the British took place in the village of Kheri, near the Mandla district in Madhya Pradesh. Kheri was less than 100 kilometers away from Ramgarh. Rani Avanti Bai led her contingent, and though the British expected an unchallenged victory, they were stunned at their defeat. Rani Avanti Bai controlled Mandla for a few months, from December 1857 to February 1858.

After assembling their full force, they launched a full-fledged attack by setting fire to Ramgarh. Rani Avanti Bai escaped with her family to Deogarh, in Chhindwara district, Madhya Pradesh. After Ramgarh was besieged, the British turned towards Deogarh to attack Rani Avanti Bai. She was a master in guerrilla warfare, led her small force to combat the large British army, and a fierce battle followed.

Eventually, on 20 March 1858, when she was fenced-in by the British forces and knew defeat was certain, she pierced herself with her sword, declaring, "Our Durgavati vowed to never let the enemy get their hands on her while she lived. Don't forget this." There is limited reference to Rani Avanti Bai in mainstream history books. However, her courage lives on through theatre performances and folklore. The Narmada Valley Development Authority honoured the courageous Rani by naming a dam in Jabalpur as Rani Avanti Bai Lodhi Sagar. The Department of Posts and the Maharashtra Government issued stamps on Rani Avanti Bai's honour. Her story of bravery is included in school textbooks. In a park in Meerut stands the magnificent statue of Rani Avanti Bai of Ramgarh, the warrior queen astride a horse, commanding attention as she looks on!

CHAPTER FIVE
THE FEARLESS MAHARANI

In a vast country stretching from the Khyber Pass to Kashmir, with Lahore as its capital was the Sikh Empire. And an exquisite Jindan Kaur was born there in Gujranwala, in 1817. Her father, Sardar Manna Singh Aulakh, was a supervisor of the royal kennel for Maharaja Ranjit Singh, the first Maharaja of the Sikh Empire and known as Maharaja Sher-e-Punjab. The Maharaja heard of Jind Kaur from Manna Singh and sent his 'arrow and sword' for her hand in marriage. She became his youngest wife in 1835 and their son Duleep Singh, the last Maharaja of Punjab, was born in 1838.

The British signed a treaty with Maharaja Ranjit Singh. The treaty stated they will keep trade relations with Punjab and will protect Punjab, and on Maharaja's death, his sons will be the legal heir. However, they added a clause stating if there is no heir apparent to the throne, the British would take over Punjab.

Maharaja Ranjit Singh died on 27 June 1839, though under mysterious circumstances. His eldest son Kharak Singh became the Maharaja. Dethroned a month after his coronation, taken prisoner, and poisoned to death by the British. His son Nau Nihal Singh who was nineteen was to be crowned. However, while returning from his father's cremation, a big brass chandelier hanging from the gate fell on him and he died on the spot. Moreover, many descendants of the throne died one by one within a short duration. These royal assassinations and power struggles destroyed the Sikh unity and the throne passed between four different rulers over four years.

After the death of Maharaja Ranjit Singh, Maharani Jindan Kaur and her son Duleep Singh moved to Jammu and lived in anonymity under the care of Raja Dhian Singh. He was the longest-serving Prime

Minister of the Sikh Empire during the reign of Maharaja Ranjit Singh. When the heir apparent Sher Singh and Karivar Pratam Singh were assassinated on 15 September 1843 the Sikhs requested the Maharani to return to Lahore. After her return, on the forthcoming day six-year-old Duleep Singh was crowned. He was the only one left in line for the throne.

Maharani Jindan Kaur became the ruler on her son's behalf and ruled the Sikh Empire from 1843 until 1846. The new Prime Minister, Hira Singh, took little notice of young Duleep Singh and the Maharani. As time went by, he was restless and wanted more control. The Rani appealed to the regimental committees to protect her son's position and his rights. She wanted to make sure that the young Maharaja was not a nondescript ruler. The young Maharani faced several hurdles, Duleep Singh's half-brother was looking to replace him as the Maharaja and the Sikh cliques were negotiating with the East India Company. The feudal chiefs wanted a reduction in taxes and restoration of their jagirs and land grants. The army wanted a pay rise. Young but knowledgeable, the Maharani stood her ground against the British and actively took charge of her kingdom.

Defying all traditions, Jindan Kaur cast aside the veil to attend court, and even rode out to address her forces. She reconstituted the Supreme Council of the Khalsa and reinstated a balance between the army and the civil administration. Holding formal meetings with the court and reviewing the business in public. The Maharani had many able advisers in the newly appointed council of leaders and military officials who guided her well in matters of running the empire. She soon became the sign of governance. Sharp to acknowledge that she needed internal support, the young Duleep Singh was engaged to the daughter of the Governor of Hazara province, Chatar Singh Atarivala, a prominent member of the Sikh nobility and a military commander in her army.

The British launched a vicious smear campaign against Jindan Kaur from the fear she created in them! A threat to the British, they did everything in their power to ruin the Maharani's reputation. However, she stood strong!

On 13 December 1845 the Governor-General of India Henry Harding, declared war on the Sikhs citing there was escalated tension in the region. The Maharani sent for help to Kathmandu, but there was a Divided court in Kathmandu, which meant that the opinion or decision in a particular case was not unanimous. King Rajendra Bikram Shah, did not respond favourably to her request.

A war followed, which the Sikhs lost because of the betrayal of their commander-in-chief, Lal Singh and Tej Singh. Both the chiefs failed to attack the British during the Battle of Ferozeshah, fought on 21 and 22 December 1845. The Sikhs lost this decisive battle, known as the First Anglo-Sikh War. Though the British came close to a defeat at the Battle of Ferozeshah, they were eventually victorious because of the internal betrayal.

The British army marched unopposed towards Lahore on 20 February 1846. After the defeat of the Sikh Empire, the then Governor-General of India, Henry Harding, and the young Maharaja Duleep Singh signed a peace treaty, called the Treaty of Lahore on 9 March 1846, marking the end of the First Anglo-Sikh War. According to the Treaty, there were restrictions on the size of the Lahore army, and the British confiscated the armoury. The control of the rivers, Sutlej and Beas, and part of the Indus went to the British and they took over Jammu. The British rewarded the leaders who had helped them, including the deceitful Lal Singh and Tej Singh. As a quid-pro-quo, the sale of all the hilly regions between River Beas and Indus, including Kashmir was handed over to the East India Company who at a later date handed the same to Gulab Singh, the Raja of Jammu for his help in fighting the war with the Sikhs.

To put in context, a part of the Treaty of Lahore read 'In consideration of the services rendered by Raja Gulab Singh of Jammu, to the Lahore State, towards procuring the restoration of the relations of amity between the Lahore and British Governments, the Maharajah agrees to recognize the Independent sovereignty of Raja Gulab Singh, in such territories and districts in the hills as made over to the said Raja Gulab Singh, by separate agreement between himself and the British Government, with the dependencies thereof, which may have been in the Raja's possession since the time of the late Maharajah Kharak Singh, and the British Government, in consideration of the good conduct of Raja Gulab Singh, also agrees to recognize his independence in such territories and to admit him to the privileges of a separate Treaty with the British Government.'

The terms of the Treaty of Lahore, allowed for Duleep Singh to stay, as Maharaja and Maharani Jindan Kaur as regent. 'There shall be perpetual peace and friendship between the British Government on the one part and Maharaja Duleep Singh, his heirs, and successors on the other.' However, at the end of the year, in December 1846, the British Resident, Henry Lawrence, replaced Maharani Jindan Kaur. She was given an annual pension of 150,000 rupees.

After the Second Anglo-Sikh War between 1848 and 1849, the Sikh Empire fell. Followed by the Punjab annexation on 29 March 1849, the British forced the ten year old Maharaja Duleep Singh to sign a formal Act of Submission, a legal document amending the Treaty of Lahore. This amendment required Duleep Singh to give away all claims to sovereignty and the valuable Koh-I-Noor diamond belonging to his father, Maharaja Ranjit Singh.

Maharani Jindan Kaur's influence was so intimidating that the British not only feared her, but her impact on her son Duleep Singh. They separated Duleep Singh from her and sent him from Lahore to Fatehgarh on 21 December 1849.

Maharani Jindan Kaur wrote to the British Resident, Henry Lawrence, imploring him to return her son to her. "He has no sister, no brother. He has no uncle, senior or junior. His father he has lost. To whose care they have entrusted?" To imagine that no Indian except trusted servants could meet Duleep Singh in private. Staying away from his mother, the young boy did not keep well, often sent to Landour, Mussoorie, to recoup.

The Maharani was still very influential and considered a serious threat to the British. To counter this Henry Lawrence, imprisoned Maharani Jindan Kaur in her former home. Later they dragged her from the court of Lahore by her hair and exiled her first in the Samman Tower of the Lahore Fort. And ten days later; she was moved to the Sheikhupura Fort Lahore in September 1847. Reduced her pension to 48,000 rupees and took away her jewellery. Maharani Jindan Kaur's imprisonment in the Sheikhupura Fort Lahore had not demolished her resolve or ability to affect the matters of Punjab. She carried on with her contacts with the Sikh leaders. The following year, the new British Resident Frederick Currie described Maharani Jindan Kaur as 'the rallying point of rebellion,' and exiled her from Lahore to the Chunar Fort, about 45 km from Varanasi. Her treatment by the two British Residents caused deep resentment and bitterness among the Sikhs. Even the ruler of Afghanistan, Mohammad Khan, objected to the treatment of the Maharani.

A year later, Maharani Jindan Kaur disguised herself as a servant and escaped from the Chunar Fort. Travelling 800 miles north, she reached Nepal on 29 April 1949. On reaching she asked the authorities of Nepal for asylum. She sent a letter to the British mentioning that she had escaped by 'magic!' William Dalrymple and Anita Anand have also written about Maharani Jindan in the book, 'Kohinoor: The Story of the World's Most Infamous Diamond.' 'Dressed in beggars' rags, she fled under cover of darkness, taunting her British captors as she went. Scattering money on the floor of her cell, Jindan scrawled a note for the guards to find: You put me in a cage and locked me up. For all your locks and your sentries, I got out by magic. I had told you not to push me too hard—but don't think I ran away. Understand well that I escape by myself unaided… don't imagine I got out like a thief.' The British certainly could not crush her will!

The Maharani lived at the home of Amar Bikram Shah, son of General Chautariya Pushkar Shah, the erstwhile Prime Minister of Nepal. The General was one of the key officials who had forged an alliance between Nepal and Punjab against the British when Maharaja Ranjit Singh was alive. They extended her hospitality befitting royalty. While in hiding, she would disguise herself as a servant in front of outsiders and a maid from Hindustan! She lived in hiding for a few months before re-emerging and approaching the then Prime Minister Jung Bahadur Rana, for asylum and lived in Nepal for the next decade.

The Nepal government built a palace called 'Charburja Durbar' in the Thapathali Durbar complex, in Kathmandu for the Maharani. She received an allowance from the Nepali government. The British were still apprehensive about the Maharani and instructed the British Resident in Kathmandu to spy on her. They believed she was powerful enough to revive the Sikh dynasty.

The British converted Duleep Singh to Christianity in 1853 and anglicized him in every way and the following year they sent him to England. The Maharani did not see her son again for twelve years! Raised as an English boy, he had friends like Queen Victoria, among others. To imagine, that Queen Victoria wrote: 'I always feel so much for these poor deposed Indian princes … once destined to so high and powerful a position and now reduced to so dependent a one by our arms.' Later, Queen Victoria offered peerages to his sons, Victor Albert and Frederick Victor, Duleep Singh graciously declined, writing: I claim myself to be royal; I am not English, and neither I nor my children will ever become so. Such titles – though kindly offered – we do not need and cannot assume. We love the English and especially their monarchs, but we must remain Sikhs.'

The Maharani never regained the empire for her son. In January 1861, Duleep Singh was 'allowed' to meet his mother in Calcutta as the British believed she was no longer a threat to them. During that time, many Sikh regiments were returning home via Calcutta from the civil war in China. The news and presence of the Maharani in the city soon spread across Calcutta. The Sikh regiments wanted to pay their respects to the Maharani and reached the hotel where she was staying.

Charles John Canning the Governor-General of India was uneasy with the response the Maharani's presence had in Calcutta and asked Duleep Singh to leave for England with his mother by the next boat! Such was the Maharani's spirited aura and influence.

In Private Correspondence relating to the Anglo-Sikh Wars, written by Dr. Ganda Singh the Punjabi historian he quotes Edward Law who served as the Governor-General of India 1842 -1844, that, "The mother of the boy Maharaja Duleep Singh seems to be a woman of determined course and she is the only person apparently at Lahore, who has courage."

Duleep Singh left Calcutta with his mother, and on the way to England, he wrote to John Spencer Login, a Scottish surgeon, entrusted with his guardianship and also the protection of the Koh-I- Noor. He requested his guardian to find a home for his mother near Lancaster Gate. Soon after her arrival, John Spencer Login's wife visited the Maharani. She had heard wonderful stories of the Maharani's beauty and was curious to meet the woman who was, at one time, described as the most influential woman in the Sikh Empire. When she met the Maharani, she was surprised to see a half-blind woman with faded beauty and in ill health. She mentioned that 'despite her advancing age and deteriorating health, the Maharani spoke with interest in subjects that she was passionate about.'

Maharani Jindan Kaur lived in Kensington, London until her death on 1st August 1863, she was just forty-six. She was initially laid to rest in Kensal Green Dissenters Chapel in west London as cremation was illegal in Britain at that time. During restoration at the Chapel in 1997, an uncovered marble headstone inscribed with her name in Gurmukhi and English was discovered. Her remains were repatriated to India in 1864. Later Duleep Singh's daughter took Maharani Jindan Kaur's ashes and placed them next to the samadhi of Maharaja Ranjit Singh in Lahore. Duleep Singh later converted back to Sikhism, reversing the work of the British who had indoctrinated the young Maharaja. In 1886, after over 30 years in Britain, Duleep Singh wished to return to India and renounced Christianity and converted back to Sikhism. His return created uneasiness among the British authorities, just as it did when Jindan Kaur was in Calcutta way back in 1861! The British felt that his presence in India was likely to have a 'disquieting effect' and cause 'much anxiety to the government.' Orders were issued to detain him at Aden. Queen Victoria wrote, 'This is rather sharp practice,' but concluded that 'better than if he went to India.'

CHAPTER SIX
THE BEGUM IN CHARGE

Born in 1820 in Faizabad, Awadh, Hazrat Mahal's maiden name was Muhammedi Khanum and she was married to the Nawab Wajid Ali Shah, the ruler of Awadh. The Nawab called her Iftikarun-nisa, 'the pride of women.' Later she was addressed as Begum Hazrat Mahal after the birth of their son, Birjis Qadr.

Awadh was in the heart of North India and by 1801 half of Awadh came under the control of the East India Company. The Nawab had to disband the military forces as per the Subsidiary Alliance (the alliance meant the princely state maintain British troops in the state and a British resident.) The Nawab was now dependent on the British troops to maintain law and order in his state!

By 1850 the East India Company had taken over most of the princely states and the takeover of Awadh would complete their territorial annexation. Hence on 7 February 1856, James Outram, the Resident of Lucknow went ahead and annexed Awadh. Nawab Wajid Ali Shah was exiled to Calcutta, with the excuse that the region was being misgoverned. And as per the Doctrine of Lapse, the Begum had to surrender Lucknow, the capital of Awadh.

A year later on 10 May 1857, the sepoys in Meerut rebelled, followed by Delhi and on 30 May 1857, the sepoy regiments revolted in Lucknow. After this, a series of mutinies took place in Sitapur, Faizabad, Bareilly, Kanpur, and Jhansi.

Looking at the turn of events, with the insurgency in various states, on 5 June 1857, Begum Hazrat Mahal went ahead and crowned her eleven-year-old son Birjis Qadr as the ruler (Wali) of Awadh and proclaimed him as the new Nawab. The Begum had the biggest army of rebel leaders, and a majority of the sepoys were recruited from the villages of Awadh. During the revolt, the loyal taluqdars of the Nawab of Awadh and the sepoys carried out an intense and long-lasting rebellion in Lucknow. After encountering a well-organized rebellion at Chinhat on the morning of 30 June 1857, the British were forced to take refuge in Lucknow Residency. The Residency was the headquarters of the Chief Commissioner and within the compound of sixty acres, there were buildings for the administrative, financial, and judicial departments, as well as a hospital and jail. A series of events took place in Lucknow and is known as the 'Siege of Lucknow.' The Siege of Lucknow was one of the most tragic events of the Indian Mutiny and lasted for nearly 6 months.

The British captured Musa Bagh, Char Bagh, and Qaiser Bagh in Lucknow. Musa Bagh was the Begum's stronghold. She held the place with Maulvi Ahmadullah, the leader of the rebels from Faizabad until 18 March 1858. Begum Hazrat Mahal encouraged the brave soldiers to fight and warned her people not to have faith in the promises of the British, 'for it is the unvarying custom of the English never to forgive a fault, be it great or small.'

William Forbes-Mitchell in Reminiscences of the Great Mutiny, 1857 records, 'From the heights of the Dilkooshá in the cool of the early morning, Lucknow, with its numerous domed mosques, minarets, and palaces, looked very picturesque. I don't think I ever saw a prettier scene than that presented on the morning of the 3rd of March, 1858, when the sun rose, and Captain Peel and his Blue-jackets were getting their heavy guns, 68-pounders, into position. From the Dilkooshá, even without the aid of telescopes, we could see that the defences had been greatly strengthened since we retired from Lucknow in November, and I called to mind the warning of Jamie Green, that if the enemy stood to their guns like men behind those extensive earthworks, many of the British force would lose the number of their men before we could take the city; and although the Indian papers which reached our camp affected to sneer at the Begum, Huzrut Mahal, and the legitimacy of her son Brijis Kuddur, whom the mutineers had proclaimed King of Oude, they had evidently the support of the whole country, for every chief and zamindar of any importance had joined them.'

After capturing Lucknow, several hundred were hanged for the rebellion and the British declared that the rebels and their leaders must give themselves up for conspiring against them. Moreover, they confirmed they would spare the lives of those who did not kill British officials. This applied from the Begum, down to those of the lower ranks. They further affirmed that the Begum will receive all the considerations which are because of her as a woman and a member of royalty. However, Begum Hazrat Mahal did not surrender to the British and instead asked for help from the Nepalese authorities as a last resort after her efforts to defeat the British failed. She along with her son Birjis Qadr and a few followers escaped to Bithauli, Bihar on their way to Nepal.

Rana Jang Bahadur, the Prime Minister of Nepal and the Nepalese authorities, was hesitant to give the Begum asylum. In a letter to the Begum he wrote, "If you should remain or seek asylum within my territory and frontier, the Gorkha troops will, in pursuance of the treaty agreed upon by both the high States, attack, and make war on you." They later reversed their decision, and they gave asylum to her on conditions that she would not communicate with the rebel leaders or with the people of India.

In 1877, the Begum tried to return to India, but the British denied her entry. The order further mentioned that if she entered any of the states in India, they would watch the state and put it under the magistrate of the district, making sure the Begum never returns to her own country.

After living in Nepal for twenty long years, the Begum died on 7 April 1879, in exile and is buried in a nameless grave in Kathmandu's Jama Masjid. After her death, the British Government 'pardoned' her son Birjis Qadr. On the jubilee of Queen Victoria in 1887, Birjis Qadr was 'allowed' to return home! The Government of India issued a Postage Stamp on 10 May 1984, in honour of the invincible Begum who fought the fiercest battle with the British in the first war of Independence.

CHAPTER SEVEN
THE GUTSY

Uda Devi was born in a small village Ujriaon, in Awadh. She was also known as Jagrani and grew up resentful of the atrocities by the British. During the Revolt of 1857, Uda Devi formed a women's army, and as the commander led them to Secundrabâgh, Lucknow. Her husband Makki Passi who was a soldier in the Avadh army was killed in the battle at Chinhat on 30 June 1857.

Secundrabâgh, a villa, and garden enclosed by fortified walls on four and a half acres of land was built as the summer residence of the Nawab. During the revolt, it was used to protect a small garrison of 2200 soldiers and was the centre or refuge of the mutineers during the siege of the Lucknow Residency. It stood on the way of Colin Campbell's planned route to relieve the besieged Residency. Uda Devi instructed the soldiers to attack the advancing British army from all directions. She then climbed on a pipal tree with pistols in both her hands and concealed within the leaves of the tree.

William Forbes-Mitchell in Reminiscences of the Great Mutiny, 1857-59, records, 'In the centre of the inner court of the Secundrabâgh, there was a large peepul tree with a very bushy top, round the foot of which were set a number of jars full of cool water. When the slaughter was almost over, many of our men went under the tree for the sake of its shade, and to quench their burning thirst with a draught of the cool water from the jars. A number however lay dead under this tree, both of the Fifty-Third and Ninety-Third, and the many bodies lying in that particular spot attracted the notice of Captain Dawson. After having carefully examined the wounds, he noticed that in every case the men had evidently been shot from above. He thereupon stepped out from beneath the tree, and called to Quaker Wallace to look up if he could see anyone in the top of the tree, because all the dead under it had apparently been shot from above. Wallace had his rifle loaded, and stepping back he carefully scanned the top of the tree. He almost immediately called out, "I see him, sir!" and cocking his rifle he repeated aloud, I'll pay my vows now to the Lord Before His people all.' He further writes, 'He fired, and down fell a body dressed in a tight-fitting red jacket and tight-fitting rose-coloured silk trousers.' It was the brave Uda Devi. 'She was armed with a pair of heavy old-pattern cavalry pistols, one of which was in her belt still loaded, and her pouch was still about half full of ammunition, while from her perch in the tree, which had been carefully prepared before the attack, she had killed more than half-a-dozen men.' 'By this time all opposition had ceased, and over two thousand of the enemy lay dead within the building and the centre court.'

Throughout the summer of 1857, many women soldiers lost their lives during the 'Siege of Lucknow.' Along with the brave Ranis, Uda Devi was the face of the Mutiny of 1857. Today in the centre of an intersection outside Secundrabâgh, in Lucknow, stands Uda Devi's statue, carrying a rifle and walking forward with a determined glare. The Pasi community has existed for over a thousand years and they are very much part of Indian history. The community observes 16 November as Uda Devi's anniversary and she is remembered as 'Dalit Veerangana,' a gallant woman. Women from remote villages travel long distances to attend her Martyrdom Day and through folk songs, the community narrates Uda Devi's bravery.

CHAPTER EIGHT
THE REBELLION IN UNIFORM

Born in a distinguished Brahmin family in Benares on 19 November 1827, Manikarnika was affectionately called Manu. Her mother, Bhagirathi Sapre, died when Manu was four. Her father Moropant Tambe, worked as an adviser in the royal court of Peshwa Baji Rao II of Bithoor, Cawnpur. Manu spent her childhood in the household of the Peshwa ruler, who considered Manu as his daughter. Growing up in the company of Nana Sahib Peshwa and Tatya Tope ensured Manikarnika access to education as well as horsemanship, fencing, and shooting.

In 1842 Manikarnika was married to Maharaja Gangadhar Rao the ruler of Jhansi. As was a common practice, she was renamed Lakshmi Bai after marriage. The couple had a son in 1851, but he died four months after his birth. Two years later Gangadhar Rao's health started to deteriorate. Hence they adopted a relative, five-year-old Damodar Rao, to groom him as a successor. The adoption took place on 20 November 1853, in the presence of a British officer and the Maharaja wrote "I trust that in consideration of the fidelity I have evinced toward government, the favour maybe shown to this child and that my widow during her lifetime may be considered the Regent." The papers and a will naming Damodar Rao as heir and the Rani as regent were presented to the assistant political agent in Jhansi.

In the letter, the Maharaja further wrote that the British treat his son with respect, and on his death, hand over Jhansi to his wife, Rani Lakshmi Bai, and their son Damodar Rao for their lifetime. The following day Gangadhar Rao died. After his death on 21 November 1853, the British East India Company applied for the Doctrine of Lapse. They ignored the Maharaja's letter, and they rejected Damodar Rao's claim to the throne, stating that he was the adopted son of Maharaja Gangadhar Rao with no right to the throne of Jhansi.

Dalhousie refused to acknowledge the young Damodar Rao as an heir and declared that since the adoption was not approved by the government, the state would pass by "lapse" to the British. This was immediately followed by Captain Alexander Skene, the British superintendent, taking control of Jhansi. The Rani was allowed to live in the palace and given an annual pension of 60,000 rupees.

Lakshmi Bai submitted a letter contesting the Doctrine of Lapse, on 3 December 1853, and a second letter on 16 February 1854. This was followed up with several petitions, however, no response was ever received.

The 1857 mutiny propagated quickly across cantonments of north India and by the end of May 1857, the most important region of the country was boiling with anger. Soon violence spread through north and central India and transformed the mutiny into an organized resistance. The revolt reached Jhansi in June 1857. The British suspected Rani Lakshmi Bai of conspiring with rebels to revenge for their refusal to recognize her heir. Though Rani Lakshmi Bai was initially not part of the rebellion, the British blamed her for it. On 6 June 1857, the troops at Jhansi mutinied. They shot their commanding officers and occupied the Star Fort, where the garrison's armoury was stored. When Rani Lakshmi Bai got to know of the revolt, she requested the British political officer for protection.

There are several versions of the rebellion in Jhansi. There is a mention that the rebels of the 12th Bengal Native Infantry seized the Jhansi Fort and asked the British to give up their arms, promising them no harm. Instead, they killed 60 British officers of the garrison along with their families. The army's field surgeon, Dr. Thomas Lowe, in his book, 'Central India during the Rebellion of 1857 and 1858,' wrote that Rani Lakshmi Bai played a role in the killings. Accounted by the British, though! Lowe called her the 'Jezebel of India, the young rani upon whose head rested the blood of the slain.' and wrote, 'Heaps of dead lay all along the rampart and in the streets below.'

Soon the British invaded Jhansi. Supported by the forces of the British subsidiary allies, Maharaja Hamir Singh, the ruler of Orchha, and the royal family of Datia. However, they were defeated by Rani Lakshmi Bai's army in August 1857. The British ignored her request for aid as the Governor-General of India Charles Canning believed she could handle the events in Jhansi. Rani Lakshmi Bai quickly guarded the fort and assembled her forces, including the former feudatory of Jhansi and mutineers who had defeated the British forces.

From August 1857 to January 1858, Jhansi was peaceful under Rani Lakshmi Bai. This established Rani's position and her advisers who demanded independence from the British. When the British forces eventually arrived in Jhansi, to their surprise, they found the fort well protected, with heavy guns and ammunition. The fort was well-designed to resist a siege. 'The guns could fire over the town and the countryside! Hugh Rose, who was the Commanding Officer of the British forces, demanded the surrender of the city and they would destroy it if refused.

It is at that juncture that the Rani issued a proclamation: "We fight for independence. In the words of Lord Krishna, we will, if we are victorious, enjoy the fruits of victory. If defeated and killed on the field of battle, we shall surely earn eternal glory and salvation." She reached out for help to Tatya Tope and an army of over 20,000, headed by Tatya Tope himself, reached Jhansi. They defended Jhansi against the British forces till Hugh Rose besieged Jhansi. By 30 March 1858, most of the guns had been disabled and the fort's walls were breached. And on 3 April 1858, the British forces attacked Jhansi, met with equal retaliation and a heavy return of fire however they captured the palace and stormed the fort. Determined resistance in every street and every room of Rani's palace continued till the siege of Jhansi. Dr. Thomas Lowe wrote, "No maudlin clemency was to mark the fall of the city."

Rani Lakshmi Bai soon realized that resisting the British forces in the city was futile. With her son Damodar Rao on her back, she jumped on her horse Badal and rode away in the night, surrounded by her troops, and escaped from the fortress. They reached Kalpi, a small town between Jhansi and Kanpur. Here they were joined by Nana Sahib, Rao Sahib, and Tatya Tope. Their plan was to capture Gwalior from Maharaja Jayaji Rao Scindhia who continued to side with the British. They reached Gwalior on 30 May 1858, attacked Morar, Gwalior, and took most of the Maharaja's forces and ammunition. He had a large military cantonment of around 7000 infantry and 4000 cavalry. The Maharaja, along with his bodyguards, fled to a British garrison in Agra.

Though the rebels captured Gwalior, they did not loot the city, other than to take money from Maharaja Scindia's treasury to pay the rebel forces. They did not realize that Hugh Rose had advanced from Jhansi and a brigadier from Antari. Brigadier Smith attacked the rebels at Kota-Ki-Serai, about four miles southeast of Gwalior.

On 12 June 1858, Hugh Rose recaptured Morar, and on 17 June 1858, Kota-Ki-Serai. The British forces massacred 5,000 Indian soldiers and civilians. On the second day of the fighting at Kota-ki-Serai, a fatally wounded Rani Lakshmi Bai did not want to be captured by the British. It is said that the locals cremated her in Phool Bagh Gwalior.

Gwalior fell soon after, and the organized resistance collapsed. Rao Sahib and Tatya Tope continued to lead guerrilla attacks against the British until they were captured.

Hugh Rose, who commanded the Central Indian Field Force and defeated the armies at Jhansi and Gwalior, reported Rani Lakshmi Bai's death to William Augustus, Duke of Cumberland, 'The Rani is remarkable for her bravery, cleverness, and perseverance; her generosity to her subordinates was unbounded. These qualities, combined with her rank, rendered her the most dangerous of all the rebel leaders.' "Although she was a lady, she was the bravest and best military leader of the rebels. A man among the mutineers." Hugh Rose reported they had buried the Rani with a grand ceremony under a tamarind tree in Gwalior.

In 1890 Colonel Malleson published the book, History of the Indian Mutiny of 1857-8, and writes, 'Whatever her faults in British eyes may have been, her countrymen will ever remember that she was driven by ill-treatment into rebellion and that she lived and died for her country. We cannot forget her contribution to India.' Referred to as India's 'Joan of Arc,' the celebrated Rani Lakshmi Bai battled against the British artillery and might! Rani Lakshmi Bai's statue guards Jhansi and Gwalior. B. R. Tambe, a poet laureate of Maharashtra, while sitting in front of the 8-meter tall metal statue of Rani Lakshmi Bai in Phool Bagh, Gwalior wrote, 'She burst open the British siege. And came to rest here, the brave lady of Jhansi!' In 1942, the women's unit of the Indian National Army (Azad Hind Fauj) was named the 'Rani Jhansi Regiment.' The Government of India issued two postage stamps in 1957 to commemorate the centenary of the illustrious rebellion. We have all grown up listening to 'khoob ladi mardani woh to Jhansi wali Rani thi.' How well like a man fought the Rani of Jhansi. How valiantly and well.' She had also declared "Maain Apni Jhansi Nahi Doongi" (I will not give up my Jhansi.)

CHAPTER NINE
THE TRUSTED WARRIOR

There is very little documented on Jhalkaribai. She was born in 1830 in Bhojla, a village near Jhansi. Learned the art of weaponry and horse riding very young, it is said Jhalkari could fight dacoits and kill tigers. Her mother Jamuna Devi died when Jhalkari was very young and she was brought up by her father Sadoba Singh.

During Gauri Puja, an important festival for Marathi women, Rani Lakshmi Bai saw Jhalkaribai at the fort and was surprised by the resemblance they shared. Jhalkaribai was married to Puran Singh in Rani Lakshmi Bai's army and soon Rani Lakshmi Bai inducted Jhalkaribai into the women's wing of her army. Since Jhalkaribai resembled Rani Lakshmi Bai, it is believed she disguised herself as the Rani during the 1857 revolt. This gave Rani Lakshmi Bai time to escape.

Predictably, very little is documented on Jhalkaribai's bravery in the rebellion of 1857. A Dalit warrior, she played an important role in the 1857 revolt against the British. The Government of India issued a postal stamp in the name of Jhalkaribai. The Dalits celebrate 'Jhalkaribai Jayanti.' as her birth anniversary.

SECTION TWO

VISIONARIES

SWARAJ~SWADESH~SATYAGRAHA

As highlighted in the first section of the book, the East India Company was established in India, as a trading body for English merchants. An unregulated private company held by a couple of English business owners who surprisingly had their army, their territory, and a total hold on the trade of tea! The Company slowly consolidated its position in India. After the First War of Indian Independence- Indian Rebellion of 1857, the British government ended the company's control, and on 2 August 1858, the British Crown took direct administration of India. East India Company was shut down and finally dissolved fifteen years later.

The years from 1905 onwards, witnessed a nationwide movement emerging from a fierce sense of Indian nationalism. There was a high level of dissatisfaction with the British and dissent surfaced amongst millions of Indians. This was led by courageous, defiant, and resolute women and men of India, who shared a single focus: freedom and political independence.

The first nationalist mass movement called the Swadeshi Movement began on 7 August 1905 after the partition of Bengal. This infuriated people all over the country and is seen as an important event in the narrative of the Indian Nationalist Movement. The boycott of British goods was very symbolic, targeting salt from Liverpool, and sugar and goods from Manchester, resulting in a decline in the import of liquor, tobacco, cotton, and apparel. The Indian women, who demanded restrictions on products in their homes such as clothes, medicines, and other remote items, enthusiastically received the Swadeshi Movement.

Further, the boycott of schools, colleges, and government posts and the refusal to provide any service to the British government only grew stronger. Anti-propaganda, through the setting up of Swadeshi crafts, press, petitions, meetings, conferences, and messaging through songs and complete social rejection, became a national culture. One of the most successful initial movements against the British, it was India's rebellion response through the withdrawal of Indian support to the British and the origins of the Indian independence movement. The British did not expect such a sustained reaction to their decision and eventually agreed to reverse the partition in 1911.

What was also upsetting was that over a million Indians, the largest voluntary army, fought the World War from 28 July 1914 to 11 November 1918. However, the Indian soldiers faced racial discrimination, were denied civil rights, and were barred from positions of command under colonial domination. The sacrifice and contribution of nearly 75000 of them who died during the war went unnoticed. The soldiers sent letters to their home, which, of course, passed through the censor's office. In those letters, the soldiers mentioned the mistreatment at war and they penned this in their diaries as well. Despite playing an important role in the victory of the allies and their extraordinary bravery, they remain the unremembered voices of World War One, excluded and dismissed.

After over two decades in South Africa, Gandhi returned to India in 1915. He had launched effective Satyagrahas in South Africa and on the advice of Gopalkrishna Gokhale, he toured India to understand the country before commencing any political work. On 6 April 1919, he went ahead and launched a non-violent Satyagraha against the controversial and unjust Rowlatt Act passed on 18 March 1919. The Act allowed political cases to be tried without juries, detention by police without reason, police could search without a warrant and muzzling of the press. This led to further discontent in the nation and protests throughout the country.

On 13 April 1919, the Sikh Community gathered for Baisakhi in Jallianwala Bagh, Amritsar. The British police opened fire at the unarmed gathering and massacred over 1000 people. This was a watershed moment in Indian history and is marked as the darkest chapter in the history of the Indian Independence Movement. After the massacre, protests took place throughout the country forcing the British to send a warning letter to Gandhi on 18 July 1919. It read "Dear Mr. Gandhi, I am to inform you that the Government of India have desired His Excellency the Governor of Bombay to convey to you a grave warning of the consequences which must inevitably be anticipated from the resumption of any action or propaganda involving the disobedience of the law and of the heavy moral responsibility that must lie on those who take or advise this course. In making this communication to you I am to say that His Excellency would add a further warning that an assumption that such action can be undertaken without most serious consequences to the public security is entirely unwarranted by the situation in this Presidency. Yours A. Montgomerie, for Political Secretary to Government."

Gandhi replied, "Sir, The Government of India have given me through His Excellency the Governor of Bombay, a grave warning that resumption of Civil Disobedience is likely to be attended with serious consequences to the public security. This warning has been enforced by His Excellency the Governor himself at interviews to which I was summoned. In response to this warning and to the urgent desire, publicly expressed, by Dewan Bahadur Govinda Raghava Iyer, Sir Narayan Chandavarkar, and several Editors, I have, after deep consideration, decided not to resume Civil Resistance for the time being."

He further added, 'But this suspension while it lightens my responsibility by reason of the feared outbreak of violence, makes it incumbent upon the Government and the eminent public men who have advised suspension to see that the Rowlatt Legislation is removed without delay."

''I have thus suspended Civil Resistance to hasten the end of that Legislation. But Satyagrahis will pay for its removal by their lives if it cannot be removed by lesser means. The period of suspension is for

Satyagrahis an opportunity for further discipline in an enlightened and willing obedience to the laws of the State."

For a year, the movement was stopped however a year later the Non-Cooperation Movement was formally launched on 1 August 1920. This was a passive resistance and the backbone of the non-violent resistance adopted by Gandhi, working toward a peaceful end to British rule. He was also looking at winning the British over and persuading them to free India.

Gandhi outlined the broad objectives of the new movement at the Indian National Congress and encouraged Indians to discard the British political, economic, bureaucratic, military, and educational institutions and build a self-reliant (atmanirbhar) Nation. He urged Indians to replace government schools and courts with nationalist schools and arbitration bodies. Indian-made products and textiles-handmade goods were to be substituted for British imports. He was aware of the risks, as well as the need to motivate millions of Indians to participate in the movement. He now encouraged women to join the freedom movement, making it his mission to give significant roles and jobs to women. At a meeting in Bombay, he very tactfully put it across to the women present, 'So long as women in India do not take equal part with men in the affairs of the world, and in religious and political matters, we shall not see India's star rising.' Women took to fasting and prayer, spinning, protesting, and breaking laws, wherever possible. They picketed shops selling liquor or foreign goods, raised funds, boycotted government institutions and functions, and courted jail. Takli (a hand spindle used for spinning) and Charkha appeared in many homes. Women made spinning a daily practice and promoted Khadi. This was most definitely a notable period for women in India, as they united and brilliantly participated in the national movement.

As the Non-Cooperation Movement spread, there were riots in some places and the violence led Gandhi to call off the movement in 1922. During the Movement, several thousand Indians were put in jail. Gandhi along with other leaders was arrested in March 1922, and charged with sedition, and Gandhi was sentenced to six years imprisonment. 'In my humble opinion,' he declared at his trial, 'non-cooperation with evil is as much a duty as is cooperation with good.' Gandhi was released after two years, and the struggle against the British continued.

On 12 March 1930, Gandhi carried out an astonishing act of civil disobedience against the Salt Law. The law made it a crime for anyone in India to possess salt not purchased from the government monopoly and prohibited Indians from collecting or selling salt, hence forcing them to buy expensive imported taxed salt! In defiance of British authority, Gandhi walked nearly 375 km, from Sabarmati Ashram to the Dandi seashore in Gujarat along with his followers. When he reached Dandi, he picked up a handful of salt and broke the salt law as a symbol of the Indian's refusal to live under British-made laws and British rule. This sparked a mass movement among the people to gather and make salt. The daily newspapers reported his speeches and the impact that this march had on the people, in fact, the village officials on Gandhi's route to Dandi, resigned from their jobs. This march brought Gandhi to world attention and India received wide coverage in the International media. Women participated in large numbers and many were arrested for breaking the salt law. Gandhi was arrested and jailed with other leaders and released in January 1931.

The Bombay Chronicle reported, 'The successes that preceded, accompanied and followed this great national event, were so enthusiastic, magnificent and soul-stirring that indeed they beggar description. Never was the wave of patriotism so powerful in the hearts of mankind, as it was on this great occasion, which is bound to go down in the chapters of the history of India's national freedom as a great beginning of a great movement.' Webb Miller, correspondent to the New Freeman reported, "In eighteen years of reporting in twenty-two countries, during which I have witnessed innumerable civil disobediences, riots, street fights and rebellions, I have never witnessed such harrowing scenes as at Dharsana. Sometimes the scenes were so painful that I had to turn away momentarily. One surprising feature was the discipline of the volunteers. It seemed they were thoroughly imbued with Gandhi's non-violent creed." The scope of Satyagraha now extended to the boycott of foreign cloth, picketing of liquor shops, disobeying forest laws, and non-payment of taxes.

Horace Alexander an English Quaker who played a significant part in relations between Indian nationalist leaders and the British Government writes about what he saw in Bombay in 1930, "It was startling, when one landed in Bombay in 1930, during the then Civil Disobedience, to go round the city watching women, some of whom had till that day never ventured outside their households even veiled, now sitting openly on stools outside liquor shops, quietly, composedly plying their little hand-spinning wheels, as if they had been in public life all their lives. Yet some of them knew the city so little that they had no idea how to find their way home at the end of the day. Either they must wait for some man member of the family to fetch them, or, does it sound incredible? They would rely on the goodwill of the shopkeeper whose trade they were silently picketing. Such was the policy of Gandhi's appeal to the hearts of Indian women that scores responded to his call. When the women led processions through the streets, as they were eager to do, the unfortunate police angrily protested that the men ought not to allow such things to happen, as it made the task of the police intolerable."

Kamaladevi Chattopadhyay's account for the part played by women at this stage of the struggle, "Gandhiji's first instinct was to reserve women for some special work and not allow them to participate in the general struggle. But the movement proved too big for that. Even though only a few women were chosen officially in the salt satyagraha with which the Indian revolution opened on the morning of April 6, 1930, by sunset of that first day it had turned into a mass movement and swept the country. On that memorable day thousands of women strode down to the sea like proud warriors. But instead of weapons they bore pitchers of clay, brass and copper, and instead of uniforms, the simple saris of village India. One watched them fascinated and awestruck. How had they broken their age-old shell of social seclusion and burst into this fierce light of open warfare? Undoubtedly the women turned this struggle into a beautiful epic.'

"Unlettered, untrained, unprepared, they assumed new duties with unexpected courage. It was the women who made law-breaking universal. Following the violation of the Salt Act came effective attacks on the Forest Laws and other obnoxious taxes and regulations."

The Gandhi-Irwin Pact was signed on 5 March 1931 to release those imprisoned during the Civil Disobedience and Indians were allowed to make salt. It also marked the end of the civil disobedience movement. Congress in 1933 officially suspended the movement and withdrew a year later.

The Quit India Movement further sped up the British departure and unified Indians' resolve against British rule. On 8 August 1942, Mahatma Gandhi called for an orderly British withdrawal from India. This was a demand to end the British rule of India. The British swiftly responded with mass detentions and arrested Mahatma Gandhi and his wife Kasturba Gandhi along with other freedom fighters for participating in the Quit India Movement. Kasturba Gandhi, was imprisoned and her health seriously worsened, and she died at the Aga Khan Palace detention camp in 1944, sadly before India got its Independence.

Meanwhile, in 1942 the Indian National Army (INA), also known later as the Azad Hind Fauj, became active in Singapore. An armed force was formed by Indian freedom fighters to secure India's freedom from the British. Initially formed under Mohan Singh, an Indian military officer. Subhas Chandra Bose, arrived in Singapore, from Germany in June 1943. He planned to take foreign help with a single aim, to overthrow the British out of India. Bose's speeches in Singapore, Malaya, and Burma inspired both men and women to join the march toward Delhi. With the war cry Dilli Chalo he revived the army and renamed the INA -Azad Hind Fauj. The army of 43000, comprised Burma, Malaya, and Singapore volunteers. The British Military Intelligence began an anti-propaganda work against the Azad Hind Fauj. They did not divulge the number of soldiers in the Azad Hind Fauj, and falsely implicated Azad Hind Fauj's involvement in Japanese atrocities. The British were concerned that the British Indian army would defect. So much so that the British even restricted the Indian press from publishing accounts of the Azad Hind Fauj.

An unparalleled army because it was engaged in a global war of Indians, brought together in a foreign land. However, as a condition for independence from the British, these former soldiers of the INA / Azad Hind Fauj were barred from joining the new Indian Armed Forces. Their commitment to an independent India is noteworthy, but unfortunately, their stories are lost in history.

Within Azad Hind Fauj was the Rani of Jhansi Regiment (named after Rani Lakshmi Bai) a women's Regiment and amongst the first of its kind recorded anywhere in the military history of the world. They were trained to go into combat. Subhas Chandra Bose's vision was to empower the Ranis to fight for the equality of women. The members of the Rani of Jhansi were equal to the men in the army. The women belonged to the Indian communities settled in Malaya, Singapore, and Burma.

Lakshmi Sahgal, an officer of the Indian National Army, referred to as Captain Lakshmi, headed the combat unit of the Rani of Jhansi Regiment and was the Minister of Women's Affairs in the regiment. She was arrested by the British army in June 1945 in Burma and was under house arrest after which she was sent back to India in March 1946.

The Non-Cooperation of 1920-21, the Civil Disobedience of 1930-34 and the Quit India Movement of 1942, had a big role in hastening independence and a call for independence could no longer be disregarded. However, the British refused immediate independence. They had no intention of exiting India but realized that India was ungovernable and finally it was time to exit the country. And the Royal Indian Navy Mutiny in 1946, which lasted from 18 February to 23 February, was the last straw! Britain's Parliament passed the Independence Act in July

1947, ordering the demarcation of India through religious lines and partitioned by 14-15 August 1947.

The British administration officially ended on 15 August 1947, but only after a tragic exodus of over 15 million Hindus, Muslims, and Sikhs who fled their homes when they heard of the partition. A million people were violently massacred when British rule ended most recklessly. In their rush to exit and when they left, they displaced millions, destroyed properties, and created chaos in the country they ruled. India finally got its independence.

Fifteen women were selected amongst 299 in the Constituent Assembly, to debate and draft the Indian Constitution. Debating every Article in the Constitution, these fifteen women played an important role, sitting for 11 sessions and 167 days to frame the Constitution, over 2 years and 11 months. The Constitution of India came into force on 26 January 1950. At the time of its adoption, the Constitution contained 395 Articles and 8 Schedules and was about 145,000 words long, making it the longest national Constitution to ever be adopted.

To give a sense of how Indians felt about colonial rule, here is an excerpt from Dr. Sarvepalli Radhakrishnan's address at the Constituent Assembly. 'The first Britisher to arrive in this country was a Jesuit Missionary in 1579. He was followed by merchants who came to trade but stayed to rule. In 1765 the authority was transferred to the East India Company, later it was gradually subordinated to and replaced by the authority of Parliament and it has been continuing till now on the famous principle enunciated by Cecil Rhodes-the principle fundamental to imperialism, philanthropy plus 5 percent. On that principle, it has worked. Right through, however, there were protests against British rule. All these protests became canalized when the Indian National Congress was established in 1885. It adopted mild methods till the advent of Mahatma Gandhi when it became aggressive and dynamic.'

'In 1930 the Resolution for the Independence of India was passed at Lahore and we are now here to give effect to that resolution. The British are empirics from beginning to end. It was Lord Palmerston who said 'we British have no eternal principles, we have only eternal interests.' When they adopt any particular line of action you may take it that it is not a willing surrender of power or authority but it is a response to the historic necessities of the case. When the discontent grew up they gave us the Morley-Minto Reforms and they introduced the principle of communal electorates and these communal electorates were intended to keep the people apart. The higher mind of Britain advised the local officials that they would betray the trust placed upon them if they foisted communal electorates. They would inject a poison into the very body politic which could be removed if at all, at the cost of a civil war. We know how those anticipations are getting realized today.'

'We had after that the Montford Reforms and then the 1935 Act, the Cripps' proposals, and now the Cabinet Plan. The latest Statement of His Majesty's Government on this question indicates how it is not in human nature to surrender power easily. Playing off one section against another is unworthy of a great people. It is much too clever to be permanent and would embitter the relations of this country and Great Britain. It is essential for the British to understand that if an act is done it must be done with the utmost grace.'

'All the same we are here assembled to draw up a constitution for future India. A constitution is the fundamental law of the nation. It should embody and express the dreams and passions, the ideals and aspirations of the people. It must be based on the consent of all, and respect the rights of all people who belong to this great land,' he declared.

In this section, I highlight the early women activists. Educators, writers, strategists, and freedom fighters. Their history under colonial rule and after Independence. Women writers gave a much-required impetus to various struggles for social transformation and through their stories, they advocated and enabled other women and women's rights groups to participate in the freedom struggle.

These women activists and educators played a significant role in the fight for freedom and in creating a new India. During the first Swadeshi movement in 1905, the role of women was restricted to boycotting foreign goods, schools, colleges, and complete social rejection. From there on a fierce sense of patriotism developed among women which required them to play a much larger role in the freedom movement. Gandhi led mass movements and women took a lead by mobilizing the nation to join these movements by participating through their networks, campaigning through their speeches, and writing articles in journals. They raised their voice against colonial rule while attending international conferences and roundtable meetings.

The women's movement gathered momentum with the inception of the Women Indian Association in 1917 and the All India Women Conference in 1927, founded by Annie Besant and Margaret Cousins who were the pioneers of the women's rights movement. Moreover, these associations played an important role in the political movements of the time. The intent was to influence the states and facilitate measures during legislation dialogues affecting the welfare of women and children. The women leaders in political circles backed the feminist concerns raised by these women organisations and set forth a collective vision toward the advent of the women's liberation movement in India. The Women Indian Association was focused on lobbying with the government on policies concerning women's rights, and articulating educational and social reforms like the elimination of child marriage and other social evils.

Many women went ahead and joined revolutionary groups against the colonial regime. During the passive resistance, the Non-Cooperation Movement, and Civil Disobedience Movement, several nationalistic groups and associations were formed by women. They participated in marches, flag hoisting, and boycotts, they were arrested and imprisoned for months and years. However, the brave women survived an environment of oppression and went beyond what was dictated in the books and set by society. They directly fought to free their country, and cracked the walls of patriarchy, because they recognized, 'Swaraj is my birthright and I shall have it.'

I believe that Indian history books remain incomplete without the narratives of the inspirational women, and their journey from 'surviving to suffrage.'

In this second section I share stories of the remarkable women activists who championed a free India. As mentioned in the preface, the narratives are arranged in chronological order. Each account begins with the date of birth of the woman profiled and the events inform a broad atmosphere of the generation as well as the tone of society in that period. I have referred to the women by their given names or surnames. To avoid confusion, I have retained the colonial spellings for Indian cities; therefore, Mumbai remains Bombay, Kolkata remains Calcutta, etc. Further, I have deliberately kept a set format, for readers to context the era and for clarity to the intended message. The intent is to create a relationship between the story and the readers: the background and circumstances of why something happened: the personality of the women, and a context of how people behaved during that period in history. Quotes from memoirs for authenticity and facts that the event took place. I have tried to adopt the most commonly used spellings for individuals. Further, my focus is only on the subject matter, hence I have not written about families, future generations, and so on.

Savitri Bai Phule

Annie Besant

Sarojini Naidu

Pandita Ramabai Dongre

Bhikaiji Cama

Abala Bose

Matangini Maity Hazra

Kasturba Gandhi

Lady Meherbai Tata

CHAPTER TEN
THE REFORMER EDUCATIONIST

It is said that when Savitribai was young her father snatched a book she was looking at and instructed her not to touch one again. In those days, reading and studying were the rights of upper-caste men. Savitribai was born on 3 January 1831 at Naigaon, Satara. Her parents, Lakshmi and Khandoji Nevase Patil belonged to the socially backward Mali community (gardeners.)

Child marriage was common in India and Savitribai was nine and Jyotirao Phule, thirteen, a student in class 3 when they got married. Later Jyotirao also known as Mahatma Jyotiba Phule, became a social activist, anti-caste social reformer, and writer. After marriage, Savitribai moved to Poona and as Jyotirao was a strong believer in educating the girl child, he home-schooled his wife much against the family's wishes. Jyotirao then enrolled Savitribai in two teacher's training programs at a training institute in Poona, run by the American missionary Cynthia Farrar in Ahmednagar, and the second at the Normal School Of Ms. Mitchel in Poona. Savitribai became a qualified teacher in 1847 and on 1 January 1848, the couple established the country's first modern school for girls in Bhidewada, Poona. This school offered the students a traditional western curriculum of mathematics, science, and social studies. It was the country's first school for girls started by an Indian couple. They had to face resistance from the local community, who considered their work a sin. Brahmins were the only caste group that received an education and the 'chosen' ones who could take a lead in setting up schools. Thus the conservative, educated, upper castes in the locality pelted Savitribai with stones and dirt forcing her to carry an extra saree while commuting to her school! Eventually, when Jyotirao's father was threatened, the couple was asked to leave home. They moved out to stay at Jyotirao's friend's home and Savitribai, along with the host's sister Fatima Begum, opened a school at home. The following year, in 1850, Savitribai and Jyotirao Phule opened two educational trusts encircling many schools. And by 1851, the couple were running three different schools in Pune for girls, educating over 150 girl students and that was not all, in time they opened a total of 18 schools!

To increase attendance in these schools, Savitribai would give a stipend to the children. She engaged in parent-teacher meetings where she spoke with the parents on the importance of educating the girl child. Later the couple went beyond education and launched a care centre called Balhatya Pratibandhak Griha for destitute women. They were both advocates of widow remarriage and opposed Sati. In 1873, the couple went on to establish the Satyashodhak Samaj (The Truth-Seeker's Society) which championed broad-mindedness and the samaj arranged marriages without a priest, rituals, or dowry. Satyashodhak marriage also required the bridegroom to pledge that his wife would be given an education and equal rights.

When her husband died on 28th November 1890, in defiance of social customs Savitribai led the last rights of her husband while the family contested their adopted son's rights.

Credited for being a trailblazer in women's education and setting up India's first school for girls, Savitibai was the first native woman teacher from the backward class. As a poet she made a conscious decision to compose poetry in traditional Marathi forms, they were articulate and directed at expressing social discrimination. Most of her poems centred on the ills of the caste order and the need to put an end to bonded labour. And through word choice, she reached out and emphasized the urgency of education. Take for instance the message in her poem, 'Go, Get Education,' here she advocates values such as liberty, equality, and for the helpless to get educated in order to break the chain of suppression. She pens,

"Be self-reliant, be industrious.

Work gathers wisdom and riches.

All gets lost without knowledge.

We become animals without wisdom.

Sit idle no more, go, get an education.

End misery of the oppressed and the forsaken.

You've got a golden chance to learn.

So learn and break the chains of caste.

Throw away the Brahman's scriptures."

The language in this poem is direct and provokes the reader to think as well as act. Perhaps among the first published Marathi poets in modern India, her collection of poems is admired in the world. Her other famous poem, 'Awake, arise and educate' is highly significant of that time and era.

'Awake, arise and educate.

Smash traditions-liberate!

We'll come together and learn Policy-righteousness-religion,

Slumber not but blow the trumpet O Brahman, dare not you upset.

Give a war cry, rise fast, Rise, to learn and act.'

Common phrases in her poems advocate the significance of modern education and liberation.

When famine hit Maharashtra in 1896, it also brought with it the contagious plague. The selfless devoted Savitribai got into action during this critical epidemic as well. While working in the relief operations, she came in close contact with the plague patients and contracted the disease. Savitribai Phule died on 10 March 1897. Known as Kaku (paternal aunt) by her students, the Pune City Corporation created a memorial for her in 1983, and India Post released a stamp in her honour on 10 March 1998. On 9 August 2014, the University of Pune was renamed Savitribai Phule Pune University. Called Jananajyoti (Flame of education) and Krantijyoti (Flame of Revolution,) Savitribai Phule's birthday is celebrated as Balika Din (Little Girl Child Day) in Maharashtra. An educator, feminist, poet and social reformer, Savitribai Phule has many firsts to her name.

CHAPTER ELEVEN
THE RADICAL VICTORIAN

Born on 1 October 1847 in Clapham, London, Annie Besant née Wood lost her father Dr.William Persee Wood, when she was five, leaving his young widow Emily Morris with two children. In her memoir, 'An Autobiography,' Annie pens, 'And now began my mother's time of struggle and of anxiety. Hitherto, since her marriage, she had known no money troubles, for her husband was earning a good income; he was apparently vigorous and well: no thought of anxiety clouded their future. When he died, he believed that he left his wife and children safe, at least, from pecuniary distress. It was not so. I know nothing of the details, but the outcome of all was that nothing was left for the widow and children, save a trifle of ready money…On his death-bed, there was nothing more earnestly urged by my father than that Harry should receive the best possible education, and the widow was resolute to fulfil that last wish.' After her father died Annie visited a family friend and there she met a woman who took a liking to Annie and asked if she would like to study with her niece, 'But they urged her that the advantages of education offered were such as no money could purchase for me; that it would be a disadvantage for me to grow up in a houseful of boys - and, in truth, I was as good a cricketer and climber as the best of them - that my mother would soon be obliged to send me to school unless she accepted an offer which gave me every advantage of school without its disadvantages.' Her mother agreed and Annie moved to live with Ellen Marryat. Ellen was an evangelical Calvinist who contributed extensively to Annie's education and spiritual pursuits and at the early age of eight, Annie received a strongly evangelical education.

In the summer of 1866, Annie was engaged to Frank Besant, a young priest she had met at the mission church in the spring. They met for a week, at a small party of holiday-makers, and an hour or two before Frank left he asked Annie to marry him and they were married fourteen months later. 'We were an ill-matched pair, my husband and I, from the very outset; he, with very high ideas of a husband's authority and a wife's submission, holding strongly to the "master-in-my-own-house theory." writes Besant in her memoir.

They had two children. However it was an unhappy marriage and she looked forward to being independent, far from the burdens of a compressed married life. The marriage lasted five years and after legal separation in 1873, Annie now had to look after her daily expenses, so she began writing short stories as well as working for social causes.

During this time, Annie Besant met Charles Bradlaugh a political activist and the editor of the radical National Reformer, which published articles on trade unions, women's right to vote, national education, birth control, and the abolition of capital punishment. An atheist, he influenced Annie with his radical views on secularism. Encouraging her to discover her passion and he recognised her talent for public speaking, something she had never set out to accomplish. Later she became a co-editor of the newspaper and eventually a co-owner. They were also brought to trial for obscenity for printing pamphlets on birth control though subsequently acquitted. In 1876, she was elected vice president of the National Secular Society, which preached 'free thought', and became a prominent Fabian socialist. Inspired by Thomas Scott, one of her early influencers, a freethinker and rationalist, she drifted from being a devout Christian to a freethinker and later turned into an atheist. She began penning her views on religion and travelled in the country for lectures. Soon Besant became an important activist in the Secularist movement and an advocate of atheism and free thought in England. She wrote many articles on marriage, birth control, women's rights, the land, and free trade. Besides, Bradlaugh and Besant founded the Free thought Publishing Company.

Besant also met George Bernard Shaw and was influenced by his views on socialism and became part of the labour movement in England

and voiced her support in her newspaper through a column 'Our Corner.' She believed that socialism was a revolution that carried more force and change than any social reform could ever bring.

One of the famous movements she led was the London Match girl's strike -after it was brought to her attention the conditions of women and girls working in match factories for fourteen hours a day. She writes in her memoirs, 'The London Trades Council finally consented to act as arbitrators and a satisfactory settlement was arrived at; the girls went into work, fines and deductions were abolished, better wages paid; the Match-makers' Union was established, still the strongest woman's Trades Union in England, and for years I acted as secretary, till, under press of other duties, I resigned, and my work was given by the girls to Mrs. Thornton Smith; Herbert Burrows became, and still is, the treasurer. For a time there was friction between the Company and the Union, but it gradually disappeared under the influence of common sense on both sides, and we have found the manager ready to consider any just grievance and to endeavour to remove it, while the Company have been liberal supporters of the Working Women's Club at Bow, founded by H.P. Blavatsky.' Annie was a woman who championed everything she put her heart into and with unimaginable brilliance.

In the 1890s, Annie renounced all her social work and immersed herself in theosophy an esoteric movement co-founded by Helena Blavatsky, a Russian-born clairvoyant, whose vision of theosophy incorporated aspects of Western spiritualism and belief in reincarnation.

Besant's unanticipated desertion from socialism to theosophy astonished many of her supporters in England. Besant was convinced that her mission was to be of service to all humankind and unity in the world. As a member and leader of the Theosophical Society, she helped spread theosophical beliefs around the world.

With an intention to preach the ideals of the theosophy Besant came to India in 1893 and moved permanently in 1898. Initially in India she worked for educational, religious, and political reforms. And in 1898, she founded the Central Hindu College in Benares, this college was later converted into Benares Hindu University (BHU.) In the following years, she established a network of schools and colleges.

Besant was critical of British rule in India and along with Lokmanya Tilak she established the Indian Home Rule League, in 1916. Designed similar to the Irish Home Rule, the objective was to achieve self-governance in India. In 1917, she was put under house arrest under the Defence of India Act, however, she remained rebellious and raised the green and red flag as a symbol of the Home Rule movement. There were widespread protests in India and abroad and under international pressure, Annie Besant was released after three-month detention. The movement lasted around two years between 1916 and 1918 and is believed to have set the stage for the independence movement with the Indian Home Rule League's activities playing a significant role in enabling the freedom struggle.

One of her most important and notable contributions to the women of India is the Women's Indian Association which she co-founded in 1917, the mission was women's rights, education, and reforms related to women and children. This association went on to address social and political issues critical under colonial rule. She played a significant role in the implementation of the Child Marriage Restraint Act, widow remarriage, and abolishing the devadasi system. As the first woman President of the Indian National Congress, she presided over the 1917 Calcutta session of the Indian National Congress. In 1920, when Gandhi launched the non-cooperation movement Besant while agreeing with his objectives opposed the means adopted by him! Sarojini Naidu, who became the second woman President of the Indian National Congress in 1925 mentioned, "Had there been no Annie Besant there would have been no Mahatma Gandhi." She certainly was one of the most admired leaders of the pre-Gandhi period.

Besant changed her ways often and did what she felt was true to her conscience and persisted in her quest for a purpose. Subjected to social segregation by her community for confronting the religious shallowness of Victorian England, she questioned the superficiality of human actions and the oppression of the subdued and the poor. She had written in her autobiography, "I'm not what you think of me, and your verdict does not change myself. You cannot make me vile whatever you think of me. I have never, in my own eyes, be that what you deem me to be now.'

Editor of Madras Standard, a daily newspaper, later she bought the publication and called the newspaper New India. In 1918, she declared in her paper, "I love the Indian people as I love none other, and… my heart and my mind… have long been laid on the altar of the Motherland." The British later banned the newspaper! Besant wrote over 380 books and pamphlets and co-authored twenty-six books.

Born in England, Annie Besant's story is of determination. A courageous woman and an active participant in the freedom struggle of a country she made her home and where she died on 20 September 1933, shortly before her 86th birthday. Gandhi in his tribute to Annie Besant wrote, 'Whilst the people will thank the Almighty for relieving Dr. Besant from lingering illness by sending to her the Angel of Death, thousands will, at the same time, mourn the event. So long as India lives, the memory of the magnificent services rendered by Dr. Besant will also live. She had endeared herself to India by making it the country of her adoption and dedicating her all to her country.' M. K. Gandhi The Bombay Chronicle, 21-9-1933.

CHAPTER TWELVE

THE NIGHTINGALE OF INDIA 'BULBUL-I-HIND'

'But I believe that I must disprove the age-old proverb that woman has not only the last but the longest word. I have the last word not because I am a woman but because I am acting today as the hostess of the Indian National Congress which has so gladly invited those who are outside its fold to come and participate with us in framing the constitution, that is to be the immortal charter of India's freedom,' Naidu announced at the Constituent Assembly of India.

Sarojini Naidu, née Chattopadhyay, was the first Governor of the United Provinces. Accomplished in Urdu, Telugu, English, Bengali, and Persian, Naidu was a poet, lecturer, women's rights activist, and politician. Born on 13 February 1879, in Hyderabad Sarojini was the eldest daughter of Varada Sundari a Bengali poet, and Aghorenath Chattopadhyay a distinguished Bengali scholar, and linguist. He founded two Indian colleges and was additionally the principal of the Nizam College, Hyderabad.

At twelve, Sarojini completed her matriculation (10th) from the University of Madras. During that time she fell in love with Govindarajulu Naidu, a doctor, disapproved by her parents as she was far too young to marry, they sent her to England in 1895, to study at the King's College, London. Later at the Girton College, University of Cambridge. Naidu began to write poetry very early in England and though she followed an English poetic tradition, she developed her own poetic style. She soon became friends with well-known English critics and writers, Edmund Gosse and Arthur Symons. Both appreciated her outstanding technical craft and mastery of English metrical forms as well as the imageries that she included in her poetry and went ahead to write forewords for her books.

Upon her return to India in 1898, Sarojini married Govindarajalu Naidu. She was nineteen and after marriage moved to Hyderabad.

Her early poetry had a powerful western bent, with a focus on themes and images from the western world. Edmund Gosse recognized Naidu's capabilities as a poet and advised her to include Indian issues and content in her work. Naidu accepted his advice and in her first volume of poetry, published in England in 1905, 'The Golden Threshold,' she integrated both the traditional poetic form with rich images of India. The book was an immense success in England with readers applauding Naidu's proficient grasp of the English language, as well as her native perspectives of mysterious Indian imageries. Her poems were well-received by the critics as well, because of the way she used rich sensory images in her writing and this encouraged her to publish more of her works. Her second collection of poems 'The Bird of Time' was published in 1912. This collection focused on grief and death and communicated her religious leaning and patriotic disposition.

In a foreword to this volume, Edmund Gosse wrote, 'It is only at the request that is to say at the command of a dear and valued friend that I consent to write these few sentences. It would seem that an "introduction" can only be needed when the personage to be "introduced" is unknown in a world prepared to welcome her, but still ignorant of her qualities. This is certainly not the case with Mrs. Naidu, whose successive volumes, of which this is the third, have been received in Europe with approval, and in India with acclamation. Mrs. Naidu is, I believe, acknowledged being the most accomplished living poet of India—at least, of those who write in English, since what lyric wonders the native languages of that country may be producing.'

In 1915, Sarojini Naidu met with Mahatma Gandhi and became a follower of Gandhi's idea of self-governance. She supported him in several demonstrations and protests and joined him in the Indian

National Congress movement for India's independence. An excellent public speaker with a grasp of the subject, and a great sense of humour she often travelled overseas to lecture on self-governance for India, and women's rights.

In the middle of the First World War Naidu wrote the poem, 'The Gift of India, as a tribute to one million Indian soldiers who were part of the British India Army, and nearly 75000 Indian soldiers died in the war.

'Is there aught you need that my hands withhold,

Rich gifts of raiment or grain or gold?

Lo! I have flung to the East and West

Priceless treasures torn from my breast,

And yielded the sons of my stricken womb

To the drum-beats of duty, the sabres of doom.

Gathered like pearls in their alien graves

Silent they sleep by the Persian waves,

Scattered like shells on Egyptian sands,

They lie with pale brows and brave, broken hands,

They are strewn like blossoms mown down by chance

On the blood-brown meadows of Flanders and France.

Can ye measure the grief of the tears I weep

Or compass the woe of the watch I keep?

Or the pride that thrills thro' my heart's despair

And the hope that comforts the anguish of prayer?

And the far sad glorious vision I see

Of the torn red banners of Victory?

When the terror and tumult of hate shall cease

And life be refashioned on anvils of peace,

And your love shall offer memorial thanks

To the comrades who fought in your dauntless ranks,

And you honour the deeds of the deathless ones

Remember the blood of thy martyred sons!

In this poem, Naidu is not only paying tribute to the Indian soldiers but also making a statement that their sacrifice should be recognized. Over one million Indian soldiers fought as Allied forces in the First World War. They fought in different locations throughout the war, however, their contributions were overlooked and nearly 75000 of them sacrificed their lives without being acknowledged. A powerful war poem, directed at the loss wars bring, the grief, as well as a dare. When the poem was published it stirred up a feeling of pride and nationalism in the hearts of the countrymen. Many believe that it was Naidu's greatest poetic master-work and the last volume of poetry published by Naidu after which she was preoccupied with politics. Thus from literary pursuits, she transited to a political one. And when she did start to write again, she wrote mainly patriotic poems with a contemplative voice.

When the British enacted the controversial Rowlatt Act, Sarojini Naidu moved the following resolution against the Act in Madras on 7th March 1919, "This public meeting of the citizens of Madras once again earnestly urges on His Excellency, the Viceroy and the Government of India, that they should drop the Rowlatt Bills at least at this stage in as much as they are unjust, subversive of the principle of liberty and justice with which the safety of the community as a whole and the state itself is based." The Act was later repealed in 1922.

Naidu succeeded Gandhi and was appointed as the President of the Indian National Congress at Kanpur in 1925 and she became the second woman to preside over the Congress after Annie Besant. During her presidential address, she said 'How shall I stir your hearts, how shall I light that flame that cannot die, so that your slavery, so that your disunion, so that all the things that make you hungry and naked and forlorn, oppressed and battered will be burnt in that undying fire?'

Arrested by the British authorities frequently for participating in several protests she was jailed from 1930 until 1931, 1932 to 1933, and again from 1942 to 1943. However, she remained steadfast and continued to campaign for freedom not only in India but also on her tours overseas where she lectured on self-governance demand for India. On March 12, 1930, when Gandhi embarked on a Salt March from Sabarmati Ashram to the seashore of Dandi to protest against the steep tax the British levied on salt, Naidu supported Gandhi.

During the boycott call of foreign merchandise for Indian goods, Naidu penned a very impressive and intriguing poem urging the world to notice the richness in the products of India, 'In the Bazaars of Hyderabad,' she describes the various stalls in the bazaars of Hyderabad. The poem is comprised of questions and answers.

In The Bazaars of Hyderabad:

What do you sell, 0 ye merchants?

Richly your wares are displayed,

Turbans of crimson and silver,

Tunics of purple brocade,

Mirrors with panels of amber,

Daggers with handles of jade.

What do you weigh, 0 ye vendors?

Saffron and lentil and rice.

What do you grind, 0 ye maidens?

Sandalwood, henna, and spice.

What do you call, 0 ye pedlars?

Chessmen and ivory dice.

What do you make, 0 ye goldsmiths?

Wristlet and anklet and ring,

Bells for the feet of blue pigeons,

Frail as a dragon-fly's wing,

Girdles of gold for the dancers,

Scabbards of gold for the king.

What do you cry, 0 ye fruitmen?

Citron, pomegranate, and plum.

What do you play, 0 musicians?

Cithar, sarangi and drum.

What do you chant, 0 magicians?

Spells for the aeons to come.

What do you weave, 0 ye flower-girls?

With tassels of azure and red?

Crowns for the brow of a bridegroom,

Chaplets to garland his bed,

Sheets of white blossoms new-gathered

To perfume the sleep of the dead.

In the poem, Naidu wanted to convey a message to the world about India's diversity in products and that there was little need for Indians to buy foreign merchandise. Cleverly, she outlined in the poem a picture of a bazaar where the merchants sell traditional Indian products. The magnificence of the Indian bazaar is expressed through the colours, sounds, smells, and sights. The technique she used for this poem, was forms of questions and answers, where the poet asks the questions and the merchants answer them, creating visible pictures of the bazaar.

Naidu was among the fifteen women members of the Constituent Assembly, in a meeting to frame the constitution and establish a free independent India, she said. 'Standing in the immemorial house with its roof of snow and walls of sea, once again in the history of humanity, she will rekindle her lamp of wisdom and inspiration to illuminate the world on its onward march to freedom. So will she be justified of her children and the children be justified of her.'

After independence in 1947, Sarojini Naidu accepted the governorship of the United Provinces and was the first woman to hold the office of Governor in the Dominion of India. (Officially the Union of India, was an independent dominion in the British Commonwealth of Nations.) She remained in office till her 70th birthday on 13 February 1949. She had a head injury which resulted in severe headaches and her health deteriorated. She was hospitalized and died on 2 March 1949 in Lucknow.

At the Constituent Assembly of India meeting on 16 May 1949, President Dr. Rajendra Prasad opened the house with a homage to the great poet leader, he said, 'Honourable Members, this is the first time that we meet in this Assembly since the passing away of Shrimati Sarojini Devi. Her life had been dedicated to the service of the country and her steadfastness during the great struggle through which we had to go was exemplary. She had been one of the makers of the India of today, and the loss which the country has sustained cannot be easily repaired.'

An opponent of imperials, and an advocate of civil rights and women's independence, Naidu played a significant role in India's struggle for independence. Often referred to as 'The Nightingale of India', or 'Bharat Kokila,' because her poetry spoke of many emotions, and the lyrical quality of her poetry connected people on many levels. Her poetry was about hope, life, death, beauty, love, power, past, future, and dreams. Sarojini Naidu had once commented 'Oh the patience of India! How I hate her patience!'

The English writer and philosopher Aldous Huxley had said about Sarojni Naidu, "It has been our good fortune, while in Bombay, to meet Mrs. Sarojini Naidu, the newly elected President of the All-India

Congress and a woman who combines most remarkably great intellectual power with charm, sweetness with courageous energy, a wide culture with originality, and earnestness with humour. If all Indian politicians are like Mrs. Naidu, then the country is fortunate indeed."

CHAPTER THIRTEEN
THE PANDITA

In 1878, the faculty of the University of Calcutta conferred the titles Pandita and Sarasvati on Ramabai Dongre. This was in acknowledgment of her knowledge of Sanskrit works. Born on 23 April 1858, in Karavali, Karnataka, Ramabai's father Anant Shastri Dongre, and mother Lakshmibai were Sanskrit scholars and wandering professional reciters of Hindu mythological texts. Her father read the Puranas in public and at a very young age, Ramabai learned Sanskrit and the Puranas from her parents. By fifteen Ramabai was herself a puranika and was able to recite Bhagavata Purana which has 18000 verses from memory! Having wandered with her parents across India she was conversant with Hindi, Marathi, and Kannada.

Ramabai's parents succumbed to the famine of 1876-78 and she continued the family tradition of reciting texts, along with her brother. Both the brother and sister wandered for nearly two years until they reached Calcutta. This is where Ramabai received the titles of Pandita and Sarasvati from the most learned scholars of the city. However, she soon felt let down by Hinduism because of the deeply entrenched caste system and became a follower of Brahmoism. She then gave up reciting the Puranas and became a lecturer, taking up causes relevant to social reforms for women. The audience was mesmerised by her impressive learning, her broad understanding of subjects and her gracious demeanour.

Ramabai's brother died of cholera while they were in Calcutta and soon she married a lawyer, Bepin Behari Das Medhavi, a Kayastha which of course caused an uproar in the orthodox community! Unfortunately, her husband died, leaving her as a young widow with an infant daughter. From Calcutta, Ramabai moved to Poona, a city known for its social reforms. And within a year of her arrival, Ramabai formed a women's society on 30 November 1882, called the Arya Mahila Samaj (Aryan's Women's Society) to advance female education. The same year Viceroy Ripon, appointed an Education Commission to review the progress of education in India. Ramabai met with the education examination committee and suggested to them, that there was an urgent need for training teachers, appointing women school inspectors, and admission of women to medical colleges. In an address to the Education Commission, she said, "In ninety-nine cases, out of a hundred, the educated men of this country are opposed to female education and the proper position of women. If they observe the slightest fault, they magnify the grain of mustard seed into a mountain, and try to ruin the character of a woman." Her inputs to the committee were well received and the commission agreed to promote female education and most of the recommendations of the commission were accepted. From Poona, Ramabai would travel to several cities within the Bombay Presidency advocating education of women.

In 1883, Ramabai went to England to study medicine believing that it would help her serve the women who found health care, even the traditional kind, hard to access. While in England, she taught Sanskrit to support herself and stayed with the Anglo-Catholic Sisters of St. Mary the Virgin, whose missionary community she had known in India. A month later she converted to Christianity, after which she was ostracized from the Indian social reforming field and faced fierce criticism from her fellow reformers.

Ramabai was hoping to complete a medical degree, however, because of her battle with deafness, she could not and that put an end to her dreams of becoming a physician. After two years in England, Ramabai travelled to the United States to attend the graduation of a relative Anandibai Joshi, the first Indian female doctor of western medicine. She stayed back for two years, translated textbooks, and delivered lectures in the United States and Canada. It is in the United States that she envisaged the idea of creating a school for Hindu widows in India. And to fund the project, she wrote the book, The High Caste Hindu Woman in 1888, which was widely sold and helped in the formation of the American Ramabai Association. Impressed by American feminism she reached out to the women highlighting the sorrowful state of the distressed widows in India, as very few in America were aware of the conditions of the widows in India. She travelled around America, lecturing and organizing 'Ramabai Circles,' to finance the school. This then provided the funds and support for the opening and continued maintenance of the Widow's Home in India.

Dedicating the book to her mother, she writes, 'the light and guide of my life,' and highlights the lives of the Hindu widows in the book. Most were young girls from high caste families. She brings forward the mistreatment of the widows by their families and society, as well as the social evils of the time, such as child marriage, the plight of child widows, and the repression of women under colonial rule. While in America she also penned notes and put them together in the Marathi book, Conditions of Life in the United States.

Ramabai had by now achieved what she had set out to do on her travels, raised funding for feminist social reforms, and written two very critical books highlighting the state of the women of her country. She returned to India, and founded Sharada Sadan a school for child widows in Bombay, and later moved the school in 1890 to Poona and changed the name to Mukti Mission. Committed to supporting destitute women and children, Pandita Ramabai Mukti Mission is still active today, providing housing, and imparting vocational training to widows, orphans, and those with sight impairments and other difficulties.

She suffered the loss of her daughter who died when she was forty, in 1921. Pandita Ramabai followed, nine months later and died on 5 April 1922. Ramabai's contribution to the education and welfare of Indian women is very worthy. On 26th October 1989, the Government honoured her life and works with a commemorative stamp. Pandita Ramabai was the first woman to be awarded the title of Pandita and Sarasvati as a Sanskrit scholar and she wrote as a social reformer, an activist, a traveller, and a spiritual being.

CHAPTER FOURTEEN
MOTHER OF INDIAN REVOLUTION

An advocate for women's rights and a woman who unfurled the first version of the Indian national flag at the International Socialist Congress held in Stuttgart, Germany, in 1907, Bhikaiji Cama, was a rare woman living in exile most of her life. Born on 24 September 1861, in Bombay, her father Sorabji Framji Patel was an influential and wealthy Parsi merchant, and her mother, Jaijibai Sorabji Patel a homemaker.

Bhikaiji studied at the Alexandra Girls' English Institution and grew up predisposed toward socio-political issues and a nationalist mind set. On 3 August 1885, she married Rustomji Cama who was a lawyer. He was an ardent supporter of British culture and Bhikaiji a staunch nationalist, hence the couple had their share of differences. She spent most of her time on philanthropic activities and social work after the marriage.

When famine struck Bombay, along with the plague in 1899, Bhikaiji helped in the relief operations at the Bombay Grant Medical College to care for the plague victims and also help citizens get inoculated. In all of this, she got infected. Bhikaiji Cama then had to travel to Europe for treatment and lived in Germany, France, and Scotland for a year each, finally moving to London in 1905.

The British administration in India sent a letter to her in London stating that her return to India would be subject to the promise that she would not take part in the Nationalist Movement. She of course refused to make any such promise and remained in exile. In London, Bhikaiji met Shyamji Krishna Varma. Early 1905, Krishna Varma had established India House, a hostel for students, and this became a centre for meetings and the dissemination of revolutionary ideas. Varma introduced Bikhaiji to Dadabhai Naoroji, the then President of the British Committee of the Indian National Congress. She later became Naoroji's secretary and began working for the Indian National Congress. Cama also came in contact with other Indian nationalists, including Vinayak Damodar Savarkar and she would address several meetings in London's Hyde Park with Dadabhai Naoroji and other nationalists and strong critics of British policy in India. From London, Cama moved to Paris, compelled to live outside of Paris and report to the police station once a week because France and England were war allies. Unperturbed, she co-founded the Paris Indian Society, along with S. R. Rana and Munchershah Burjorji Godrej.

By 1907, Cama, had become a very well-known Indian woman in European revolutionary circles. She was a delegate at the International Socialist Congress at Stuttgart held on 22 August 1907. With the support of the Social Democratic Federation, she proposed a resolution on India. She demanded the withdrawal of British rule, 'no people should be subject to any despotic or tyrannical form of government.' However, the British delegates present opposed and prevented its adoption. Cama was then allowed to address the delegates. In a speech, she unmasked the 'terrible tyrannies' under British rule. Bhikaiji appealed to the delegates, for human rights, equality, and independence from Great Britain. She went on to share the devastating famine that had struck India. She concluded her speech by unfurling the Indian National flag, a tricolour with Bande Mataram printed on the middle band, and eight lotuses representing the eight provinces. She called it the Flag of Indian Independence, 'Behold, the flag of independent India is born! It has been made sacred by the blood of young Indians who sacrificed their lives in its honour. In the name of this flag, I appeal to lovers of freedom all over the world to support this struggle.' She went on to add , 'This is the flag of independent India. I appeal to all gentlemen to stand and salute the Flag.' The delegates then stood and saluted the first flag of Independent India. This was the first time an Indian flag had been displayed in a foreign country, which she had designed with Shyamji Krishna Varma.

Following Stuttgart, Cama travelled to United States and then to London, and Paris, where she settled, however, ensured direct contact with India House. Early September 1909, in response to the ban put by the British on Bankim Chandra Chatterjee's famous nationalist poem, 'Vande Mataram,' she founded Bande Mataram, an Indian nationalist newspaper. She financed the paper, which appeared regularly till 1913, as well as funded the party, contributed money to print its literature and helped to smuggle revolutionary literature into India through the French colony of Pondicherry. Bhikaiji would also assist the revolutionaries with money. Later she published another revolutionary newspaper called The Talvar, published in Berlin. This was named after Madan Lal Dhingra, one of the heroes of the Indian independence movement, executed for the political assassination of William Hutt Curzon Wylie. Despite their best efforts, the British Government was unable to find out how she was able to send the material to India.

She was in touch with Indian revolutionaries in different parts of the world as well as maintained contacts in French socialist circles. Her home in Paris was a meeting place for nationalists and revolutionaries. A few years later while speaking at the National Conference in Cairo, Egypt in 1910, Cama asked the delegates, "Where is the other half of Egypt? I see only men who represent half the country! Where are the mothers? Where are the sisters? You must not forget that the hands that rock cradles also build persons." Bhikaiji believed in the serious role women played in building a nation. In 1920, when she met Mithan Tata Lam and her mother Herabai Tata, women suffrage campaigners on the issue of the right to vote, Bikhaiji told them, 'Work for Indian's freedom and independence. When India is independent, women will not only have the right to vote but all other rights.'

She continued to fight for freedom while she lived away from her own country. During the First World War in 1914, Bhikaiji even influenced the Indian soldiers fighting for the British forces. On her visit to an army camp in Marseilles, she asked the Indian forces, "Are you going to fight for the people who have chained your motherland?" England and France were allies in this First World War.

In 1935, Bhikaiji suffered a paralytic stroke. She requested the British to let her return to India. Aware of her serious health condition, they knew she would not be able to take part in any revolutionary activities. They permitted Bhikaiji Cama, now 74-year-old, to finally return to her country after 33 years of living in exile. She was hospitalized and, nine months later died on 13 August 1936 at the Parsi General Hospital, Bombay.

She donated most of her assets to the Avabai Petit Orphanage for girls. A trust was established in her name. The government named several streets and places in India in her honour and her contributions to the fight for freedom. On the 11th Republic Day of India, the Indian Posts and Telegraphs Department issued a memorial stamp to commemorate her. 'India must be free, India must be a republic, India must be united,' declared the Mother of the Indian Revolution and while she did not live to see a free India, she worked her entire life fighting for it.

Socialist leader Indulal Yagnik later smuggled the flag hoisted by Madam Bhikaiji Cama to India, and it is put on public display at the Maratha and Kesari Library in Pune. In 1997, the Indian Coast Guard commissioned a Priyadarshini-class fast patrol vessel named ICGS Bhikaiji Cama, in remembrance of Bhikaiji's tremendous participation in the freedom struggle and her continued efforts to achieve self-governance for her country.

CHAPTER FIFTEEN
THE TRAVELLER

Abala was born on 8 August 1865, in Barisal, Bengal. Her father, Durga Mohan Das, was a Brahmo Samaj leader, and social reformer. Her Mother Brahmamoyee Devi worked to improve the status of widows. Inspired by her parents, Abala Bose née Das inherited a reformist mindset. Though the family was ostracised by the community for advocating widow remarriage, they continued with a single focus. Through their work, they enabled widows to be financially independent as well as made it possible for young girls to go to school.

Abala studied at the Bangla Mahila Vidyalaya and later Bethune School which her father had assisted financially to build. She was one of the earlier batches to pass out of the school. She was denied admission to Calcutta Medical College as female students were not accepted in the college then. She then enrolled at the Madras University in 1882 on a Bengal government scholarship to study medicine, but could not continue her studies because of ill health.

At twenty-three, Abala married Jagadish Chandra Bose, the 'Father of Radio Sciences.' An Indian physicist who is considered the father of Bengali science fiction and the first Indian to get a US patent. He is best known for his research into the life of plants. During her overseas travels with her husband from 1896 to 1933, Abala Bose had the opportunity of meeting several women and in the interactions, she learned about their way of living and culture. Exposed to contemporary education, she was able to implement these later, in several institutions she opened in India.

Abala Bose was purposeful in her travels and documented all her experiences. Her travel narratives represent her feminist identity and ambition, especially in India's backdrop under colonial rule. Some of her works include 'England Bharaman' (Travel to England) which is in three parts and published in 1897. In 1901 she wrote Italy Bhraman (Travel to Italy) and in 1908 she published her book titled Americar Balakbalikader Katha (About the Children of America.) And a travelogue about Japan, Japan Bharaman (Travel to Japan) in 1915. Later, in 1928, she published a travelogue called Bangali Mohilar Prithibi Bhromon (World Tour of a Bengali Woman.) This was published in the periodical Prabasi, a monthly Bengali language literary magazine.

Abala Bose was committed to advancing educational opportunities for women and the betterment of disadvantaged widows. In 1910, she was elected as the Secretary of the Brahmo Balika Shikshalaya (Brahmo Girls' School) in Calcutta and was at the helm for 26 years, from 1910 to 1936. She transformed the school into a top-ranking institution at that time and introduced the Montessori system of teaching, which meant developing natural interests and activities in children, rather than formal teaching.

Jagdish Chandra Bose received a knighthood in 1916 and Abala Bose came to be known as Lady Bose. She was also at the forefront of fighting for the voting rights of women in India. Women in India were granted voting rights for the first time in 1921 after a prolonged struggle by Lady Abala Bose and Kamini Roy, the Bengali poet, and social worker.

She also established the Nari Shiksha Samiti, in 1919, with the objective of educating children, girls and women. The organisation advocated female representation in educational bodies and reforms for women at the mass level. Abala Bose set up 88 primary schools and fourteen adult training centres in Bengal, along with Sister Nivedita, who was Swami Vivekananda's disciple and a close friend. They set up training centres for kindergarten teachers, trained girls in self-defence, and along with this, emphasised the importance of replacing the Brahmin pundits with female teachers so that the girl students did not feel uncomfortable.

The Vidyasagar Bani Bhawan was set up in 1925, with the objective of experience-based learning for multifaceted development and professional preparation of educational leaders; teacher training for the widows. Abala Bose also set up the Mahila Shilpa Bhavan in Calcutta and Jhargram to provide vocational training to distressed women and widows. A training institute in Kamarhati that skilled and trained poor women in weaving, tailoring, leather-work, and pottery making. In 1928, she started the Bengal Women's Educational League, an institution that campaigned for gender sensitivity in the syllabus. She channeled her privileges toward the improvement of the marginalised sections.

Highlighting the importance of women's education Abala Bose advocated, 'women should have a deeper and extended education, not because we may make better matches for our girls, not even that the services of the daughter-in-law may be more valuable in the home of her adoption, but because a woman like a man is first a mind, and only in the second place physical and a body.' She believed that a woman deserves a right to be educated because, 'she too consists of the same human condition that makes up a man.'

Lady Abala Bose died on 25 April 1951. She spent most of her life advocating women's rights and education and the rehabilitation of displaced and economically disadvantaged girls and women. She understood that in order to bring changes in society, just setting up schools would not be enough, teacher training was as important to impart the right quality of education.

CHAPTER SIXTEEN
GANDHI BURI

Matangini Maity Hazra was born in 1869. Her parents were poor peasants from Tamluk, Midnapore, Bengal. Married at an early age to Trilochan Hazra, a man in his 60s with a young son, she was widowed when she was eighteen. After which she returned to her paternal home.

Devoting her time to the Indian freedom movement, she became an ardent follower of Gandhi and actively took part in the Indian independence movement. In and out of prison several times in her lifetime, she was arrested for petitioning for abolishing the salt tax and imprisoned at the Hijli detention camp which was used by the British to lodge women prisoners of Midnapore. The British considered Midnapore as a serious threat to their rule, as several freedom fighters and women revolutionaries came from this part of Bengal.

After her release, Hazra joined the local branch of the Indian National Congress. She was arrested once again and imprisoned for six months, this time in Berhampore, Orissa. After her release, she became even more active in the freedom movements and when John Anderson, Governor of Bengal, visited Tamluk in 1933 to address a public gathering, Matangini reached the dais and waved a black flag at him! She was immediately taken into custody and spent the next six months yet again in jail.

Despite her age and frail eyesight, she continued to spin the charkha and be of service to her country. During the Quit India Movement, Congress planned to take over police stations in the Midnapore district and other government offices. They planned to hoist the flag at the Tamluk police station on 29 September 1942. Hazra approached the local leadership that she would like to lead the procession of 6000 supporters, to hoist the flag. Concerned with her age they dissuaded her. When the procession reached the outskirts of the town, they were ordered to end the procession under Section 144. However, Hazra stepped forward to request the police not to shoot at the crowd. The police shot her while she was speaking to them. She kept moving forward with the tricolour held high and asked others to do the same. While she continued toward the police station, two more bullets hit her, and she eventually died of the bullet wounds, with the flag held high and still flying.

The local Biplabi Newspaper, reported Hazra's last moments, 'Matangini led one procession from the north of the criminal court building; even after the firing started, she continued to advance with the national flag, leaving all the volunteers behind. The police shot her three times. She continued marching despite wounds to the forehead and both hands.'

Matangini Hazra came to be known as Gandhi Buri, Bengali for old lady Gandhi. The rendering of a woman with her white hair streaming, carrying the Indian flag, and directing a crowd of people, that image is of Matangini Hazra. A national figure of the Indian Independence Movement, the Hazra Road in Calcutta is named after her. And in 1977, the government of West Bengal built her statue in Calcutta as well as in her native Tamluk. A fierce protester, an extraordinary woman she exhibited courage and perseverance in her life which was truly a journey of sheer determination.

CHAPTER SEVENTEEN

BA

Kasturbai was born on 11 April 1869. Her father Gokuladas Kapadia was a Gujarati merchant and the Mayor of Porbandar. Her mother Vrajkunwerba Kapadia was a homemaker. The family was close friends with the family of Dewan of Porbandar, Karamchand Gandhi, and the father of Mohandas Gandhi. Kasturbai and Mohandas were engaged when she was seven and she was thirteen when they got married in 1882. She moved to Rajkot from Porbandar after marriage.

Shortly after their son's birth, Gandhi left to study law in London while Kasturba Gandhi remained in India. After his return from London, in 1891, Gandhi practiced law for two years and in 1893, the family moved to South Africa where Mahatma Gandhi worked as a legal counsel. And soon he became the leader of the South African Indian Community. His involvement in the non-violent movement in South Africa started after he was thrown out of a train by the authorities because a white man complained of an Indian sitting in the same first-class compartment. In response to this, he formed the Natal Indian Congress in 1894 to draw international attention to the predicament of Indians in South Africa. The members fought against the oppression of native Africans and Indians, they took part in Gandhi's Satyagraha campaigns.

By 1896 Gandhi had established himself as a political leader in South Africa and returned to India in 1901 before deciding to move back to South Africa in 1903. In 1904, Gandhi along with Kasturba established a communal living community called Phoenix Settlement near Durban. The settlement was an experiment in communal living. After over twenty years in South Africa, in 1915, Gandhi decided to return home. By now Gandhi was fairly well known, for the work he had done in South Africa. He founded a similar settlement like Phoenix in Ahmedabad and called it the Sabarmati Ashram and the Gandhis lived there for sixteen years.

Kasturba Gandhi dedicated most of her time to the ashram. She was referred to as Ba or Mother because she served as the mother of the ashram. She reached out to women in India with her message that women could play a critical role in their homes and be self-sufficient by learning to spin the charkha and weave.

Although her health did not permit her, she continued to take part in many civil disobedience campaigns and marches, resulting in several arrests and imprisonment, and would go on a fast whenever her husband was in prison. In 1939, she joined the Rajkot Satyagraha, to support the women who requested her help against the rule of the local prince. Arrested during this Satyagraha, on 3 February 1939 she was kept in solitary confinement for a month, and here her health deteriorated. However, that did not stop her from taking part in the various movements.

During the Quit India movement, the British imprisoned Mahatma Gandhi before he could address a public meeting near Bombay. He wanted Kasturba to take his place. She realized the police would stop her and imprison her too. Within moments, she dictated a message to the public. Her message read, 'Gandhi poured out his heart for two hours at the All India Congress Committee meeting last night. What can I add to that? All that remains for us is to live up to his ideals. The women of India must prove their mettle. They should all join in this struggle, regardless of caste or creed. Truth and non-violence must be our watchwords.' The British stopped Kasturba on the way to the meeting, where more than a lakh people had gathered to see her, arrested her and sent her to jail.

She was imprisoned in the Aga Khan Palace Detention Camp in Poona. While in prison Kasturba Gandhi had two heart attacks. When her health worsened she asked the prison authorities to allow her to be treated by an Ayurvedic doctor however the British did not permit this for a long time and eventually let a specialist in traditional Indian medicine treat her. She responded to the treatment initially, however, suffered a relapse. Being in and out of prison, her health had severely worsened. On the evening of 22 February 1944, Ba died and was cremated in the compound of the Aga Khan Palace Detention Camp on 23 February 1944. She was seventy-four.

Mahatma Gandhi watched the funeral pyre until the end. A few gathered at the funeral and asked him to leave and take some rest. 'This is the final parting, the end of 62 years of shared life. Let me stay here till the cremation is over,'he said. And the same evening, after a prayer meeting, he remarked, 'I cannot imagine life without Ba,' and in his biography, he penned, 'According to my earlier experience, she was very obstinate. Despite all my pressure, she would do as she wished. This led to short or long periods of estrangement between us. But as my public life expanded, my wife bloomed forth and deliberately lost herself in my work.'

Sarojini Naidu who was very close to Gandhis described Ba as 'The living symbol of Indian womanhood. Never once did her feet falter or her heart quail on the steep path of perpetual sacrifice, which was her portion in the wake of the great man whom she loved and served and followed with such surpassing courage, faith and devotion. She has passed from mortality to immortality and taken her rightful place in the valiant assembly of the beloved heroines of India's legend, history, and the song.'

Gandhi declared, 'If anything, she stood above me. But for her unfailing co-operation, I might have been in the abyss. She helped me to keep wide awake and true to my vows. She stood by me in all my political fights and never hesitated to take the plunge. In the current sense of the word, she was uneducated; but to my mind, she was a model of true education. She was a devoted Vaishnav. But she had obliterated all feelings of caste from her mind and regarded a Harijan girl with no less affection than her children. She personified the Kasturba Gandhi ideal, which Narsimha Mehta has sung in the Vaishnavajana hymn. Sometimes

I was engaged in a grim wrestle with death. During my Aga Khan Palace fast, I came out of death's jaws. But she shed not a tear, never lost hope or courage, but prayed to God with all her soul.' Kasturba Gandhi National Memorial Trust Fund was set up in her memory. Gandhi requested that the fund be used to help women and children in villages in India and her legacy carries on. Kasturba Gandhi's determination to challenge bereavement, crisis and difficulties equalled that of Mahatma Gandhi.

CHAPTER EIGHTEEN
THE MEHRI

Meherbai Tata was born on 10 October 1879. Her father Dr. Hormusji Jehangir Bhabha, was the Inspector-General of Education of Mysore State and took keen interest in his daughter's education. Mehri studied at the Bishop Cotton Girls School, in Bangalore, appreciated literature, and was fond of playing the piano. An avid sportswoman, she won many tennis tournaments and was probably the only lady who played professional tennis wearing a sari, to make a point to the British!

Dorabji's father, Jamshetji Tata had visited Mysore State on business and met Meherbai at her father's home. Returning to Bombay, he sent his eldest son Dorabji to Mysore purely to visit the Bhabha family and on 14 February 1898, Meherbai was married to Dorabji Tata! An Indian business owner and a key figure in the history and development of the Tata Group.

Married into a leading industrial family, Meherbai had access to the influential societies of Europe as well as the royalty of India. She observed the social work that the European women were taking forward in their respective countries and was confident that women in India could do similar work and help resolve many social issues. She reached out to women in forums and associations, urging the women to get actively involved in charity work, such as visiting slums and grassroots-level work as she was quite opposed to passive charity. And as a first step, she urged men to support female education.

Active in the formation of the Bombay Presidency Women's Council in 1919, and was on the executive committee of the National Council of Indian Women (NCIW) founded in 1923. The objective of the Councils was to improve the status of underprivileged women and children through education and vocational skills : aware that social customs were a hindrance to women's emancipation. After NCIW several Women's councils emerged in different parts of India with similar agendas and goals. The NCIW founded in 1923 became the parent body for the affiliate State Councils, with a shared goal to facilitate knowledge sharing and unity in intent.

Through her networks, Lady Tata influenced women to play active roles in the prevailing social issues, advocating for women's rights and voicing her opinion on purdah. The International Women Suffrage News in London reported in 1921, that 'A big public meeting in favour of women suffrage was held in the Wilson College Hall, Bombay, under the Presidency of Lady Tata, and a resolution calling on the Legislative Council to enfranchise the women of Bombay was passed and sent to every member of the Legislative Council. We rejoice in this second big victory for Indian women.'

During the economic crisis in the 1920s, TISCO was struggling to pay outstanding salaries to the employees. Sir Dorab Tata pledged the family wealth of over 1 crore to Imperial Bank, which included a 245-carat Jubilee Diamond, he had gifted his wife. The diamond was part of Lady Tata's collection, bigger than the Kohinoor Diamond. She did not think twice before giving it away to raise funds for employee salaries. According to the Tata Group, they sold the Jubilee diamond after the death of Sir Dorabji Tata towards the creation of Sir Dorabji Tata Trust.

An opponent of the caste system and child marriage, she played an important part in the deliberations to outlaw child marriage. The Child Marriage Restraint Act was a milestone act later passed in 1929 that fixed the marriageable age for girls at fourteen years and eighteen years for boys. In 1930 she demanded equal political status for women at the All India Women's Conference.

Lady Meherbai was 50 when diagnosed with leukemia and died in Ruthin, North Wales, on 18 June 1931. Buried at Brookwood Cemetery, Woking, England alongside her husband, Sir Dorabji Tata who died exactly a year later on 3 June 1932 in Germany. Shortly after her death, Sir Dorabji Tata established the Lady Tata Memorial Trust to help advance the study of cancer. Tata Memorial Hospital was established in her honour, in 1941. This is India's first and the leading hospital to treat cancer. Lady Meherbai Tata was the first Indian woman to play the mixed doubles in the Paris Olympics of 1924.

Kamala Satthianadhan

Padmini Lilian
Sengupta

Kamalini Sengupta
Kumar

Begum Rokeya

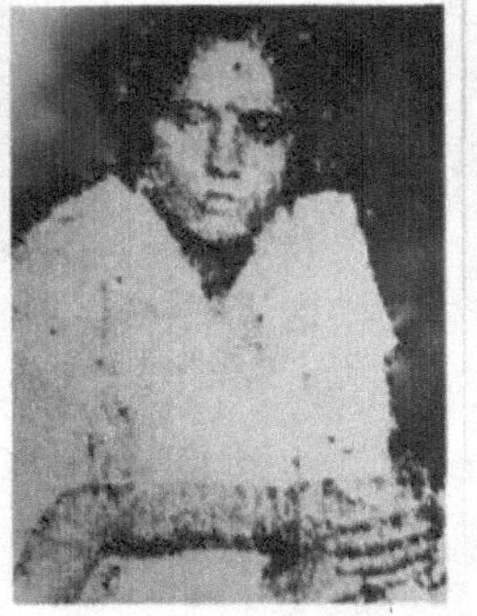

Bhogeswari Phukanani

R. S. Subbalakshmi

Dr. Muthulakshmi
Reddy

Rajkumari Amrit Kaur

Perin Captain

CHAPTER NINETEEN
THE CATALYST

Satthianadhan's achievement and contribution to education and writing in India are commendable. Three generations of powerful women writers believed India was destined for greatness. Kamala Satthianadhan was born Hannah Rathnam Krishnamma in 1879, a Telugu Christian and the first female graduate in South India, an educator, writer, and editor of the Indian Ladies' Magazine.

Hannah lost her mother at an early age after which her father OSR Krishnama who was a barrister in Masulipatnam, Andhra Pradesh remarried. He ensured both his daughters received an excellent education and would say, 'I will never deny economic independence to my daughters. It will give them the security which the women of our country badly need.' An intelligent girl and very focused, Hannah's only goal in life was education. She completed her graduation from Masulipatnam's Noble College and even before completing her master's in 1901, Hannah was already an established writer and the first woman English novelist in south India.

A family friend introduced her father to Reverend WT Satthianadhan who was a well-known missionary of Madras and his son Samuel Satthianadhan was being groomed to take over from his father. Samuel had graduated with an LLD (Dr. of Law) from Oxford University. On his return to India, they appointed him the Professor of Logic and Moral Philosophy at the Presidency College, Madras. In 1894 Samuel had lost his wife Krupabai, who is credited with being one of the first Indian women to write in English and is known for her book, Kamala: A Story of Hindu Life. An aspiring doctor, she died as her tuberculosis, diagnosed in Bombay, was certified beyond cure.

The Satthianadhan family was active in the literary sphere. Hannah was 20 years younger than Samuel and was one of his students at the Presidency College. He was not very keen to marry but the couple finally got married in 1898 and moved to Madras. Hannah and Samuel wrote and published a book, Stories on Indian Christian Life in 1899, contributing six stories each, chiefly comprising religious parables. Hannah's pseudonym was Kamala and the central character in Krupabai's book was also called Kamala and that's how Hannah came to be known as Kamala!

The couple's son Bill was born in 1900 and a year later, their daughter Padmini. Kamala looked after her home, gardening, tending to Irish linen, and fine cutlery in the house. She also learned horse riding, played tennis, and learned to drive cars. Hannah completed her master's degree in 1901, the first woman in South India to do so. Samuel understood Hannah's potential and encouraged her to bring out a magazine for women. And in 1901 established, the Indian Ladies Magazine, India's first women's magazine in English, was edited and published by a woman in the south of India. The intention was to record and write about reforms relating to women's rights through print and to a larger audience. In the early 1900s periodicals and magazines, written for and by women were one of the earliest channels for women to interact in public as both a contributor and a reader. Encouraging writers to contribute to the magazine and enlighten other women on their collective responsibility for the nation as well as political activism.

The magazine had a fairly large readership of English-educated judicious readers. Women who wished to better their condition, required an honest and hands-on journal to advocate their achievements. Kamala edited the magazine first with her husband, from 1901 until 1906 when Samuel died. She continued to publish the magazine after his death and between 1901 and 1918 the magazine was published monthly and between 1927 and 1938 it was bi-monthly.

Kamala was not an active politician, but her friend Sarojini Naidu, was and Naidu contributed to the Indian Ladies Magazine. Including the writer and educator Begum Rokeya, lawyer and writer Cornelia Sorabji, and politician and Theosophist Annie Besant. The feminist and educator Pandita Ramabai, Satthianadhan's niece, missionary, and teacher Mona Hensman and Margaret Cousins also wrote columns for the magazine. The magazine had short stories, columns by political activists, and pictures of sari-clad women playing tennis while holding on to their babies. There were cartoons from 'drumsticus,' a pseudo-name for probably someone known to Kamala.

Her editorial, called Friendly Chats, highlighted issues concerning women and their status in society. There were articles on fashion, needlework, cookery, a detective series, science, skits, and fiction. Profiles of woman achievers were included in the magazine, for aspirational readers to connect with their narratives. She also published poems by Carlyle, Ruskin, Keats, Shelley, and Wilcox. There were articles explaining Aurora Borealis on one end and articles on how to maintain silverware on the other side. She also published the English translation of Sultana's Dream, India's first science fiction written by a woman, Roqaiya Begum, in 1905. She wrote skits and published series, like Detective Janaki, Bibi a Muslim Girl, and Surya Rao's Ordeal.

In 1905, Kamala gave birth to a still-born baby Katie, and the following year, her husband Samuel Satthianadhan died during a voyage to Japan. Samuel had deposited the entire family's savings in Arbuthnot Bank of Madras, which crashed in the last quarter of 1906. The worst financial crisis hit the city of Madras. Of the three best-known British commercial banks in the 19th century, one crashed, a second had to be resurrected by a distress sale and the third had to be bailed out by a benevolent benefactor. This completely wiped out the savings of many generations.

Kamala was left with no money or savings, a young widow, with two small children and penniless, but she was a resolute woman. A young widow, she had to support her children financially and emotionally when most widows were struggling because of their class and religion. Five years after the death of her husband, Kamala accepted the post of a tutor to Rani Chinnamamba Devi of Pithapuram, a town in the Kakinada district, Andhra Pradesh. Kamala then travelled with her two young children and spent 6 years there, teaching English to the young Rani. As well as her children Bill and Padmini. She continued to publish the Indian Ladies Magazine, editing it from Pithapuram. The London Times wrote in their magazine that 'ILM was one of the best Indian women's magazines.'

In, The Portrait of an Indian Woman, published in 1951 by her daughter Padmini who mentions, ''The mofussil town in which my brother and I spent a number of years of our childhood with Kamala, our mother, was in reality no better than a poverty-stricken village. From the midst of its decrepit mud-walled huts and evil-smelling drains, however, rose the five-storeyed white palace of a Raja. The opulent edifice springing out of a chaos of squalor and dust always resembled to my childish eyes the delicate tiers of a wedding cake. The palace was protected by a high mud wall, known as the fort. The only entrance leading into this large circular structure was an imposing gate with turrets on either side, in the dark arches of which elephants stood, forever swaying their heavy bodies and twitching their large ears. It was inside this fort, cut off from the outer world, so to speak, that we stayed for six years.'

The Rani later told Padmini, that Kamala, 'showed me that there was a world outside the palace and a duty for us women to perform from our homes even though we keep our purdah.' Kamala taught the young Rani, English and Sanskrit literature, and matters of the public world. Later Chinnamamba Devi's husband, the Raja, who was an authoritarian, expelled Kamala from the palace when Padmini developed a rash. Despite Kamala protesting against the eviction, they were asked to leave. In her last moments of life, Chinnamamba Devi wished to see Kamala, but the Raja refused to let her.

Kamala was jobless now and went back to Madras with her children. In Madras, she continued publishing her magazine and teaching children. She decided to sail to England with her children, for their education. She started saving money for her voyage and sold her home. In 1918, with whatever little saving she had accumulated, she sailed away to England! Since she had little money to manage her day-to-day expenses, she took in paying guests and cared for the Indian students who lived in England. She became a member of the Royal Asiatic Society and was inducted into the Committees of YWCA and the Indian Students' Hostel. When her son Bill passed his ICS, the family set sail back to India in 1923. On her return to India, she became active in the Indian independence movement.

In 1924 Mrs. E.S. Appasamy, a visionary in the field of all-around education for girls started Vidyodaya, with 6 students, in a tiny bungalow, three resident pupils, and three Day Scholars. She invited Kamala to be the first principal of the new school. By the end of 1925, the school had grown with a few more students. After a short stint of a year in Vidyodaya, Kamala joined her son Bill in Tanjore, where he was the Assistant Collector and from there on, she travelled with him wherever he got transferred. She then wrote the book, Lives of Great Men and Great Women of India. She also wrote a series entitled, My impressions of England, in The Hindu newspaper for a year.

In 1927, Kamala re-started The Indian Ladies Magazine. This time around, there was a greater focus on politics along with regular editorial features supporting early feminist movements in India. Her daughter was now the assistant editor for the magazine. Padmini, in her mother's biography, The Portrait of an Indian Women, mentions that Kamala published three novels, including one titled Detective Janaki, about a young female detective. The book has a foreword by Sarvepalli Radhakrishnan, a distinguished professor of philosophy, and then Vice-President of India. Padmini's biography of her mother highlights the dynamic friendships between Indian and British women in the educational and reformist spheres.

The Indian Ladies Magazine shut down in 1938. Sarojini Naidu mentioned to Padmini Sengupta, 'The Magazine was once one of the most important publications in the country. It was needed to awake the women of India, to right their wrongs, and announce the clarion call of reformers; but it is needed no longer now. The women of the country think they know everything. They do not wish to be taught any longer. I am glad Kamala stopped the Magazine when she did.'

Kamala Satthianadhan died in 1950, on India's Republic Day, her contribution to women's groups, and social service organizations are noteworthy. She is a profound example, both in her writing and in her life. With diverse interests, Kamala formed the Women's Cooperative Societies in Anantpur and Madras. She also helped in establishing a child care facility at Tirunelveli aimed at providing care for pregnant women and children. She established nine co-operative societies for women in Andhra Pradesh and the Madras Presidency, to help women become financially independent. Kamala worked with Red Cross and YMCA and supported anti-discrimination measures aimed at the caste hierarchy. She was a Senate member of Madras University and Andhra University.

Dr. S. Radhakrishnan wrote 'After Dr. Samuel Satthianadhan died in 1906, an Endowment created by her in the Madras University in his name and the income from that was utilized to award a gold medal to the candidate who obtains the highest mark in Ethics in the BA degree examination. I was the first recipient of that medal. It would be a mistake to think that her activities were limited to her own family. In a quiet way, by running an ideal home and by editing a Ladies Magazine, she prepared for the emancipation of women, which is the most significant feature of our time.'

CHAPTER TWENTY
THE AUTHOR

Padmini Lilian Sengupta was born on 26 March 1906, in Madras. Her parents Samuel and Hannah (Kamala) Satthianadhan were both intellectually oriented and believed in social reforms. A creative thinker like her mother, she authored and published thirty-five books. Many of her works are non-fictional as well as biographical in nature and delve into histories of Indian women's education, formal and informal.

Her works which were written after Indian Independence provides for the evolution of the multidisciplinary study of the societal contributions of women. Her works have been translated into over five languages.

In 1938 Padmini married the famous trade unionist Sen Gupta, Ranendra Mohan Sen Gupta, who specialized in labour matters and worked at the Bengal Chamber of Commerce. Their daughter, Kamalini, was born in 1942. In Padmini's biography of her mother, The Portrait of an Indian Woman, published in 1951, she honours her mother Kamala Satthianadhan's social and literary works. She later wrote a Biography on Sarojini Naidu, titled A Biography, which was published in 1966. She mentions in the book, that despite Sarojini Naidu being home schooled, she went on to get a First Class in the matriculation exams. 'Her success was all the more surprising as the examination in 1891 was by no means easy. Neither were girls accustomed to attending school in the higher classes. Sarojini's syllabus consisted of English, a second language, Science, Mathematics, History, and Geography. Some of the questions were of the B.A. standard of today.'

Commissioned by the Pandita Ramabai Centenary Committee, Padmini published a book in 1970 on the life of Pandita Ramabai Saraswati titled, Her Life and Works. In the book, Padmini said, 'it is not easy to present the life of a saint to the public.' An important book of hers titled 'Everyday Life in Ancient India' has 36 editions and was published between 1950 and 1957, and Women Workers of India, has 17 editions published in 1960.

Padmini reviewed the position of women in Indian society through different eras in history in book, The Story of Women of India, published in 1974. She states that every era has produced extraordinary women scholars, poets, and administrators and with their talent contributed to the nation. While there are known women, countless unknown women have influenced their families to navigate the nation's destiny. Through various references to mythology and mythical figures, Padmini justified the position of women in ancient India as honourable and independent and that of a wife who shared an equal status. Only much later and gradually there was a decline in the position of women in society. In most of Padmini's writings, she delved into the history of Indian women's education. Highlighting regional and national associations and the importance of women's networks and friendships between activists in India and Britain.

Red Hibiscus is her only novel which she published in 1962. In the novel, she writes of the riots between different communities in Bengal from 1946 onwards and the demand for Pakistan, a separate homeland for Muslims.

Later in her life, Padmini wrote a history of the Indian Y.W.C.A. She writes that she arrived in Calcutta to edit the magazine called India Monthly Magazine, funded by the industrial house, Mahindra and Mahindra, 'I lived a very happy life in Gallway House and was thankful for its shelter and hospitality. I lived in the Hostel until the end of 1936 when I returned to my home in South India. Often, during my stay in the Hostel with my mother, Mrs. Kamala Satthianadhan, would come and stay with me.'

Padmini Sengupta died at 81 on 5 March 1988, in Calcutta. Her grandson Dev Khare says, 'My grandmother was very close to my great-grandmother. She was a decisive, matter-of-fact person. She was action-oriented and a socially active woman in the community. Did a lot of charity work, extremely idealistic about India, an inclusive person who took many people along with her.' He further mentions in our conversation, 'My grandmother was part of a family whose older members fought for India's independence and she passed on this belief in a strong India where everybody deserved to succeed, no matter what religion or socio-economic background people came from.'

CHAPTER TWENTY ONE
THE BANYAN TREE

Kamalini Sen Gupta Kumar, also Known As "Lini" was born on 13 June 1942, in Krishnanagar, Bengal. Her mother Padmini Sengupta and grandmother Kamala Satthianadhan were both authors, so it was not surprising that Kamalini followed. A writer, documentary film-maker, and freelance journalist and editor, Kamalini studied at the London School of Journalism. She freelanced for newspapers and magazines published in India, the UK, and Hong Kong. As the head of The Surya Trust, an organisation which focused on education, she filmed documentaries that aimed to correct misconceptions about Indian life. Kamalini was a member of the Indian Administrative Service.

Dev Khare mentions, 'My mother was selected to the Indian Administrative Service after her graduation and a couple of other jobs, in 1965. My father, Santosh Kumar, worked with the Indian Foreign Service, in 1971. They lived long periods in Hong Kong, China. I was born in Beijing, and my brother Dushyant was born in Brussels. The Government also posted my parents in Pakistan, Germany, Yemen, Korea, and South Africa.'

'My mother's first novel was The Top of the Raintree, published, in December 2006 and she wrote and published another book titled A Seasoned Couple.' The Top of the Raintree (Rajmahal) is an exploration of post-colonial Indian life through 'engagingly embroidered stories that leave us replete and delighted,' reported, The Sunday Tribune, India. In this beautifully crafted tale, the intertwined fortunes and personal battles of the characters become a mirror of the country's struggle for possession of its future. 'The encompassing achievement of the novel is its penetration of the life of the post-colonialist and post-colonized living on, somehow together,' mentioned Nadine Gordimer, winner of the Nobel Prize in Literature.

Kamalini was creating a series called the Banyan Tree, to highlight language and migration issues. However, she could not complete the series due to a lack of funding. Through the series, she wished to increase awareness about the diversity of cultures in India. The Banyan Tree project was to be a twenty-part series and would have served as an educational tool in India. Kamalini Sengupta hoped that the Banyan Tree documentary series would give vital information about India and counter widely held misconceptions based on mindsets.

The first episode 'In the Beginning', traced the emergence of humans and introduced the historical evolution of the cultures, traditions, and religions in India. The series did not challenge theories but sought to present various views, encouraging the people to delve deeper into the subject. 'It was the riots between communities in India in the 1990s that inspired me to undertake this series so that we can begin to understand each other better,' Sengupta told IANS. 'I discovered we don't have proper information about the country. It is educationally essential for us to know these things.'

She also presented a collection of papers titled, Endangered Languages in India, at an international seminar organized by INTACH. The publication aimed to spread awareness of the existence and dangers of the loss of endangered languages and to determine a place for minority and regional languages in education and society. Further, it recommended viable solutions for a future course as well. Kamalini Sengupta died in 2011 when she was 69. Her son Dev Khare mentions in our conversations, 'When I got married, my mother invited a friend from each religion to read a page from their holy book, such was her belief in equality.' Sengupta had planned, researched, and written the script of the Banyan Tree series and worked hard to put it together as a film. We hope a film-maker completes the remaining episodes in time to come.

CHAPTER TWENTY-TWO
THE EMPOWERED WRITER

During the Mughal regime, her family served in the military and judiciary. Roquia Khatun was born on 9 December 1880 in Pairaband, Rangpur, Bengal. She was later known as Begum Rokeya and RS Hossain in literary circles and was an educationist and social reformer. Her father, Jahiruddin Muhammad Abu Ali Haidar Saber, was a multi-lingual intellectual zamindar, and her mother, Rahatunnessa, a home-maker.

Rokeya's eldest brother, Ibrahim Saber, and her elder sister, Karimunnesa, would secretly teach the young Rokuia Bengali and both of them had a considerable influence on her. While her brother Ibrahim studied at St. Xavier's College in Calcutta and later went to England for higher studies, Rokeya along with her sisters were not allowed to attend school. Her father considered Urdu as the language of royal Muslims, and he hoped they study Arabic and Persian. The family expected them to learn the skill of reading the Quran and be an ideal wife and mother. After Ibrahim returned from England, he took it on himself to teach Rokeya and Karimunnesa English, secretly of course!

Rokeya was married in 1898, at eighteen, to Khan Bahadur Sakhawat Hossain whose first wife had died. He was twenty years older than Rokeya. A deputy magistrate of Bhagalpur, Bihar, he had a degree from England and was a member of the Royal Agriculture Society of England. A progressive and liberal thinker, he encouraged Rokeya to continue her studies. Encouraging her to write and on his advice, she adopted Bengali as the principal language for her literary works. Sakhawat Hossain earnestly supported his wife's literary activities and even after he died, he ensured he put aside a large amount of money for Begum Rokeya to start a school for girls.

Rokeya began her literary career when she was twenty-two, with a Bengali essay titled Pipasa and soon she started writing in a progressive paper Nabanoor and other literary magazines and journals under the name of Mrs. R S Hossain. She also wrote in Satthianadhan's Indian Ladies Magazine. Writing on an expansive range of subjects, through her poems, short stories, essays, novels as well as satirical writings, she highlighted social repression and prejudice. Advocating women's rights, the effect on the lives of Muslim women because of purdah, and why women's education was paramount. She also wrote against child marriages and patriarchy. Rokeya had a particular literary style, where she expressed herself through imagination, logic, and dry humour. Her writings are categorized as influential satire.

Her book Matichur (A String of Sweet Pearls) was published in 1904 and 1922. This was a collection of essays in two volumes expressing her feminist thoughts and why women's education was integral to defeat not only patriarchy but also the imperialists, racism, and fanaticism.

In a feminist science fiction titled, Sultana's Dream, Rokeya writes about reversing the roles of men and women, in which women were dominant and the men were subordinate. Originally published in the Indian Ladies' Magazine, Madras, in 1905 she writes, 'How do you cook?' I asked. 'With solar heat,' she said, at the same time showing me the pipe, through which passed the concentrated sunlight and heat. And she cooked something then and there to show me the process. 'How did you manage to gather and store up the sun-heat?' I asked her in amazement. 'Let me tell you a little of our history then. Thirty years ago, when our present Queen was thirteen years old, she inherited the throne. She was Queen in name only, the Prime Minister really ruling the country. 'Our good Queen liked science very much. She circulated an order that all the women in her country should be educated. Accordingly, many girls' schools were founded and supported by the government. Education was spread far and wide among women. And early marriage also stopped. No woman was to be allowed to marry before she was twenty-one. I must tell you that, before this change, we had been kept in strict purdah.'

Through her writings, Rokeya highlights the oppression of Muslim women. In particular, their rights, the patriarchal traditions, and why education was central to women's liberation and the lack of it was responsible for the social position of women.

Her later work, Padmarag (Essence of the Lotus,) written in 1924, depicts the difficulties faced by Bengali wives. In the book, she conveys to the women to form associations for protecting women. In 1931, she published Abarodhbasini-The Confined Women, which was an attack on the extreme forms of purdah that were detrimental to women's lives and self-image. She writes, 'the system reminds me of the lethal carbonic acid gas, which is a painless killer, its victims are never alert to its hazards. Women kept confined to the home die a slow death by the effect of this fatal gas known as purdah.' Rokeya was not against Islam but questioned the archaic and out-of-date tradition that suppressed women only to limit their future and rights.

Begum Rokeya promoted women's education through the language she used in her works. She spoke in public, vocally opposing the practices, particularly among the voiceless Muslim women of her time. Her criticism of issues related to Muslim women ruffled many men, but that did not stop her from her calling, which was to establish the rights of Muslim women. She urged women to be independent and reached out through her writings to the men, to encourage the women to work outside of their homes. This was way back in the early 1900s when the world was conservative and critical of campaigners for women's rights. She continued writing and pressing for a dignified position for Muslim women.

Five months after her husband's death in 1909, Begum Rokeya established the first high school for Muslim girls in Bhagalpur, a traditionally Urdu-speaking area. It is said that she went from house to house, persuading parents to send their daughters to her school, and started with only five students. Later, a dispute with her husband's family over property matters forced Rokeya to move the school in 1911 to Calcutta. Despite the criticism and many obstacles, she ran the school for 24 years till she died in 1932.

In 1916, Begum Rokeya founded the Anjuman-e-Khawateen-e-Islam (Islamic Women's Association), an organization focused on women's education and also their employees. She actively held debates and conferences focussing on the status of women and education.

With a distinctive logical literary style and a satirical sense of humour, Rokeya urged women to break the social barriers and protest injustice that discriminate against them. She was a firm believer that extreme orthodoxy was the reason for the relatively slow development of Muslim women. Her politics was a politics of gender and gender injustice.

Over 100 years ago, Begum Rokeya depicted an alternative feminist vision of science, in which inventions like solar ovens, cloud condensers, and flying cars were used to benefit society. Shortly after presiding over a session during an Indian Women's Conference, she died on her birthday on 9 December 1932. Bangladesh celebrates her birthday as 'Rokeya Day' to commemorate her work and legacy. In 2004, Begum Rokeya was ranked number 6 in BBC's poll of Greatest Bengali of all times. Google celebrated her 137 birthday on 9 December 2017, with a google doodle.

CHAPTER TWENTY-THREE
THE FLAG BEARER

The women of Nowgong, Assam were actively engaged in the freedom struggle. Like other parts of Assam, they faced terrible police cruelty and at times had to stay in the deep jungle, during the night for fear of police brutality. Many joined the women's force or Nari Bahini of which one of the prominent nationalist member was Bhogeswari Phukanani. Born in 1885 in Barhampur, Nowgong, Assam, she was married at a young age to Bhogeswar Phuket. They had eight children. An earnest crusader she even encouraged her children to take part in protests and in the freedom movement! She was arrested in 1930 for picketing, however that did not deter the passionate nationalist.

During the Quit India movement, in September 1942, the Barhampur office of the Indian National Congress (INC) was seized by the British. A successful attempt was made to reopen the Congress office and locals from nearby villages came out with National flags to celebrate. The British came to know of this and sent their forces to close the Congress office.

Bhogeswari Phukanani along with another nationalist, Ratanmala, joined the celebrations and led a group of women toward the Congress office. Soon they were confronted by Captain Finch, who snatched the flag from Ratanmala's hand. Caught off balance, Ratanmala fell. Angry at the disrespect shown to the national flag Bhogeswari snatched the flag from Finch and hit his head with the flagpole. Enraged, Finch pulled out his revolver and fired at Bhogeswari Phukanani, while she was trying to save the national flag from being dishonoured. She succumbed to her injuries two days later, on September 20, 1942. In her memory, the Civil Hospital in Nagaon is named Bhogeswari Phukanani Civil Hospital and a stadium in Assam is named after the remarkable freedom fighter, it's called the Bhogeswari Phukanani Indoor Stadium. However very little is documented on Bhogeswari Phukanani the ardent flag bearer of Nowgong. The nationalist women of Assam and particularly Nowgong played a critical role in the freedom struggle. They sacrificed their lives for the country and their courage is noteworthy and to be recognised.

CHAPTER TWENTY-FOUR
SISTER

At five, when girls were not allowed to go out to study, Subbalakshmi was enrolled in a primary school in Madras. Born in 1886, her mother Visalakshmi was a homemaker and her father R.V Subramania Iyer was an agriculturist scientist, and teacher. As per custom very reluctantly they had to get Subhalakshmi married when she was eleven, though she was widowed shortly after her marriage. Her father was a very progressive man and despite all the criticism, he did not follow any customary ritual of tonsuring his daughter's head or even allowing her to wear a white sari.

He was determined to educate his daughter and was equally supported by his wife and his sister Chitti, who was a young widow. Subbalakshmi continued with her education despite her grandmother opposing a young widow from going out of the house unchaperoned. Which was soon resolved as the family moved to a house opposite the school.

Subbalakshmi completed her high school at the Presidency Convent, Madras, and stood first in the entire Madras Presidency. Winning two gold medals at the end of the second year. For her graduation, she enrolled at the Presidency College, where again she passed her bachelor's in Botany with a first class. She also happened to be the first Hindu woman and a child widow, to have ever graduated from the entire Madras Presidency in 1911. It is said that she would see other girls put up with jeers from the male students and their anger worsened in May 1911, when the national daily newspapers reported that a young widow, Subbalakshmi, stood first in the BA examinations, eclipsing all the boys in her year!

After this accomplishment, Subbalakshmi received several job offers from the region. However, she was determined to work for the widows in her city. The thought and idea to open institutes for girls and widows and empower young widows to be independent and self-sufficient came to Subbalakshmi when she was studying in school. She first took up a teaching post at the Presidency Teaching School, and simultaneously studied for the Licentiate in Teaching. From there on Subbalakshmi went on to launch several institutions, in the Madras Presidency region, Cuddalore, and Madhuranthakam. The important institutes she was instrumental in setting up, were the Sarada Illam (Widows Home,) Queen Mary's College, Lady Willingdon Training School, Kuppam School, Sarada Cheri School in Cuddalore, Sarada Vidyalaya, Sri Vidya Kalanilayam, Mylapore Ladies Club which subsequently became Vidya Mandir, Mylapore. The woman addressed her as Akka (elder sister) and she came to be known as Sister Subbalakshmi. She would set up the schools and institutes and graciously hand over the running of institutions without attaching her name to the institution.

After the War, the Government restricted scholarships for widows, and only widows under fifteen years were admitted to the hostel. However, there were older widows and girls whose husbands had deserted them. Sarada Illam (Widows Home) was opened to rehabilitate and educate the widows, with the intent to nurture these women to be self-sufficient and stay relevant in society. In 1917 the first batch of trained girls from the Sarada Illam joined Queen Mary's College. Many passed out with degrees to become lecturers, headmistresses, and inspectors of girls' schools. A few even became doctors and auditors. Over the next two decades, Sister Subbalakshmi's Sarada Illam expanded and so did her voluntary commitment to women. Later she started the Kuppam School in 1920 for the children of fishermen families. She opened the Lady Willingdon Training College and Practice School, in 1922, and was the first Principal. It was an institution for teacher training. The college offered post-graduate training for potential high school teachers, secondary training for teaching through the eighth grade, and training for elementary teachers.

Wherever Subbalakshmi was posted she would take the initiative to start schools, for the local communities and once the school or institution was running she would hand them over to a local organization to run them. Attempts by politicians to smear her work as narrow-minded and that the Government was developing Brahmin organizations resulted in a reduction in financial grants to the institutions she started. Subbalakshmi however did not exclude any woman on caste alone.

When the Women's Indian Association and the All-India Women's Conference began their campaigns in support of the Child Marriage Restraint Bill, she spoke against the custom before the Joshi Committee. The Act, was later passed in 1929. While she was in Government service, she was not permitted to join the Women's Indian Association though did everything in her capacity to create awareness for women's rights. She travelled widely on lecture tours and as a Member of the Madras Legislative Council from 1952 to 1966, voiced her opinion on issues that were related to both social reforms and education. She appealed for a less academic and more realistic approach to education. Sister Subbalakshmi was honoured with the Kaisari-Hind Gold Medal for public service in 1920, and in 1958 the Padma Shri. She was not interested in personal attention and continued to shelter and educate widows, several of whom went on to become leaders in diverse fields and join the mainstream. She opened institutions which are relevant even today and impart excellent education. Sister Subbalakshmi died on 20 December 1969. By now widows did not need special homes. Those whom she had educated had become teachers, nurses, and doctors and carried forward her vision.

CHAPTER TWENTY-FIVE
FIRST EVER

Muthulakshmi was born on 30 July 1886. Her mother Chandrammal was a former devadasi and her father Narayanaswamy, was the principal of Maharaja's College in the small princely state of Pudukkottai, Tamil Nadu. Homeschooled and brilliant she refused to get married as she wanted to pursue her studies. This was a bit shocking to the orthodox community, however, with her parents' support she passed her matriculation exam as a private student and applied to the Maharaja's College, which of course denied her admission despite her excellent academic record. Protests escalated among the Hindu conformists. The parents of the boys studying in the college angrily protested and even threatened to withdraw their children from college. However, Martanda Bhairava Thondaman, the Raja of Pudukkottai was an evolved ruler and intervened and Muthulakshmi was very resentfully accepted by the college. Becoming the first woman to be admitted to a men's college in Pudukottai!

The local Pudukottai gazette reported, 'It must be said to the credit of the vision and independence of the Martanda Bhairava Thondaman that he overruled all objections and permitted Muthulakshmi admission.' The Durbar Records of Pudukaottai has evidence of her application dated 4 February 1904, for fine arts and it reads, 'éager to commence the collegiate course.'

She then went onto study medicine at the Madras Medical College again the first and only woman to be admitted to a Medical College and of course later the first woman House Surgeon in the Government Maternity and Ophthalmic Hospital, Madras! Muthulakshmi married Dr. Sundara Reddy in 1914. Her conditions for marriage were 'equal respect for each other and to allow her to work independently,' to which he agreed.

The Women Indian Association which she had established along with Annie Besant and others, in 1917, sent a list of leading women social workers, to the Government of India to be nominated as a Member of the Madras Legislative Council which included the name of Muthulakshmi Reddy. Though initially hesitant to accept the membership since it would impact her medical profession, she understood there were pressing issues related to women's rights and children, and she agreed. She was elected as the Vice-President of the Madras Legislative Council in 1927 again making her the first Indian woman member of a Legislative Council in Madras. In her capacity as a legislator, Muthulakshmi advocated the Child Marriage Restraint Act which came into effect in 1929. As well as she pushed the Council to pass the crucial Immoral Traffic Control Act and urged the government to abolish the devadasi system. She believed that 'laws and legislation are there only for sanction, it is up to us women to energize these and implement them into action.' She lobbied for reservation of seats for women in districts, municipalities, local boards and the police force.

In her book, My Experience as Legislator, published in 1930, she accounts the conflicts of being the only woman legislator in a council full of men. She writes, 'In presenting this book to the public, I have two objects in view. The first one is to show to such of my sisters and others who still hold the view that women are created only for the home and men for the state, how women's activity could be profitably extended from the home to the city and how in the administration of the state as in the management of a household, women could co-operate with their men in promoting the well-being of that large family, the nation.'

In 1930 she resigned from the Council to protest the arrest of Gandhi but continued with her political and social activities. The following letter was addressed to Muthulakshmi Reddy on 13 May 1930 by the People of India when she resigned as the Deputy President of the Legislative Council, 'in resigning to help India's Struggle for freedom, you have conveyed a wireless noble message to every man and woman in the Legislatures in British India at the critical stage to do likewise. The people of India send their warmest congratulations for pointing the way to members of the existing Legislatures.' And in a farewell address, the Legislatures and Citizens of Madras stated, 'You had to cut a pioneer's path. Your task was not an easy one. You had no precedents to follow. You created instead an independent path, a precedent for other women legislators, as the champion of many causes, needs, and rights of women and children of all communities.'

Muthulakshmi was aware that despite abolishing the devadasi system, bias against the devadasi women would continue. In 1930, there were only two hostels in Madras to shelter Hindu girls, one for Brahmin and the other for non-Brahmin women. While she was arguing the bill for the abolition of the devadasi system, three young girls who did not want be dedicated to the temples, reached her home as their relatives did not want them back. Since Muthulakshmi was a medical officer of these two hostels, she sent them there. However, they were abused at the hostel and returned the same night to Muthulakshmi's home. She then realized she needed to support the helpless young girls. She opened a home for them and called it the Avvai Home, it continues to function. The three girls she had invited to her home went on to become a teacher, a doctor, and a nurse. Initially started as a home for the protection and education of the devadasi community, the Avvai Home later became a shelter for women, unwed mothers, widows, destitute orphans, and children.

In 1925 she went to England, on a government scholarship for her postgraduate study on the diseases of women and children. As a young medical graduate, Muthulakshmi had witnessed the premature death of her sister due to misdiagnosed case of rectal cancer. There were no facilities for the treatment of cancer at that time. Hence she decided to establish a cancer hospital for anyone who needed treatment without caring about their social or economic background. When she approached the Government for land, they wanted to know why there was a need for a cancer hospital, since cancer was incurable. In 1954, after several hindrances, the Cancer Institute, the first in South India at the time, was born. It was also the second specialized cancer centre in India. Called the Adyar Cancer Institute it has a research division, along with the Dr. Muthulakshmi College of Oncologic Sciences. In April 1966, The Hindu wrote, 'In the history of women's movement in India, in the struggle for women's rights and in the campaign for the eradication of some of the social evils of which women had been victims, Dr. Reddy's name will find honourable mention.'

Awarded the Padma Bhushan in 1956, Dr Muthulakshmi Reddy died on 22 July 1968 at the age of 81. On the occasion of Dr. Reddy's birth anniversary Google described her as "Constantly breaking barriers throughout her life, Reddi was a trailblazer, who devoted herself to public health and the battle against gender inequality, transforming the lives of countless people, especially young girls." The Tamil Nadu government celebrates, Dr Reddy's birthday as 'Hospital Day.'

CHAPTER TWENTY-SIX
THE VISIONARY PRINCESS

The first Health Minister of the country and the far-sighted princess behind the foundation of All India Institute of Medical Sceinces (AIIMS.) The New York Times befittingly called her, a princess in her nation's service! Rajkumari Amrit Kaur was born on 2 February 1887 in Badshah Bagh, Lucknow. Her father Raja Sir Harnam Singh Ahluwalia was a member of the Kapurthala royal family and was on the Legislative Council of Punjab. He had converted to Christianity, renouncing his right to the Kapurthala succession after marrying Rani Priscilla Kaur Sahiba, the daughter of a Bengali Presbyterian convert. Amrit Kaur studied at Sherborne School, North Dorset, England, and returned to India after her undergraduate degree from Oxford University.

Her father was a nationalist and the young princess was inspired by his ideas about politics and the independence struggle. She supported her mother with social work and acted as unofficial secretary to both parents. However her decision to join the freedom movement came when she met Gopal Krishna Gokhle who was her father's close friend. A senior leader in INC, and a campaigner for self-rule and social reforms Gokhle had a considerable impact on Kaur with his ideals of patriotism. He was also a mentor to Gandhi in his early years. In a letter, she wrote, 'I tried to learn about Gandhiji from Mr. Gokhale and when Bapu came to India for good in the winter of 1915-1916. I had the privilege of meeting him at the session in Bombay and Lucknow. Later I met him in Jullundur after the Jallianwala Bagh disaster.' Though associated with the freedom movement and helping Gandhi, she continued supporting her parents' activities until they died in 1924 and 1930, and then she got actively involved in the freedom struggle and joined Gandhi.

When Gandhi marched to the coast of Dandi, in response to the salt laws imposed by the British, he encouraged his followers to defy the law and she followed! She was imprisoned for her participation. After this, Kaur became Gandhi's secretary for 16 years. Combining work on the ashram with other nationalist activities which included social reforms and resolutions put forward by the All India Woman's Conference (AIWC) which was founded in 1927 to improve women's education in the country. Many of the women who contributed to AIWC were women involved in the freedom struggle and politics. In 1928, Kaur along with Rameshwari Nehru founded the Delhi Women's League, the Delhi branch of AIWC which played a significant role in mobilising support for the Child Marriage Restraint ACT- Sarda Bill. A committee was formed to note down all child marriages that were being registered during that time and send circulars to parents warning them of the evils of child marriages. A significant achievement of their work was the passing of the Sarda Act in 1929. To get the Act passed in a span of roughly two years after the formation of AIWC and DWL, was commendable. Soon AIWC developed into an internationally discerning institution, working jointly with international associations on issues related to women's rights. Kaur also served as the Chairperson of the All India Women's Education Fund Association, which, amongst other things, set up and maintained the Lady Irwin College, a women's college founded in 1932. The college was set up under the Education Fund of the Conference.

In June 1933 Amrit Kaur visited London as part of the Indian women's delegation to highlight and address issues related to social and educational reforms in India. The Manchester Guardian described Kaur as, 'intensely interested in the welfare of women in India. A member of a noble Sikh family and a Christian. Having spent many years in England, she is well able to understand the points of view held here about the problem of India. A woman of distinguished appearance and of great intellectual ability, she produced a marked impression on the members of the Joint Select Committee when she pleaded the case for her countrywomen before them early this month.'

At the end of her visit, Rajkumari Amrit Kaur said, 'Before we left India people said what was the use of sending us to England since English people knew so little about India and did not care. It is a joy to be able to tell our organizations that there are some women here who do care about India and that we have their entire cooperation.' Upon her return to India, Kaur ensured cooperation with women's organizations the delegates had interacted with and later Kaur herself was elected as the President of AIWC.

At the annual meeting of the AIWC in December 1937, Kaur in her Presidential Address said, 'With what voice, can we raise a protest against the Italian conquest of Abyssinia or Japanese ruthless aggression in China if we cannot condemn the bombing of villages on the north-west Frontier or speak out against imperialistic designs where so ever they be? How can we deplore the civil war in Spain if we may not condemn those who stir up communal strife in our own country? Violence has brought mankind to the terrible state in which we see it today through 'selfishness, exploitation, oppression, imperialism, and cruelty.'

Kaur was a believer in 'one national language' in the country and concerned with the wide use of foreign languages she once remarked, 'It has been one of the many tragedies of foreign rule that the medium of instruction in our educational institutions has, except in its initial stages, been English. The result has been a lack of real knowledge of our own languages. Needless to say we cannot reach the large mass of our people through English and nor can we produce suitable literature for our women, if we have not more than a working knowledge of our languages…It needs encouragement on the part of all of us so that we may grow to our full stature.'

In 1942 Kaur resigned from her post as a member of the advisory board of All India Women's Education Fund Association to take part in the Quit India Movement. Very active during the movement, organising protests and in one of the several demonstrations that she led, she was severely lathi charged, imprisoned in Ambala, and later put under house arrest in Shimla.

Despite her being under house arrest, Kaur was nominated to represent India for an official delegation to UNESCO in November 1945. 'Culture and civilization stand today at the brink of disaster,' she declared at the Conference, 'still bent on the exploitation of weaker peoples, each country solicitous of his own freedom but indifferent to that of others. There can be no true freedom and consequently, no genuine culture in a world which is half bond and half free, half-fed and half-starved, where exploitation and social injustices flourish side by side with pious expressions of good intentions and high-sounding policies. Educational and cultural forces if directed in the right channels, save humanity. And a spirit of understanding and world fellowship must transcend the national interest: No longer must children be taught to think in terms only of the glory of their own country; they must think of their country as being no more than a unit in and dedicated to the service of the larger whole of a world state.'

She added, "No structure of society can be stable one that has not the roots deep in moral and spiritual values of life; our children must be educated to appreciate which is of permanent worth. Geographical barriers may have been conquered but oceans of hate and misunderstanding still divide us. If education is to play the part, it should play in the refashioning of the world it must itself be refashioned.'

After independence, Kaur built connections with international organizations such as the World Health Organisation and was the first woman who chaired the Indian Red Cross Society for fourteen years. Since her mother was Vice-President of the Young Women's Christian Association, the YWCA was an equally important network and later she became the President of the YWCA in India as well.

Kaur was amongst the 15 other women members in the Constituent Assembly and was part of the Sub Committee on Fundamental Rights and Minority Rights. She was also a member of the Finance and Staff Committee and Provincial Constitution Committee. She advocated for universal voting rights, protected religious rights, and also supported the Uniform Civil Code. Like many women members of the Constituent Assembly, she opposed women's reservation in the Lok Sabha. She said, 'In the matter of representation it was felt that if practical equality were secured for women in the domain of franchise, they would be able to find their way into the legislative and administrative institutions of the country through the open door of an ordinary election, and no special expedients such as reservation of seats, nomination, co-option or separate electorates would then be necessary.' She was optimistic that equality in the political domain would bring many more women into the assembly.

Gandhi wrote to her requesting her to become India's first Health Minister and she became the first woman Cabinet Minister of Independent India and held the portfolio of the Department of Health from 1947 to 1957. She piloted the All-India Institute of Medical Science (AIIMS) Bill in Lok Sabha on February 18, 1956. While speaking in Parliament, about the availability and convenience of health services for all, she said, 'I want this to be something wonderful, of which India can be proud, and I want India to be proud of it.' And the Bill was approved. Through her influence, she arranged funds and donations for equipment from different countries around the world to set up AIMS!

She requested full freedom for the institute and for those who would run it, she said, 'The future of the Institute will lie ultimately in the hands of the Director, the Professors, and other members of the teaching staff and students, and I believe it will be their devotion to duty, their desire to promote their work, and the spirit of altruism that will actuate them to subordinate personal considerations, as I believe the noble profession of medicine should do, to the fulfillment of the objectives to be achieved that will eventually create and maintain the atmosphere which is necessary for an institute like this.'

In 1956, Princeton awarded her an honorary degree of Doctor of Laws. From 1958 to 1963, Amrit Kaur was the President of the All Indian Motor Transport Congress in Delhi. An accomplished tennis player, she was also the President of the All India Lawn Tennis Association and the Table Tennis Federation of India.

In 1961, Kaur received the René Sand Award for Social Service, an international accolade that celebrated her long career in the imperial, national, and international public spheres. Named TIME Magazine's Woman of the Year in 1947, the magazine wrote, 'In leaving her life of luxury, Kaur not only helped build lasting democratic institutions, but she also inspired generations to fight for the marginalized.'

Amrit Kaur served as the first President of AIIMS and remained in that position until she died on 6 February 1964, at seventy-five. She chaired her last governing body meeting of AIIMS on 14 August 1963, where she donated her residence Manorville, in Shimla, to AIIMS as a holiday retreat and a rest home for its nurses and doctors. AIIMS was the first hospital in Asia to prohibit its medical practitioners from practicing in the private sector. It was expected of Doctors to spend their time treating patients, teaching students, and doing research. Kaur's contribution to the healthcare system continues to be significant even today.

Her private papers are part of the Archives at the Nehru Memorial Museum and Library in Delhi. After independence, India was struck with malaria. This affected seventy-five million Indians and killed eight lakh people. Kaur actively kept track of the execution of a strong anti-malaria public campaign. Because of her efforts, 400,000 deaths were prevented. This helped India enter the Eradication Era between the 1950s to the 1960s. New York Times obituary remembered her, 'At the height of the campaign, in 1955, it was estimated that 400,000 Indians who otherwise would have died had been saved by mitigation of malaria in their districts.' Besides promoting the health care system, Rajkumari Amrit Kaur worked to free India from foreign domination, advance equality and justice. Her commitment to social service was deeply rooted in her upbringing.

CHAPTER TWENTY-SEVEN
THE CONSCIENCE KEEPER

Her grandfather Dadabhai Naoroji had declared to a London journal in August 1895, 'I prophesy, that this constant violation of pledges, this persistent opposition to Indian interests, and the deterioration and impoverishment of the country by an evil administration, must lead, sooner or later, to a rebellion.' He also remarked, 'Never can a foreign rule be anything but a curse to any country, except so far as it approaches a native rule.'

Perin Captain was born on 12 October 1888 in Mandvi, Kutch, Gujarat. Her father, Ardeshir, was a medical doctor, and her mother, Virbai Dadina, a homemaker. She was five when her father died in 1893 and the family relocated to Bombay. After completing her schooling in Bombay she went to Paris for her graduation and studied at the University of Paris III, Sorbonne Nouvelle. It was during her stay in Paris she was introduced to Bhikaiji Cama. At the time Cama was trying for the release of Vinayak Damodar Savarkar who was in prison in London for defying the British. Perin was associated with small-scale acts of freedom in Paris before she moved back to India in 1911 and married Dhunjisha S. Captain, a lawyer, in 1925.

Perin Captain worked with Gandhi during the Rowlett Act Satyagraha. This act was hurriedly passed in March 1919, by the British government, which gave them repressive powers through arrests and deportation of any person on mere suspicion of sedition and revolt. It further allowed the detention of political prisoners without trial for two years. Gandhi launched a nationwide Satyagraha against the act and opposed the law with civil disobedience movements across the nation. Perin took part in the strikes on 6 April 1919 and shopkeepers were asked to close down their shops and workers to go on strike. Protests across the nation led to the Jallianwala Bagh massacre on 13 April 1919. People had gathered in the enclosed ground for Baisakhi and some were in silent protest as well. The British troops entered the Jallianwala Bagh, blocked the main entrance behind them before opening fire on the crowd. Though the British claimed that 350 people were killed in the massacre, the number was at least 1,000. This led to even more angry protests in the country.

Later Perin Captain was elected as the first female president of the Bombay Provincial Congress Committee, in 1930 and was part of many councils of the Indian National Congress. Her sisters Goshi and Khurshid were also involved in all party activities in Bombay and great support to Gandhi. During Gandhi's salt march from Sabarmati to the Dandi seashore on 12 March 1930, he encouraged his followers to join the campaign against the salt laws. Captain along with the women in Bombay organised rallies, supporting Gandhi's defiance. Women brought seawater and made salt on chullahs at the Congress House, and multiple locations. They then sold the salt that they had made and many were arrested. Desh Sevika Sangh (National Women's Volunteer Organisation) was established in various regions of India and Perin Captain along with Hansa Mehta and Avantikabai Gokhale formed the DSS in Bombay. The focus was to ban foreign cloth, and liquor, and promote khadi-hand-spun and woven cloth. It played an active role during the civil disobedience movement and the British declared it an illegal association! The Sevikas organised picketing in Bombay, going from shop to shop requesting the shop owners not to sell imported fabric as well as take part in the Swadeshi movement. Downing shutters were against the law, hence shopkeepers were arrested along with the women for boycotting foreign goods. The members of the Desh Sevika Sangh also influenced the shopkeepers to take a pledge that they would not employ any labourers who were addicted to consuming liquor.

On the fourth day of the Boycott Week in Bombay, people gathered on the streets shouting slogans and volunteers ran with flags and pamphlets to boycott British goods. They were going from house to house collecting Swadeshi pledges (2, 00,000 pledges had been signed). Members of Desh Sevika Sangh were herded into police vans after their arrest. Perin received a cable from Gandhi to 'alert Congress to scrupulously avoid all violence, direct indirect passive or active,' and Perin was arrested.

The Bombay Chronicle of 4 July 1930 reported the arrest of Perin Captain 'She cheerfully submitted to the officers who came to her home when she was leaving for work.' On hearing of her arrest, the Municipal Corporation of Bombay was adjourned. The Sugar Merchants Association passed a unanimous resolution to boycott British refined sugar, and other merchant associations joined the boycott. They then passed a resolution that 'Mrs. Captain was an accomplished lady and was a granddaughter of the late Dadabhai Naoroji, popularly known as the Grand Old Man of India. Mrs. Captain was a lady of sound and sober views and took her education in England. It was Mr. Dadabhai Naoroji who first started the idea of Swaraj for India and Mrs. Captain took her education in England under the guidance of her revered grandfather. Self-sacrifice and service were the mottos of her life and she was acting up to her honest conviction with courage.'

On 5 July 1930, the Bombay Congress Bulletin wrote in their journal, Bombay's Homage to Perinbehn. 'Yesterday after the close of the trial which resulted in the conviction of our president and four comrades a procession of ladies filed past the prison door to pay their tribute of love and respect to our dear leader. It was only physical exigencies that prevented the whole of Bombay from tendering this loving homage. Today, there is none dearer to the heart of every man, woman, and child in Bombay than our incarcerated leader. She in her frail shown symbolised the true spirit of Satyagraha. During the days we had the privilege to working with her, her presence had been a perennial source of inspiration and courage to us all. And now that the Government has so cruelly spirited her away, sadly as we feel the void in our midst, our determination is yet stronger to keep alive the flame she has kindled in us. There is one phrase which Perinbehn always loved to repeat when referring to our saintly leader, Bapuji, whose name was always on her lips and whose ideals has ever been the guiding motive of her conduct. With those words we now greet her and remain confident that even from behind prison bars we shall still continue to draw that great strength that alone can be given by the 'terrible meek.' A procession was organised on 21 July 1930 to protest her being imprisoned.

When Perin Captain was released, the Sevikas welcomed her and the other imprisoned women activists. 10000 women were at both ends of the parade. They not only surprised the British but also the men in their family. It is reported that 17,000 women were convicted within the first 10 months of 1930 for their brave role in protesting against colonial rule.

Khadi had become the symbol of India's resistance and self-reliance. This led to the formation of Gandhi Seva Sena which was to sell swadeshi goods and promote khadi through their stores. Perin became the honorary General Secretary of Gandhi Seva Sena, a post she held till she died in 1958.

Gandhi believed that a common language was necessary to unite the nation and bring people together. He had said,' Hindustani should freely be able to admit words from other native languages and foreign languages too, provided it mixes well with the language.' For communicating this, the 'Hindi Prachar Sabha' was formed in Bombay and Perin Captain was made the Honorary Secretary. Perin herself was a strong believer in one national language for the country and in her capacity made every effort to campaign for Hindustani as the obvious choice for the national language of India. Perin Captain died in Jahangir Nursing Home, Poona in 1958. She was honoured with the Padma Shri in 1954 in recognition of her efforts in the fields of social service towards the nation.

Gulab Kaur

Anasuya Sarabhai

Ponaka Kanakamma

Mithubehn Hormusji
Petit

Ammu Swaminathan

Nalinibala Devi

Ashalata Sen

Ramadevi Choudhury

Kamala Nehru

CHAPTER TWENTY-EIGHT
THE LIONESS OF PUNJAB

Bibi Gulab Kaur, born in 1890 in Bakshiwala village, Sangrur district, Punjab, was a woman with exceptional courage. Not much has been documented about her life, though. After her marriage to a farmer in Punjab, Mann Singh, the couple left for Manila, Philippines, hoping to migrate to America from there. As was the practice during colonial rule, farmers were driven off their lands because of the British policies.

During their stay in Manila, the couple met with the local leaders of the Ghadar Party, an Indian revolutionary organization. In India's freedom struggle, the Ghadar movement has a distinctive identity because it mainly comprised of immigrants from America, Canada, and East Asia countries.

After a decade of fighting against racism in North America and Canada, the party was founded in 1913 by Punjabi immigrants in North America. Sohan Singh Bakhna, Pandit Kanshi Ram, and Lala Hardyal a former professor of Indian Philosophy at Stanford. They were determined to free India from the colonist rule and aimed to wage a nationwide struggle against British colonialism. Most members of the Ghadar party came from the peasantry who migrated from Punjab to cities like Hong Kong, Manila, and Singapore in the early 20th century. Later many moved to North America. Ghadar's had a common belief that they were forced to leave India due to the British colonists and they were now disgraced and known as colonial subjects around the world.

Within a year of the formation, several branches were set up and Manila was one of them. Although some accounts state the couple intended to return home and fight the British, Mann Singh refused to take part in the revolution and left for America while Gulab Kaur remained in Manila, and joined the Ghadar party.

The party owned a newspaper called Hindustan Ghadar and published profiles of martyrs, excerpts of rebel leaders, the 1857 revolt, and through the newspaper informed the Indian immigrants about their rights and the need for equality. They also published a weekly compilation of poetry and songs called Ghadar ki Goonj. In its inaugural issue, the paper boldly declared 'A war against the English Raj. What is our name? Ghadar. What is our work? Ghadar. Our name and our work are identical.' With this, the news of a newly-born revolutionary party spread like wildfire. An advertisement with the following lines was carried in the inaugural issue of the newspaper, Wanted: Brave soldiers to stir up revolution in India. Pay: Death. Prize: Martyrdom. Pension: Liberty. Field of Battle: India. Within a few months, the party grew to about a thousand members and recruitment continued. Despite efforts to intercept Hindustan Ghadar, the paper still made its way into India.

At a meeting with Indian immigrants in 1914, the Ghadar party leaders urged the immigrants to fight for the country's independence. It is documented that towards the end of the meeting, Gulab Kaur started singing the patriotic song 'Ghadar ki Goonj.' She noticed some people were hesitant to register their names as revolutionaries, she immediately took off the bangles she was wearing and declared, 'those of you unwilling to join this rare opportunity should wear these bangles and sit aside and women will fight in their place.' Kaur then boarded the ship to India with fifty other Ghadar leaders.

The Rowlatt Act and the massacre that followed at Jallianwala Bagh in 1919 had an impact on the Ghadar movement too. On her return to India, Kaur reached out to people in Punjab, appealing to them to join the movement. She played a key role in secretly distributing arms and Ghadar literature and supervised the party printing press by impersonating a journalist along with a press pass to carry out operations. She was also at the forefront of recruiting members through her daring speeches as well as inspiring the women to take part in the freedom against injustice. The British got to know about her activities and she was eventually sentenced to prison and tortured for insurgent activities. She died in 1931.

In Kesar Singh's book, Ghadar Di Dhee or The Daughter of Ghadar, he documented Gulab Kaur's life, on how she was influenced by the talks of Ghadar Party members in Manila, which directed her to join the movement. Gulab Kaur is remembered every year, at the Ghadari Babian Da Mela held in Jalandhar, Punjab from 30 October to 1 November. At the mela, cultural programs are held, along with talks by progressive writers, thinkers, and activists who come together and pay homage to revolutionaries like the brave Bibi Gulab Kaur, and the legacy of the Ghadar continues.

CHAPTER TWENTY-NINE
THE MOTABEN TO EVERYONE

Anasuya Sarabhai was born on 11 November 1885, in Ahmedabad in a progressive and illustrious business family of Sarabhai. They were among the pioneers of the mechanized textile industry in Ahmedabad. In 1894, during a trip to Kashmir, Anasuya's father died very suddenly, and her mother followed three months later. The three children, Anasuya was nine, her brother Ambalal was five, and the youngest Kanta was a year old. They were left in the care of their father's brother Chimanbhai Sarabhai.

Born when child marriage was practiced, Anasuya was married at thirteen most reluctantly to a boy from the Jain community. She was unhappy staying away from her siblings and was unable to adjust to her new family. With no interest in her husband who was not brilliant in his studies, Anasuya would find excuses to keep returning home. Her married life was short. She separated and later divorced her husband. Unacceptable in India in the early 1900s.

After returning to her maternal family, a friend suggested that she become a doctor. With her brother's support, she went to England in 1912 to study medicine. For someone who had never lived on her own, London was a big change. For six months she studied at a tutorial college and finished her basic education. When she realized that animal dissection was required for a medical degree, which was against her Jain beliefs, she switched to the London School of Economics. She studied labour and social welfare instead. After meeting with Fabian, socialists like Bernard Shaw, she was influenced by the idea of socialism and the social equality of the suffragette movement, and her path changed!

The following year, in 1913, her youngest sister Kanta died of meningitis. She rushed home to India, to be by her brother's side and never went back to England to resume her studies. Anasuya started working with the marginalised communities in the region. At first, she opened a school for poor students from all castes. She created toilets for women, a maternity home, and a hostel for Harijan girls.

Despite her efforts to improve the lives of women workers in Ahmedabad, things got worse during the plague. The devastated cotton mill workers were the hardest hit. In 1918, a conflict had arisen between cotton mill owners, who wanted to scrap the plague bonus, and workers who wanted a 50% wage hike. Thousands joined in the protest and did not attend work. They requested Anasuya to take the lead and she did, addressing the mill workers and mill owners. She demanded better wages and better working conditions and gave an ultimatum to the mill owners that the workers would go on strike. Her brother Ambalal, was the president of the Mill Owners' Association and was upset with her views. However, Anasuya stood her ground. The strike lasted for 21 days, and the owners ultimately conceded a 35% raise.

Soon afterward, Anasuya played a formidable role in Kheda Satyagraha which began on 11 March 1918, in the Kheda district of Gujarat. The region was hit by famine, cholera, and plague destroying the local economy. The British increased the taxes in the region, in spite of a crop failure and breakout of plague and cholera. The peasant, Patidar community of Kheda refused to agree to a 23% tax hike that was imposed on them. Anasuya travelled the region with other congress leaders, making sure that the farmers were aware of their rights and stood with them firmly for the cancellation of taxes that year. The British government refused the demands and asked the area administrations to seize the land, homes, and cattle of the peasants. As their homes and cattle sheds were seized, the farmers donated everything to the Gujarat Sabha! Eventually, the British authorities realised that the farmers were firm on their stand, and a solution was reached whereby only the richer Patidars would pay tax, while the poor farmers got an exemption.

Anasuya was also one of the first signatories of Gandhi's Satyagraha pledge against the Rowlatt Bill, a legislative council act passed by the Imperial Legislative Council in Delhi on 18 March 1919. The act extended the emergency measures of preventive indefinite detention and imprisonment without trial. The Rowlatt Act gave powers to the police to arrest any person for no reason. The purpose of the Act was to curb the growing nationalist upsurge in the country. And this created protests across India, it was later repealed in 1922.

Anasuya took the lead to establish the Majdoor Mahajan Sangh, Gujarat's oldest labour or the Ahmedabad Textile Labour Association (TLA) on 25 February 1920. This was formed for the betterment of the mill workers. The first meeting of the association took place at Anasuya's Mirzapur bungalow, where Gandhi declared Anasuya a lifelong president of the union. In 1950, Ela Bhatt, who was a young college graduate, joined the Textile Labour Association. Anasuya was her mentor and inspiration. Bhatt started the Self-employed Women's Association (SEWA) in 1972, the same year on 1 November 1972, Anasuya Sarabhai died.

In 1934 Munshi Premchand wrote the script for a movie named 'Mill Mazdoor' inspired by her life. Anasuya led a union of nearly two lakh workers, and a life devoted to the improvement of the workers. In 2017, Google honoured Anasuya Sarabhai with a doodle on her 132 birth anniversary. Anasuya Sarabhai was the warm 'Motaben' to everyone and to her brother, Ambalal, too! They may have had different political opinions, though. A trailblazer of the women's labour movement in India and the first woman trade union leader she altered the social and economic image of Ahmedabad.

CHAPTER THIRTY
THE BENEVOLENT

Ponaka Kanakamma was born on 10 June 1892 in the village Minagallu, near Nellore. Her father Marupuru Kondareddi, was a wealthy landlord, and her mother Kaamamma a home-maker. As was customary she was married at eight in an orthodox family. Her husband Subbarama Reddy was also a landlord. Ponaka was not allowed to go to school, however, the young Ponaka learned Sanskrit, Hindi, and Telugu on her own.

When Ponaka was sixteen, she hosted, Bipin Chandra Pal an assertive nationalist and one of the main architects of the swadeshi movement. He was on a tour of Coastal Andhra in April 1907. He visited Nellore to create awareness among the locals of the political and national developments in the country, through the Swadeshi and Vandematram movements.

From there on very inspired by the freedom struggle, she started a literacy drive among the locals by initiating two libraries, the Sujana Ranjani Samajam in the village Potlapudi near Nellore and later the Vivekananda Granthalayam. The Library movement had gained momentum in Nellore, developed mainly through private enterprise and patronage. This movement was also connected at one end with the freedom struggle and at the other end a campaign for adult literacy. The libraries and reading rooms of Nellore acted as places where conversations ranged around and against colonial rule. The libraries encouraged the locals' to develop a habit of reading newspapers and take interest in their language, literature, and history. These centres were established besides night schools for adults and for circulating books among women to read.

In 1923 Ponaka went on to establish a girls' school, Sri Kasturidevi Vidyalayam (Kasturi Devi Girls School) in Nellore, to ensure that girls in the region were educated, as their parents were unwilling to send them to co-educational schools. Later Gandhi laid the foundation stone for a permanent building for this school in 1929. Ponaka raised her voice against the powerful Zamindars for the abolition of the zamindari system. She contributed to the Zameen Ryot a Telugu weekly at Nellore started during the Zameendari Ryotwari movement in 1930. The zamindari system was introduced by the British, the zamindars were made owners of the land and had the right to evict the peasants as they wished and a number of peasant movements started thereon. Ponaka donated 13 acres of land of the 22 acres to build the Pinakini Satyagraha Ashram in the Pallipadu village. The ashram was completed in 1925 and was built on the lines of Sabarmati Ashram.

Ponaka Kanakamma was the first woman President of the Nellore Congress Committee and actively participated in the non-cooperation movement. During one of the dharnas in 1932, she was arrested and imprisoned for thirteen months in Raya Vellore prison. In 1934 Ponaka lost her only daughter, Venkatasubbamma, and to cope with the loss, Kanakamma devoted much more of her time to spirituality. She became a follower of Ramana Maharshi a sage of the twentieth century and wrote poems on the sage, as well as translated the Bhagavad Gita into Telugu. Her short stories, essays, and poems were published in several magazines and newspapers. Ponaka Kanakamma died in Nellore, on 15 September 1963, her contribution to the education of girls in Nellore is notable and she is remembered as a kind and generous soul. In her honour a bronze statue of hers has been installed at the Pinakini Satyagraha Ashram Pallipadu.

CHAPTER THIRTY-ONE

MAIJI

Mithu Hormusji Petit was born on 11 April 1892. Her father Sir Dinshaw Maneckjee Petit was the founder of the first textile mill in India, an industrialist, philanthropist, and the first Petit Baronet. As a child, Mithu was influenced by her maternal aunt Jaiji J Petit, who was a member of the Bhagini Samaj, a women's welfare organization in Bombay, a follower of Gandhi, and Secretary of the Rashtriya Stree Sabha.

She would often accompany her aunt on her visits to meet Gandhi. Her aunt believed, 'Gandhi was a great link between the poor and the rich, the small and the great, the illiterate and the literate, between those of advanced views and conservative ones, as well as between different communities. Such a link uniting one another led on a divine path the country and humanity.' At one of the meetings Jaiji J Petit declared, it was not possible to gain any insight into the condition of India by observing the state of cities like Bombay and it was quite misleading to get an idea of the condition of village people by observing the state of people living in cities. If the women, who, by living in cities got more independence and other advantages, attempted to reform the condition of women living in villages, then only it could be said that they understood and assimilated the ideals of Mr. Gandhi. There were innumerable ways for women to render some sort of useful service in Bombay. They could impart knowledge to those of their sisters, who knew less than they. They could also help those who had not sufficient means to obtain an education. And if they were not able to render such kind of help themselves they could give pecuniary help to those who wanted to do such work.' Soon Mithubehn influenced by Gandhi's principles moved out of her home and took a pledge to visit villages and educate the rural people. Dedicating her life to the tribal and the underprivileged people of Gujarat she started to follow a strictly disciplined life.

Mithubehn joined Sardar Vallabhbhai Patel during the Bardoli Satyagraha, a no-tax campaign in 1928. The farmers in Bardoli were shocked when they heard that an officer had recommended an increase in land revenue by 30% when the ground reality was the opposite of what was being cited. The farmers decided to withhold tax payments, resulting in the authorities confiscating the farmers land and cattle. And thus the Satyagraha started. When officials passed through villages, women looked through window panes but did not respond to the instructions of the authorities in the area to come out. The British then reversed their decision and agreed to increase the taxes by 5.7% and the confiscated land was returned to the farmers. Those who had resigned from their government jobs in agreement with the satyagrahis were reinstated. An editorial comment in Pioneer remarked, 'No impartial observer of the Bardoli dispute, possessed of the plain facts of the case, can resist the conclusion that the peasants have got the right on their side, and their claim for an examination of the enhanced assessment by an impartial tribunal is just, reasonable and fair.'

Mithubehn was also at the forefront of this National prohibition campaign in Gujarat when Gandhi made prohibition a priority of the Indian National Congress. He believed it was a social evil and a cause of domestic violence. She also played an important role during the Salt Satyagraha. This was another act of civil disobedience led by Gandhi. Mithubehn was assigned a critical role to be present at Bhimrad, Surat when Gandhi along with 78 satyagrahis walked from Sabarmati Ashram on 12th March 1930 and reached the Dandi village on 5 April, and the next day he walked to the Dandi seashore where he picked up some natural salt in his hands and said, 'with this, I am shaking the foundation of the British Empire.' The Mahatma broke the Salt Law by the simple yet symbolic act of picking up a fistful of salt. Mithubehn stood with Mahatma Gandhi when he repeated the violation at Bhimrad later. Gandhi utilized the salt march to breach the caste divide in the villages on route. In some villages in Gujarat, he went to the untouchable quarters and drew water from the well, making sure his village hosts, often from higher castes, take part.

The same year, Mithubehn set up an ashram in Maroli and it was named as the Kasturba Vanat Shala or Kasturba Sevashram. The ashram was built to support the children from families of Adivasis, Harijans, and local fishing communities. To ensure that they were economically independent, they were taught to spin the charkha, weave, dairy farming, leather work, and so on. The women were skilled, especially at sewing. On Gandhi's suggestion, she also set up a mental hospital in the ashram, to treat the mentally disturbed prisoners who suffered physical torture in jails. Many of them improved at the ashram, encouraging Mithubehn to later create a centre for scientifically treating mental ailments.

When Mithubehn's family had asked her to give up her activism or risk disinheritance, she had said, 'It is your business to sit with the government and mine to remain with the nation.' Later they understood her love for the country and transferred funds with which she met her expenses. Mithubehn understood medicines, especially home remedies. The villagers could walk in with a complaint and she would be ready with the cure! She would only send them to the hospital if the home treatment failed.

Mithubehn Petit was known as Maiji. She died on 16 July 1973, refrained from power when the country won independence, and kept away from politics. People across the villages and in the region where she lived, respected and worshipped their Maiji.

CHAPTER THIRTY-TWO
MOTHER OF THE YEAR

Ammu Swaminathan was born in 1894, in Palakkad, Kerala. Not wealthy, however, her father Govinda Menon focussed on educating the children and Ammu received an informal education at home. Govinda Menon died when Ammu was very young and since he was the only earning member in the family, her education came to a standstill. After her father's death, Subbarama Swaminathan, a close associate of her father, expressed his desire to marry one of Menon's daughters. Ammu had no choice but to accept Swaminathan's marriage proposal. She put some preconditions before agreeing to marry Swaminathan though! Her first was to move to Madras to learn English from an English woman. Ammu was aware that illiteracy in the English language would be an obstacle for her in the future. Her second condition was not to be asked when she was going out or when she would return home. Her logic was, that no one questioned the boys in the house. Swaminathan agreed to both her demands and the two married in 1907!

During those days the Nairs followed the Sabandam system which meant, informal marriages. Swaminathan and Ammu found the practice offensive and were against it. They had a proper wedding, which was, however, boycotted by Swaminathan's family. They registered their marriage in England later. The couple had four children, all of whom were given equal opportunities to peruse professions of their choice. Lakshmi Sahgal, their daughter, famously known as Captain Lakshmi, was the head of the Rani Jhansi regiment of the Indian National Army formed by Subhash Chandra Bose. We have a chapter on Captain Lakshmi later.

When Annie Besant founded the Women's India Association (WIA) in 1917, Ammu became the honorary secretary. WIA was a feminist organisation with a large agenda to advocate women's rights and education. The earliest women's organization in the country, its focus was to bring women out of their homes and into the political and social framework. This group grew into a formidable force in the struggle against child marriage, female illiteracy, the Devadasi system, and other societal issues.

Ammu was influenced by Gandhi and joined the Indian National Congress in 1934. A fierce supporter of universal adult franchise and equal constitutional rights for women she actively took part in the freedom struggle. She opposed discriminatory caste practices and supported equal status, adult franchise, and removal of untouchability. There's an interesting story about her at the Vellore prison. Imprisoned for a year during a protest, she heard someone refer to sanitary workers as shudrachi (untouchable.) Hearing this, she angrily walked up to the person, and said, 'I am a shudrachi too. Tell me.' Such was her position on the caste order. She was perturbed that Jawaharlal Nehru responded to being called Panditji. According to her, this was a sign of caste superiority.

Having gone through a child marriage herself, Ammu campaigned for the Child Marriage Restraint Act. The various Hindu Code Bills aimed at reforming succession, inheritance, and marriage regulations and pushed for reform in Hindu religious laws. She was part of the fifteen women elected to the Constituent Assembly from the Madras constituency in 1946. In one of the discussions, while drafting the Indian Constitution, Ammu said, 'People outside have been saying that India did not give equal rights to her women. Now we can say that when the Indian people themselves framed their Constitution they have given rights to women equal with every other citizen of the country.'

Although pleased with the final text of the constitution, she had several concerns. She was worried about the length of the constitution and that it had become a long and bulky volume when in effect it should have been compact enough to be carried in a pocket or purse, 'I always imagined a constitution and still believe, to be a small volume which one could carry in one's purse or pocket and not a huge big volume. There was no necessity to go into so many details as has been done here,' she had said!

After independence, Ammu Swaminathan was elected to the first Lok Sabha in 1952 and subsequently to the Rajya Sabha in 1954, representing Madras. She had an interest in movies and became the Vice President of the Federation of Film Societies and the Censor Board. Between 1960 and 1965, she was the President of the Bharat Scouts and Guides. At the inauguration of International Women's Year in 1975, Ammu was selected as 'Mother of The Year.' An advocate for pro-women legislation, Ammu Swaminathan died on 4 July 1978. Her address in the Constituent Assembly was in about 1000 words, the shortest amongst all the women who spoke in the assembly, yet the ideas she spoke of were the ones she worked towards in her life. During the constitution-making process, she had said, 'What is written on a paper would have meaning only when people desire to pay attention to it? Let us hope that in the years to come this Constitution will be considered something worthy of our country.'

CHAPTER THIRTY-THREE
AUTHOR AND NATIONALISTIC POET

Her father, Karmaveer Nabinchandra Bardoloi, was a lawyer and the leader of the Assam Congress Association and her mother, Hemanta Kumari Devi, assisted him in political activities. Nalinibala Devi was born in Guwahati, Assam, on 23 March 1898, and grew up with a sense of responsibility towards the nation. At 10 she wrote her first poem, Pita!

Married at twelve her husband Jeeveshwar Changkakoti died when she was nineteen. Being a widow with four children to take care of was a challenging phase in her life. Another tragedy struck her, and she lost two of her sons early in life. The British jailed her father for eighteen months in 1921 for taking part in the freedom movement. Directing her emotions towards writing, in many of her poems and books, Nalinibala penned the tragedy of her life. At first, she wrote letters to her father in jail to deal with her sorrow. She would also send her writings to literary journals for publication. Her first collection of poems, Sandhiya Sur, was published in 1928 this brought her recognition and it was later included in the curriculum of the universities of Calcutta and Guwahati.

Nalinibala's autobiography, Eri Aha Dinbor (The Days Passed) published in 1976, is a critical read. It traces her life and also the history of Assamese society at the end of the 19th century. She has recorded different aspects of social life and the Indian Independence Movement from an Assamese point of view. In the book, she pens the hopes of the people, their hardships, and the role of the Assamese leaders and students. She writes in detail about her father as a freedom fighter and the influence he had on her. How he actively took part in building a modern Assam and initiated Assam's status in mainstream India. And though his perspectives were Indian, she writes, he was conscious of his Assamese identity.

The reforms outlined in the Montagu-Chelmsford report of 1919, did not include Assam as a state. Her father reached England and placed before the joint parliamentary committee for inclusion of Assam's case in the Montague-Chelmsford Reforms. He refuted the report, stating that Assam was much more forward than other states and that they should count it as part of the major provinces of India and accord Assam the status as the other states.

After the Jallianwala Bagh massacre, on 13 April 1919, her father was deeply involved in the Indian freedom struggle and gave up his law practice. On his call, several hundred students joined the movement. They thought of the nation first and not their careers. Her brother who was studying medicine and her son Pabitra, who later died very young, also took part in the movement. Her father, travelled across the villages and districts of Assam to interact with the people and encourage them to join the freedom movement. In 1921, he was arrested and sent to prison and remained in jail for eighteen months. After his release, he continued with his political activities.

In her autobiography, Nalinibala mentions the visit of Mahatma Gandhi, along with Dr. Rajendra Prasad, Subhas Chandra Bose, and other leaders at their home and how she was now part of serious conversations and discussions for independence. She also writes that Mahatma Gandhi designed the Wardha Chakra on a prototype of her son Upen Changkakoti's work of a box-type spinning machine which he had gifted to Gandhi on his visit to Assam. While her father was in prison he learned the art of spinning fine threads of khadi and Nalinibala Devi created khadi dhotis of these threads. Nalinibala later opened a weaving training centre in Guwahati to increase the production of Khadi, influencing several women to learn the art of weaving.

There was no progress in women's education in Assam. The town of Dibrugarh, upper Assam, had one Assamese Girl's High School and the young girls would have to travel to Guwahati, where there was a local Bengali primary school. Nalinibala started a school in her residence for the local girls. She was elected the first President of the Kamrup Mahila Samiti in 1931, a platform she used to reach out to women urging them to be accountable for building the nation and stand in solidarity if they wanted to improve their status.

In 1950, Nalinibala established Sadou Asom Parijat Kanan, a place for children to showcase their creativity. This was later renamed Moina Parijat. As the first woman president of Assam Sahitya Sabha, she led a delegation in 1955 to the State Reorganization Commission. In the memorandum, she proved before the Commission that Goalpara which West Bengal tabled as a part of their state (since a majority of Bengalis lived there) was an integral part of Assam. She also highlighted that the Assamese language root and identity was never an off-shoot of Bengal. She said, 'as a writer in Assamese I can boldly say that the Government of India has committed a grave mistake by basing the division of states on language. This disastrous policy can achieve nothing but chaos and disunity for the country.' And she prevailed, Goalpara remained with Assam! Nalinibala was also part of the language movement of 1960, this movement recognized the Assamese language as the state language.

When China unexpectedly attacked India in 1962, and the Chinese army entered Arunachal Pradesh, the Indian army did not have the requisite arms. Nalinibala Devi, along with several leaders, reached out to the Assamese citizens through patriotic songs and poems to stay calm. In her autobiography, Nalinibala Devi writes, 'There is a time in men's lives when the urge to serve is very strong. The mind is at peace only by serving the motherland.'

Between the early 1960s and 1970s, Assam lost much of its territory to new states that emerged from within the borders. Nalinibala opposed the proposal to remove the hill districts from Assam and form an independent Hill State in 1968, which was a worry for the local Assamese people. She challenged the central government and said that a divided Assam would mean a split Assam. Her love for Assam reflects in her books and poetry. In one of her poems, she describes the beauty of Assam with much clarity, she writes, 'In the early hours of dawn when the world is still shrouded by the swirling mists of autumn, I stand at the bank of the mighty Brahmaputra to absorb the myriad beauties of my motherland. While I watch, in the hazy mornings, I see emerging one by one from the bosom of the great river, Umananda, Bhairav, Mahatirtha Bhasmachal, Urvashi, and Karmanasha... And I marvel at my good fortune that this beautiful, blessed land is my motherland.'

Nalinibala was one of the finest Assamese poets of her time. She highlighted several issues that women from the marginalised classes faced in society through her thought-provoking verses. She also wrote mystical poetry, connecting another part of herself to readers. She received the Sahitya Akademi Award for her poetry collection Alaknanda. While she pays rich tributes to her father in his biography, Smriti-Tirtha, she also documents the socio-political history of Assam.

In her autobiography Eri Aba Dimbor (Bygone Days) she mentions the three chief attributes of her life: The first, the love for her motherland, the second, her awareness of a spiritual being, and the third, her sense of duty towards her country and above all humanity. She captures the various aspects of Assamese society of that period. Life within the Bordoloi family, the religious ceremonies, lifestyle, and attitudes of the families in Guwahati. In the book, she gives an insight into the restricted lives of the Assamese upper-class women and writes, 'So many have silently withered behind the impenetrable curtains, who will account for them?'

The first woman Assamese poet to be awarded Padma Shri in 1957, she fought for the dignity of the Assamese language. Nalinibala Devi died on 24 December 1977. She inherited her father's trait to articulate and convey her messages through both speech and verse, with great aplomb. She continues to be remembered for her extensive poetry and is an important part of Assamese literature. The Cotton College, Guwahati, named its girls' hostel after her as Padmashree Nalini Bala Devi Girls Hostel in 1986.

CHAPTER THIRTY-FOUR
THE SOCIAL ACTIVIST

Ashalata Sen was born in Noakhali, Bengal on 2 Feb 1894 in an educated family. Her father Bagala Mohan Dasgupta was a lawyer at the district judge's court and her mother Monoda Dasgupta was a home-maker. At eleven she wrote a poem on the partition of Bengal and it was published in a local newspaper and the following year, she signed the swadeshi pledge to boycott foreign goods. She also went ahead and officially joined her Grandmother Nabashashi Devi's organization! Her grandmother assigned her the task of surveying houses and persuading women to join the Swadeshi movement. Married at twelve to Satya Ranjan Sen, a government employee, her husband died when she was 22, leaving behind a young widow with a four-month-son. Encouraged by her grandmother she studied as well as read books on nationalist movements of other countries.

During the non-cooperation movement, Ashalata set up several initiatives such as the 'Silpasram' a weaving centre for women at her residence in Gandaria in 1921. This centre provided women employment, as well as promoted Khadi. Her second initiative was setting up the Gandaria Mahila Samiti, to communicate Gandhi's message of swadeshi among the people, advocating the charka, khadi, and other constructive work. She followed this up by building Kalyankutir in 1927, this set up trained women volunteers to take part in the freedom movement. A separate committee called the Women's Satyagraha Committee would then enlist the trained women volunteers to protest, picket shops and so on. Next, in 1929 she visited the Juran village and established the Juran Shiksha Mandir. Here the villagers were inspired to participate in the movement through magic lantern shows which were organised for them in the villages.

The following year, during Gandhi's call to the country to defy the salt law, she helped organize a Satyagrahi Sebika Dal from among the villagers and broke the salt law. She travelled to the Noakhali coast, collected natural salt, and then demonstrated how to make salt and was arrested.

The arrest of Gandhi on 4th January 1932, further strengthened the civil disobedience movement. The country was furious and there were large scale protests. British then took action against any anti-British activities and they announced that Gandaria Mahila Samiti was illegal. The residences of the workers of Kalyankutir were sealed. While protesting, Ashalata was arrested and jailed. After her release in 1933, she was elected as vice president of the District Congress. She travelled to many districts of Bengal setting up branches of the Congress Mahila Samiti. Through these Mahila Samiti's she was hoping to send a message to women that without their engagement in the freedom movement little would be accomplished.

Ashalata actively participated in the Quit India Movement. She was again arrested while protesting against the police killing of a young man and was imprisoned for seven and a half months. After her release, famine hit Bengal in 1943. Over three million deaths resulted not from drought but from the British government's policy lapses such as prioritizing the distribution of essential food supplies to the military, civil services, and others. Not declaring Bengal famine hit was among the factors that led to the enormity of the tragedy. Ashalata closely monitored the relief work, helping the villages to sustain themselves and reached out to the country for help.

By 1946, she was popularly elected to the Bengal Legislative Assembly. At the time of partition, Ashalata stayed back in East Pakistan and in 1947 was elected the sitting MLA in the East Pakistan Assembly. She remained in her seat till 1954. During her time in the assembly, she advocated for Bangla as the language of East Pakistan and petitioned to separate the Revenue and Foreign Exchange earned by East Pakistan from that of West Pakistan.

Ashalata moved to to Delhi in 1965 to live with her son, and withdrew from public work. During the liberation war of Bangladesh, Ashalata Sen composed several songs in memory of martyred freedom fighters. After the country was liberated she visited Bangladesh at the invitation of the Bangladesh Finance Minister and in Bangladesh she met the members of the Gandaria Mahila Samiti which she had set up way back in 1924. Ashalata Sen died on 3 February 1986 in Delhi.

CHAPTER THIRTY-FIVE

MAA OF ORISSA

Ramadevi was born on 3 December 1899 in Satyabhamapur, Cuttack, Orissa. Her parents Gopal Ballav Das and Basant Kumari Devi came from an aristocratic family. At fifteen she was married to Gopabandhu Choudhury, a Deputy Collector in Cuttack and after five years of married life, the couple joined the Indian National Congress along with her brother-in-law, Nabakrushna Choudhury, and his wife, Malati Choudhury. When Gandhi visited Cuttack and addressed the women to join the freedom movement, it was the first time that women of Cuttack were attending a public gathering! Gandhi placed before them that a constructive program was an essential component of the freedom movement and to engage themselves in nation-building through constructive work. Ramadevi offered Gandhi a hand-woven cotton bundle as a gesture of Orissa's commitment to the movement. Both Ramadevi and Malati gave up their expensive sarees, clothes, and jewellery and started wearing khadi sarees to support Gandhi's ideology.

During the Salt Satyagraha in 1930, Satyagraha was prohibited in Cuttack. Ramadevi, with her husband and sister- in- law Malati Choudhury and other satyagrahis began their foot march from the Swarajya Ashram of Cuttack towards Inchudi in the Balasore district which is roughly 35 hours away from Cuttack. This Satyagraha came to be known as the Inchudi Satyagraha, where the success of mass civil disobedience in defiance of the Salt Laws occupied second place in India after Dandi in Gujarat. The very same year, she was arrested along with Malati Choudhury, however, sent to different jails. They were later released after the signing of the Gandhi-Irwin Pact.

Ramadevi was again arrested in 1932 for her nationalist activities and sent to Hazaribagh jail. On her release, she was selected as the

Joint Secretary of the Orissa Branch Asprushyata Nibarana Samiti, later named Harijan Sewa Sangh. The association focused on educating women to work against the discrimination of Harijans. During the Harijan Padyatra in June 1934, she joined Gandhi in Puri. They went from village to village educating the villagers about the need to treat Harijans with equal respect and dignity. After this tour, Gandhi remarked, "I have marvelled at how Smt. Rama Devi and her girls have discharged themselves during the tour, which was undoubtedly pleasant and easy, had undoubtedly its trials. But these ladies have not known what fatigue is? Nowhere have I seen anything quite like what Smt. Rama Devi and her little band have been found to do so gracefully and so naturally. They have never needed or claimed any special privilege."

At the end of the Padayatra, Gandhi asked workers to go back to their villages and carry on with constructive work there. Thus Ramadevi and her husband established an Ashram, Sevaghar (the abode of service) in the village Bari. This Ashram focussed on social and economic sustenance for people in rural areas and Ramadevi supervised the running of the ashram. Taking up works such as village sanitation, rendering service to the Harijans, constructing toilets, and promoting campaigns against untouchability. They taught the villagers how to plant saplings, cattle-tending, bee-keeping, and adult literacy. Ramadevi and the Choudhury family were arrested during the Quit India movement in 1942, and the British raided Sevaghar Ashram and declared it illegal. After spending 2 years in jail the Choudhury family was released in 1944. They went back to doing constructive work!

In 1945, after the death of Kasturba Gandhi, a charitable trust was instituted in her name. For the management of the trust, from each state, a woman representative was nominated and Ramadevi was nominated from Orissa. The trust established a centre in Satyabhamapur, Cuttack, to train women in the field of education, relief work and employment generation among women. Ramadevi started a Teacher's Training Centre, in Balwadi at Ramchandrapur, and Sishu Vihar Yojana for the welfare of the children as well as a Tribal Welfare Centre in 1950. During

Vinoba Bhave's Bhoodan Movement, in Orissa, Ramadevi and her husband covered over 2000 miles on foot, and through land donations from wealthy landowners, they were able to collect 1000 acres of land from people, which they later re-distributed among the landless people. In 1953, the land was distributed among the villagers and the Gramdan was the second of its kind in India.

Ramadevi protested against the Emergency and when press freedom was curtailed she launched a newspaper called The Gram Sevak Press, though eventually banned, declared unlawful by the government, and Ramadevi was then arrested with other leaders from Orissa.

Nominated for Padma Shri however, Ramadevi declined the honour along with various other recognitions from organizations as she believed that her work was a continuous effort. She also received a doctorate from Utkal University and was felicitated by the Jamnalal Bajaj Foundation for her commitment to social welfare. Ramadevi Choudhury died on 22 July 1985 in Cuttack. A museum was established in her honour at the Rama Devi Women's University in 2015. Known as Maa Ramadevi in Orissa, for her selfless constructive programs in building a nation, her contribution to the freedom movement is praiseworthy.

CHAPTER THIRTY-SIX
THE FEARLESS NEHRU

Born on 1 August 1899, Kamla Kaul Nehru was the eldest among her siblings. Her father, Jawaharmal Mull Kaul, and mother, Rajpati Kaul were traditional Kashmiri Pandits. Educated at home by pandits, Kamala studied Hindi and the Hindu scriptures. It was at a wedding function that a member of the Motilal Nehru family saw Kamala and on 7 February 1916, Kamala Nehru was married to Jawaharlal Nehru, who was then the leader of the Indian National Congress. The wedding card read, 'It is expected that you and your family members will participate in the ceremony of the scheduled marriage of my son Jawaharlal Nehru with the daughter of Jawaharmal Mull Kaul, resident of Delhi on February 7, 1916, and on February 8 and 9, 1916; and give us the privilege of your auspicious company. Regards: Moti Lal Nehru. Anticipate your kind response. Anand Bhavan, Allahabad.'

Marrying the Nehru family was a bit of a culture shock to young Kamala. She was an introvert from a straightforward conservative family, however soon she was inspired to work in the freedom struggle. She had a close bond with Kasturba Gandhi and stayed at Sabarmati ashram for a while and was drawn to Gandhian ideals. Vijay Lakshmi Pandit wrote in her memoir, 'Kamala Nehru took Gandhi's call for self-sacrifice seriously, encouraged Jawahar in this radicalism and urged him to change his way of life.'

Kamala Nehru was very popular among women throughout India. Once a shy person, she emerged as a powerful independent woman, who not only took part in the freedom movement but also persuaded a large number of women to join the movement. She would organize the women to picket businesses selling foreign clothing and liquor during boycotts in Allahabad. The British realized the threat that Kamala

Nehru posed to them and her popularity among women all over India. As a result, they detained her twice.

Kamla Nehru went ahead and established a dispensary at her home Swaraj Bhawan, converting a few rooms to treat injured activists, their families, and other Allahabad residents. When her husband, Jawahar Lal Nehru, was arrested for making a seditious public speech, she addressed the people, demonstrating her tremendous courage by standing up to support her husband. Protests against Nehru's imprisonment were held all over the country. Kamala was arrested in a public meeting while reading out the very speech for which her husband had been imprisoned! A journalist asked if she had any message to convey and she said, 'I am happy beyond measure and proud to follow in the footsteps of my husband. I hope the people will keep the flag flying.' Kamala was sentenced to two months imprisonment but was released after twenty-six days, as her father-in-law Motilal Nehru was very ill. He died a few days after her release on February 6, 1931.

Early 1936, she fell ill and her health deteriorated. She needed to go to Europe for treatment. Subhash Chandra Bose was exiled to Europe by the British, during that time, he messaged Nehru, 'If I can be of any service in your present trouble, I hope you will not hesitate to send for me.' He then accompanied Kamala from Vienna to Prague where she received her initial care. She was later moved to Badenweiler, Germany. Jawahar Lal Nehru was in prison at that time. As her health worsened, Nehru was released from prison and rushed to Germany. While she improved initially, she fell ill again. Eventually, Kamala Nehru was shifted to Lausanne, Switzerland, where she prematurely passed away on 28 February 1936 in the presence of her husband, daughter Indira, and Bose. In his autobiography, Nehru wrote that he was devastated after his wife died, 'I almost overlooked her.'

To recognize Kamala Nehru's contribution, a great number of institutions and locations of public interest in Delhi have been named after her. Notable examples include Kamala Nehru College at the University of Delhi, Kamala Nehru Hospital, and Kamala Nehru Park.

In a statement on her passing away, Gandhi remarked, "I have not known a truer, braver, or more god-fearing lady." After Kamala Nehru's death, Mahatma Gandhi transformed the dispensary founded by her in her ancestral house Swaraj Bhavan, into the Kamala Nehru Memorial Hospital. Gandhi inaugurated this hospital in memory of Kamala Nehru on 28 February 1941.

Ambujammal
Desikachari

Vijaya Lakshmi
Pandit

Leela Roy

Chandraprabha
Saikiani

Helen Lepcha

Manibehn Patel

Kamaladevi
Chattopadhyay

Malati Chaudhury

Renuka Ray

Yashodhara Dasappa

CHAPTER THIRTY-SEVEN
THE KHADI ACTIVIST

Ambujammal Desikachari née Srinivasa Iyengar was born on 8 January 1899 in a conservative family in Madras. Her father, Srinivasa Iyengar was a prominent lawyer and a well-known Congress leader. Her mother Ranganayakiammal was a home-maker. Home schooled she was taught Tamil, English, Sanskrit, and Hindi by an Anglo-Indian teacher. Married at a very young age to an advocate, S. Desikachari, Ambujammal qualified herself as a teacher and taught at Sarada Vidyala Girls School, though moved out soon to devote her time to nationalist activities.

Kasturba Gandhi and Mahatma Gandhi stayed at her father Srinivasa Iyengar's house during their visit to Madras, and in her interactions with the Gandhis, Ambujammal was influenced by their modest way of life and became an ardent follower. She began to wear Khaddar and spin the charkha and took an active part in the 1920 non-cooperation movement. Along with her mother, she visited Sabarmati Ashram soon afterwards and stayed there for a while, which reinforced her commitment to the freedom struggle.

During the Vaikam Satyagraha, Gandhi again stayed at their home on his way to Vaikam. This Satyagraha was Kerala's protest against untouchability, the Anti-Untouchability Committee had decided that the rule barring temple roads to low castes would be defied by satyagrahis. And on March 30 1924 several volunteers from different parts of Travancore arrived in Vaikom to protest. This protest lasted from 30 March 1924 to 23 November 1925.

Gandhi later presented Ambujammal a book authored by Katherine Mayo titled Mother India which was published in 1927. It was a bitter book by Mayo that criticized Indian society, culture, and religion. She wrote against India's demands for self-rule, highlighting the treatment of India's women, the untouchables, and the nationalistic politicians. The book created an uproar in India, and books were burned along with Mayo's effigy. Gandhi criticized the book as a 'report of a drain inspector sent out with the one purpose of opening and examining the drains of the country to be reported upon.' To counter her and the American's perception, several books were published to highlight Mayo's false reporting and insights into India and Indian society. Gandhi asked Ambujammal to read the book and give her opinion. He mentioned to her that there was a need for women to come forward and drive the women's rights issues and that she should take the lead.

In 1928 Ambujammal formed the Women's Swadeshi League along with K. Bashyam Iyengar. The league served as the non-political wing of Congress and the members took the swadeshi pledge, spun, and promoted khadi. They organized the youth and women to boycott foreign cloth, and picket shops selling foreign cloth. The work of this association expanded and Swayam Sevika was formed to help professionally organize meetings, and sell Swadeshi goods. Ambujammal was also a committee member of the Sarada Ladies Union, from 1929 to 1936. She worked with Sister R S Subbulakshmi who had established several educational institutions in Madras, including the Sarada Vidyalaya in 1927 and the Vidya Mandir School, Madras.

During the civil disobedience movement, Ambujammal organized protests, sold khadi, and picketed foreign cloth and liquor shops. While leading one of the boycotts she was arrested but released on health grounds. In 1932, Ambujammal was nominated by Congress as the third dictator. During the same time while leading the Satyagrahis in the foreign cloth boycott she was once again arrested and sentenced to 6 months imprisonment at the Vellore prison and released on 19th July 1932.

From 1934 to 1938 Ambujammal was a member of the managing committee, of Hindi Prachar Sabha. She played an important role in the Women's India Association (WIA) and was the association's secretary from 1939 to 1942 and Treasurer from 1939 to 1947. After

Ambujammal's father died on 19 May 1941, she donated all her jewellery for the development of the Mahila Seva Mandal, in Sevagram, near Wardha. She founded the Srinivasa Gandhi Nilayam in 1948 at Teynampet, Madras, where women were employed in its printing press, free coaching was provided to the girls. There was a free dispensary as well as free milk and rice gruel was given to the needy. She was the Vice-President of the Tamil Nadu Congress Committee from 1957 to 1962, and the Chairman of the State Social Welfare Board from 1957 to 1964. Ambujammal was a notable scholar in Hindi and Tamil and was awarded the Padma Shri in 1964. An eloquent speaker both in Tamil and Hindi, she wrote articles in Tamil magazines on issues related to women's rights and education. She wrote the books, Reminiscences of Gandhi and Reminiscences of my Father.

In her book Naan Kanda Bharatham (The Bharat I witnessed) she mentions that a new Congress was born at the 1955 Avadi session, shunning its old image. "I was hesitant to be the head of the reception committee for the conference," she wrote. "But Madras chief minister K. Kamaraj convinced me, saying I was the competent person to do it. However, I was worried, as everything had to go on well and the conference had to be successful."

Ambujammal's father's wish was that she spends time on social service and asked her to do useful work for the community which would be a great contribution to Indian freedom. She did not disappoint and dedicated her life to India's freedom struggle and inspired several women to do the same. Women's welfare was at the top of her agenda. Ambujammal Desikachari died in 1993, she donated all her jewellery to the national movement. Despite being born into a privileged family, she gave up the luxuries for a simple nationalist life and focused her energies to fight the caste order, untouchability, and women's rights.

CHAPTER THIRTY-EIGHT
THE VISIBLE DIPLOMAT

'Freedom is not for the timid,' she said when a political career was non-existent for women, Vijaya Lakshmi Pandit was way ahead of her times. Famously known for being the first female president of the United Nations General Assembly, Vijaya, was one of the highest-ranking and most visible female diplomats of her generation. "Education was not merely a means for earning a living or an instrument for the acquisition of wealth. It was an initiation into life, a training of the human soul in the pursuit of the truth and practice of virtue,' she remarked.

Born on 18 August 1900 in Allahabad, her parents named her Swarup Kumari. She was the eldest daughter of Swaruprani and Motilal Nehru, a barrister from the Kashmiri Pandit community and the president of the Indian National Congress during the Independence struggle. Vijaya had two siblings, Jawaharlal who was eleven years younger than her, and younger sister, Krishna, who in her memoirs, described her famous sister as 'docile, obedient, tactful, and eminently suited to high office. She was also beautiful, highly intelligent, at ease with people of all classes, witty, and, occasionally sharp-tongued.'

Tutors educated her entirely at home under the supervision of her English governess, Jane Hooper. The first-ever political gathering she attended was at sixteen, when her cousin, Rameshwari Nehru, arranged a protest due to the inhumane treatment of Indian labourers in South Africa. In 1921, Vijaya married Ranjit Sitaram Pandit, a Maharashtrian lawyer, and Sanskrit scholar, and changed her name from Swarup Kumari Nehru to Vijaya Laxmi Pandit.

As per family tradition, she became an active worker in the Indian nationalist movement. In the provincial elections of July 1937, Congress formed the government and Vijaya was elected Minister in the

United Provinces. This marked another milestone in her political career as the first woman to be elected to a cabinet portfolio during British rule. She resigned just two years later as a move of solidarity with other Indian ministers who resigned after the British deployed Indian troops for the Second World War without consulting the ruling government.

She was also a member of the All Indian Women's Conference (AIWC) and was its President from 1941 to 1943. Her husband, Ranjit Sitaram Pandit, a Maharashtrian barrister from Kathiawad and classical scholar, was arrested for his participation in the freedom movement and died in Lucknow prison in 1944. Vijaya was widowed at forty-two, without financial support for the first time in her life. With no sons or a will, at a time when women did not have inheritance rights, the money and property were claimed by her husband's family. She was initially offered 150 rupees for widow maintenance and 50 rupees for her daughters' education until her daughters were married. Nehru supported her from the Ahmadnagar Fort prison cell, where he was jailed, with 2000 rupees, and encouraged her to keep going. Advised by her lawyers to fight for an inheritance, Gandhi urged her saying 'we had more important things to do.' And she agreed to accept a small settlement and signed a legal document giving up her claims and that of any unborn grandsons she might have!

Gandhi approached Vijaya to speak on behalf of India in the United States. The British had confiscated her passport however she found her way to the United States without a passport. In her memoirs, Vijaya Lakshmi Pandit mentions, that the American wife of the Chinese Consul General in Calcutta, invited her to attend a consulate dinner where she was introduced to the chief of the Allied Air Command in the Eastern region. With approval from the United States, she received her visa and flew out on a US army plane in December 1944!

Pandit was already in the United States when the United Nations Conference on International Organization (UNCIO) in San Francisco, 1945 was announced and she was nominated to represent India by

Gandhi. This was a crucial diplomatic event drawing attention from around the world. During this Conference, she called out the Indian representatives as being selected by the British to represent the colonized version of India, rather than the real India. She said, "I desire to make it clear that the so-called Indian representatives attending the Conference have not the slightest representative capacity, no sanction, and no mandate from any of the responsible groups in India and are merely nominees of the British Government. Anything they say here or any vote they cast can have no binding effect or force on the Indian people." Her introduction in San Francisco could not have been at a better time. Several Congress leaders were imprisoned and Vijaya used this platform of the UN to gain support.

She went on to add that India's fate needed to be addressed by and at the United Nations. That it was an acid test of the ideals of the United Nations, and the continued denial of India's freedom by Britain was a negation of those principles and of the sacrifices that have been made.

The Times of India reported on 7 May 1945. 'The skilful timing and unremitting energy of Mrs. Vijayalakshmi Pandit and her supporters in the United States have ensured a floodlight of publicity for India's claims at a time when the peoples of the world are looking anxiously to the conference for the formulation of principles and policies which are intended to shape their destinies.' And another declared her the 'First Lady of India.'

Nehru was released from prison in June 1945, and he started negotiating the terms of the British withdrawal. He wrote to his sister Vijaya, 'You know that your work in the States has been very greatly appreciated here by all kinds of people. You have done a splendid job, as perhaps no one else could have done in the circumstances. The immediate consequences of what you have done may not be obvious but I am sure that the remoter consequences will be considerable.'

After returning to India in 1946, Vijaya Lakshmi Pandit returned to her political career. She was reinstated to her position as Minister of Local Self- Government and Health in the United Provinces. She was among the 15 women out of 299 members to be elected to the Constituent Assembly. It was the experiences of women such as Vijaya that ensured some equality in the constitution. Their recommendations included critical issues such as minority rights, reservation, women's reservation, religious education, and schooling.

During her time in the Constituent Assembly, she continued to advocate for equality and criticized the consequences of imperialism on colonized countries. In one of the speeches that she made to the constituent assembly, she presented the struggle of leaving behind the lifelong impact of imperialism, even after countries had gained independence, she said, "Imperialism dies hard and even though it knows its days are numbered, it struggles for, survival. We have before us the instance of what is happening in Burma, Indonesia, in Indochina, and we see, how in those countries, despite the desperate efforts that the people are putting up to free themselves, the stranglehold of imperialism is so great that they are unable easily to shake it off."

Vijaya Lakshmi Pandit became India's ambassador to the Soviet Union from 1947 to 1949, the United States and Mexico from 1949 to 1951, Ireland from 1955 to 1961, and Spain from 1958 to 1961. She also served as the Indian High Commissioner to the United Kingdom. She became the first female President of the United Nations General Assembly in 1953. She was also the Governor of Maharashtra from 1962 to 1964 and was elected to the Lok Sabha, from Phulpur, from 1964 to 1968.

When Prime Minister Indira Gandhi declared Emergency in 1975, Vijaya strongly criticized it, despite her being a niece. After retiring from politics because of strained relations within the family, Vijaya shifted to Dehradun. She did attempt to campaign against Indira Gandhi in 1977 after retirement but suffered defeat when Neelam Reddy was selected to run and won the election unopposed. She had said, 'A symbol is what is needed for the presidency. And several people are telling me that I am the right kind of symbol for the job.'

The government appointed her as the Indian representative to the UN Human Rights Commission in 1979, after which she retired from public life. Along with being an accomplished politician, she was an excellent writer, too. Her book So I Became a Minister, published in 1989 gives a glimpse of the contribution of women in politics in an independent India. The dilemmas she faced on assuming a ministerial post at a time when only men assumed office. She also wrote an autobiography, 'The Scope of Happiness- A Personal Memoir 'where she traces similarities between the Irish and Indians.

'Prison Days' is an account of her third and final term in Naini Central Jail in Allahabad where she was sent on 12 August 1942. In this diary, Pandit recounts her experiences in jail and the hardships she endured along with other nationalists: rations mixed with dirt and stones, a lack of water and sanitary facilities, surviving on an allowance of 9 annas a day, and only the hard ground to sleep on.

Her Speeches and writing include topics like minority rights, reservation, religious education, and reformation of schooling and the education system. "Lots of women now have done much more than I did in my time. The reason why I got publicity was because at that time women had no rights" She was against the division of genders and stressed the need to involve both men and women in the process of nation-building. "It is not only the aspect of womanhood which concerns us today but that of manhood as well. The two are not separate as some people would have us believe and we cannot place them in different compartments and deal with them separately."

Anne Guthrie, in her book, Madame Ambassador: The Life of Vijaya Lakshmi Pandit gives additional details on her family, as does the autobiography, With No Regrets written by her sister, Krishna Nehru Hutheesingh. Her daughter, Nayantara Sahgal, in the book Indira Gandhi: The Road to Power, writes about the relationship between the aunt and the niece.

Vijaya Lakshmi Pandit died on 1 December 1990. Philip Noel- Baker a British diplomat said, 'if India could produce such women, India could herself most assuredly control her national affairs. But it was the drama taking place outside the meeting halls via Pandit that predicted the nature of UN post-colonialism that would take root in the power of the General Assembly in 1946 through the Indian delegation's fight against racism in South Africa. In other words, the Vijaya Lakshmi Pandit of 1945 was the perfect future tense for both the aspiring Indian postcolonial state and the ideals of the United Nations itself.' 'Pandit had said, 'The more we sweat in peace, the less we bleed in war.'

CHAPTER THIRTY-NINE
FOR THE BETTER

She was named Leelaboti and affectionately called Leela. Born on 2 October 1900 in Goalpara, Assam, her father, Girish Chandra Nag, was a deputy magistrate and also the tutor of Subhas Chandra Bose, and her mother Kunjalata Nag, was a home-maker. Leela Roy nee Nag studied at Eden High School, Dhaka, and later graduated with a Padmabati Gold Medal in English from Bethune College in Calcutta. The college had refused her admission as it was not a co-education college, however, Leela was defiant and the Vice-Chancellor had no choice but to permit her along with three other women! The four women thus became the first women to be admitted to the college in Calcutta.

During the floods in Bengal in 1921, Subhas Chandra Bose was collecting funds for the displaced citizens. Leela formed a Dhaka Women's Committee to raise funds and relief materials. On Bose's visit to Dhaka, she handed over the funds and materials to him, and thus began her association with Subhas Chandra Bose.

After completing her education Leela build her credo and dedicated herself to social work. Her single focus was to challenge the status quo and gender bias. In 1923 she established a martial self-defence group for women and called it the Deepali Sangha, which provided physical training to women. This group with multiple branches was instrumental in creating a complete generation of fierce and passionate women activists in politics.

Rabindranath Tagore once attended a meeting of Deepali Sangha and commented that he had never attended such a large gathering of women in entire Asia. In 1926 Leela joined the nucleus of an all-male revolutionary party called the Shree Sangha. This was a progressive group founded by Anil Roy with a similar mission to activate the men.

After she joined Roy, she helped recruit women in Shree Sangha, where the women were taught to make bombs and handle arms. A few years later in 1930, Anil Roy was arrested and Leela took charge of the Shree Sangha. By now Leela had established herself in India's political landscape.

She co-founded several associations like the student revolutionary Chhatri Sangha (Girl Students' Association) in 1926 and two different schools known as Nari Shiksa Mandir (Temple of Women's Education) and Shiksa Bhaban (House of Education). As her allegiance to Muslim women, she set up one of her schools, later known as Qamrunnessa Girls' School in Dhaka. Leela was a forward-thinking woman, who understood that women needed to be professionally trained to counter the bias that conventional jobs were only for men and much less for women. That woman could go beyond spinning and weaving khadi or picketing foreign clothes and alcohol. She wanted women to challenge their capabilities by executing assignments not thought to be in their realm. In 1927 Leela set up Mahila Atma Raksha Samity (Women's Self-Defence Association), where women were taught self- defence and martial arts. Additionally, she set up the Gana Shiksa Parisad (Association for Mass Education) for women to study in mass scale. The Indian National Congress recognized Leela Roy's work and in 1928 nominated her as a representative to the Congress Session at Calcutta. At this session, she introduced a paper on the History of Women's development in Bengal. Highlighting issues and progress of women in the region.

India was at a critical juncture in the 1930s with nationalist mass movements, protests, and armed revolution. British crackdown on the press and several publications were banned, thus Leela Roy decided to publish a Bengali monthly periodical called Jayasree in 1931. Established following the Chittagong arsenal strike, the rationale behind it was to motivate the women of Bengal. Jayasree was also the voice of Netaji Subhas Chandra Bose and went through a turbulent phase during the freedom struggle. Applauded by Rabindranath Tagore who had written a few lines on the periodical, "Rise, ignoring reverence; ignoring disdain, Tread the rocky trail with unrelenting steps, Pick the tattered banner up in grimy hands." Jayasree was managed by women, an incredible feat during that time! Leela deliberately did not want any articles on household topics in the publication, just to send a message to both men and women that women were capable beyond household chores and their centre of attention during the freedom struggle was on socio-political issues.

She formed the Dhaka Mahila Satyagraha Committee and was arrested and imprisoned for six long years between 1931 and 1937. After her release, she was nominated to the National Planning Committee of the Congress by Subhas Chandra Bose who was then the president of the Indian National Congress (INC.)

In 1939, Leela and Anil Roy got married. Subhas Chandra had resigned from the Indian National Congress and formed the Forward Bloc on 22 June 1939. The couple joined their mentor SubhasChandra Bose as founding members. When Bose was arrested in July 1940 she took over as the editor of the Forward Bloc Weekly. In 1942, during the Quit India movement, she was again arrested for her patriotic editorials in Jayasree. The magazine was forced to shut down and Leela spent another four years in prison. It is said that when Subhas Chandra Bose formed the Azad Hind Fauj in 1943, he had wished Leela Roy was part of the 'Rani Jhansi' regiment of young Indian women, however, she was in prison at that time.

Leela along with her husband Anil Roy was released in 1946, that year communal riots gripped Calcutta, Bihar, and Noakhali. She was again mitigating the tension and saving lives through the rescue operations. From 1946 to 1947, she set up seventeen relief camps in Noakhali for families affected by the riots, walked for six days in the region covering over 140 kilometers, and rescued hundreds of people. Her work was acknowledged by Gandhi and in 1946 Leela was elected to the Constituent Assembly of India. She was one of the 15 women elected and the only woman to be elected from Bengal. In 1947, post the partition of India she resigned in protest against Dhaka's partition from India.

Leela Roy resigned from working actively on legislative issues in 1962. She died on 11 June 1970. Today a portrait of Leela Roy adorns the wall of the Central Hall of Parliament. Initiating associations like Chhatri Sangha (Girl Students 'Association) and the Mahila Atma Raksha Samiti (Women's Self-Defence Association,) recruiting and mobilizing strategies for the nation, Leela Roy made significant contributions to women in both their political developments and financial empowerment.

CHAPTER FORTY
THE CHAMPION

Chandraprabha Saikiani was born on 16 March 1901 in Doisingari Kamrup, Assam. Her father Ratiram Mazumdar was the gaonburha (headman) of the village and her mother Gangapriya was a homemaker. Her parents focused their energies on educating their eleven children during a time when education was not encouraged among girls.

Chandraprabha along with her sister Rameshwari were sent to their maternal aunt at Bhaluki village for their primary education as Doisingari did not have a school. After completing their elementary education the girls returned home. They were then enrolled in a boys' school in Kothalmuri village. They had to cross muddied ponds to reach the school every day. As was customary her parents wanted Chandraprabha to marry early, however, Chandraprabha declined. She was an excellent student and at thirteen founded a girls' school at Akeya village. At first, she taught without any money however her school was brought under the Local Board, and she received six rupees a month as a tutor.

While teaching the girls, she was noticed by School Inspector Neelakanta Barua. He found it quite commendable to watch a young teenage teacher giving lessons, and advised her to study at (Nowgong) Nagaon Mission School. She was given a scholarship and in 1915, along with her sister Rameshwari they were admitted to NMS. She writes in her book, Jail Kahini (Jail Stories) that some Christian Missionary teachers regarded them as lowly and inferior. "Being Hindus, I and my sister were allotted space in the newly built room for the Bible Class. Soon the Hindu Girls Hostel quickly filled up. Due to lack of space, new girls joiners would be allotted a dark storeroom to stay in.' Chandraprabha questioned this and organized protests along with other girls. She writes, 'When I objected to such an arrangement, Miss Long retorted, You Indians live in smaller and worse cottages and huts than this. I heard such insulting words for the first time and realized that though these missionaries live here, they regard us as lowly and poor. I felt a sense of anger mixed with pride. I strongly protested and said, none of our people live in goodam (store) room like this and none of us will stay here.' 'And that is exactly what happened. All our girls refused to stay in that room. I felt vindicated at our first victory against the foreigners.'Chandraprabha was fifteen then! Hindu girls had to pay for paper and pencils which were free for the Christian students and she protested against this discrimination as well.

Two years later Chandraprabha formed the Nowgong Mahila Samiti (Women's Associations.) After she passed her Normal School Training she was appointed as Headmistress of Tezpur Middle School. During this time she fell in love with a young writer Dandinath Kalita with whom she had a son in 1922, however, he was from a higher caste, yielded to social pressure, and refused to acknowledge her as his wife. While in Tezpur, her passion for women's education and empowerment took shape. Under the guidance of her local contacts, Kironmoyee and Paramananda Agarwala who she considered parents Chandraprabha formed several Mahila Samitis. The Agarwala's shaped and influenced the young Chandraprabha toward women's education and their rights, which then become her lifelong passion.

She taught physical exercise to girl students of Asom Chattra Sanmilan (Assam Students 'Association.) At the association's annual convention she was asked to address a large gathering to speak on the evil effects of opium. It was the first time a woman would address a large public meeting and this marked her formal entry into public life. Later she established the Tezpur Mahila Samiti where Kironmoyee Agarwala became the President and Chandraprabha the Secretary. The Samiti proposed a resolution against the purdah system. When Gandhi first visited Tezpur in 1921, he stayed at the Agarwala residence and they introduced Chandraprabha as the leader of the women's movement in Assam. Gandhi then met the members of Tezpur Mahila Samiti and he discussed the Proceedings of the 7th World Conference on Women's Studies and for everyone to boycott foreign goods. She wrote in 1928, 'Almost in every province of India, women have their organizations. Through such meetings, several welfare activities like the establishment of orphanages and model schools have been established…Till today the women of Assam did not have an organization encompassing the women of the entire state. It is essential to form an organization. Today Assamese women are faced with several problems and an organization is essential to redress our problems. We can save ourselves if we develop a sense of unity and cohesion amongst ourselves.'

Chandraprabha recognized that associations at the grassroots level would make a difference. At the Nowgong Sahitya Sabha in 1925 women were made to sit behind bamboo partitions, as per purdah. She was livid and followed this up with a fiery speech questioning the patriarchal norms that kept women confined, "Why in our society the women confined in a cage-like this? It is a matter of great shame for the whole nation. A woman has to hide her face from the men. There can be nothing more shameful than this custom of ours… Sisters! Why should you sit in that cage-like structure? Who dares to prevent you from sitting outside it?" This talk encouraged the women attending the Sabha, to pull down the bamboo barriers and take their place in the front seats! Looking at the fearless and motivated women, Chandraprabha asked the delegates of the Sahitya Sabha to gather the next day. A thousand women reached the venue, but the conservative section of men did not allow the meeting and dismantled the venue. However undeterred the women went ahead with the meeting in an open field and resolved to form the Asom Mahila Samiti, which was formally launched in 1926 with Chandraprabha as its Secretary. She understood the organizational power of such associations at the grassroots. These Associations brought up issues of child marriage, encouraged women's education, small-scale women entrepreneurs, and promoted khadi and local handicrafts. She was also aware of the power of language in order to reach out to more women. Thus, between 1927 and 1931 she wrote articles in the Ghar Jeuti (the light of the house) an Assamese monthly women's magazine, and later edited the Mahila Samiti`s journal called Abhijatri, for seven years.

In 1972 she was conferred the Padma Shri however Chandraprabha Saikiani died on 16 March 1972, which was also the same day that she was born and a couple of days before the Padma Shri award ceremony. In 2002, the Government of India released a commemorative postage stamp in her honour. The former Girls' Polytechnic Institute in Guwahati was named after her.

CHAPTER FORTY-ONE
THE DEVI OF THE HILLS

A prominent freedom fighter from the hills of Darjeeling, Helen Lepcha, later known as Sabitri Devi, was born on 14 January 1902 in Sangmu, South Sikkim. Her father Achung Lepcha later migrated with the family to Kurseong. She discontinued her schooling at Scott Mission School Kurseong when she heard of Gandhi's Charkha Movement and moved to Calcutta in 1918. She enrolled herself in the charkha school run by the granddaughter of the social reformer Ishwar Chandra Vidyasagar!

A proficient learner, she mastered the art of spinning the charkha, and soon represented the charkha school at the national level khadi and charkha exhibition in Muzaffarpur in Bihar. The young Helen impressed Gandhi with her volunteering work during the relief measures carried out in the Bihar floods in 1920. He invited her to Sabarmati Ashram and named her Sabitri Devi. She was asked to concentrate on constructive work in the areas of Bihar and Uttar Pradesh and worked with the Congress Labour Union, particularly at the Jharia coal fields, Dhanbad, Banikpur, Danapur, Patna, and Muzaffarpur. In 1921, she led a procession of about 10000 mine workers from the Jharia coal field against labour exploitation and the replacement of local tribal workers. Her popularity among the rural people of Bengal and Bihar was a concern for the British, and they followed her every move. They issued a warrant in her name for her anti-colonial activities. They also named her one of the most-wanted congress leaders and she escaped an assassin's bullet, unhurt! In order to escape arrest, she would be constantly on the move. For a while, she lived at Ananda Bhavan (Swaraj Bhavan), Allahabad, the residence of Nehru. Here she worked closely with the Nehru family and the local Congress leaders. Later she went back to Kurseong and worked with the Congress committee there.

Post the Nagpur Session of the Indian National Congress in December 1920, people were encouraged to renounce government titles, schools, and foreign goods, and to refuse to pay their taxes to strengthen the freedom movement. Sabitri Devi went from door to door in Kurseong and Siliguri urging people to boycott foreign goods. She gathered volunteers, bonfires were lit with foreign goods while Section 144 was imposed! She was arrested and imprisoned for three months in Darjeeling jail. After her release, she was put under house arrest with the British keeping an eye on her. And of course so fearful were they that for the next three years she could not leave Kurseong. Regarded as a leader in the region she was addressed as Helen didi.

Sabitri Devi would attend almost every political event challenging and questioning colonial rule. She was the chairperson of various associations in Kurseong like the Sherpa Association, Nagar Congress, Anjuman Islamia, and the Lepcha Association. In 1936, Sabitri Devi was elected the first woman Commissioner of Kurseong Municipality. A true Gandhi follower, she did not hanker for a political post after independence, instead, she believed in nation building without material gains. In 1972, Sabitri Devi was awarded the Tamrapatra freedom fighter award by the Government of India. She was also made Chairperson of the Freedom Fighter Award Committee of the Darjeeling district. Sabitri Devi alias Helen Lepcha died on 18 August 1980. A daring nationalist, she played a critical role during the Non-Cooperation Movement, leading mass mobilizations and conducting door-to-door campaigns against foreign goods.

CHAPTER FORTY-TWO
THE LOYALIST

Manibehn Patel was born on 3 April 1903 in Karamsad, Gujarat. Her mother Jhaverba died when Mani was six. Her father Sardar Vallabhbhai Patel, also addressed as Unifier of India, was a senior Congress leader. Mani studied at the Queen Mary High School in Bombay as a boarder, while her father studied law in London. She later graduated from Gujarat Vidyapith in 1924, this was founded by Gandhi in 1920 with the purpose to promote educational institutions to be run by Indians.

After her graduation, Manibehn started helping her father in his work and would take down notes and maintain a diary of each person her father met. She dressed in the yarn she spun and travelled only by third class facility on trains and followed a simple disciplined life. She took part in the Bardoli Satyagraha in June 1928, which was led by her father for farmers of Bardoli. The British had taken a decision to impose a 30% increase in land revenues. This Satyagraha was a big success and shortly after that her father was known as Sardar Patel and became a significant leader in the country. She was part of Gandhi's Salt March in 1930 and was arrested for taking part in the Satyagraha.

When Gandhi initiated another Satyagraha in January 1932, Manibehn, was arrested on 8 January 1932, and taken to Sabarmati jail, in Ahmedabad. She was sentenced to six months imprisonment along with Mithubehn Petit and they were made 'C' class prisoners. Twenty days later, they were moved from Sabarmati jail to Yeravada prison, Poona. After five days there was another order, to transfer them once again from Yeravada jail to Belgaum jail in Karnataka and she spent six months here and was released only on 22 June 1932.

Gandhi wrote a letter during his fast on 6 May 1933, ''Chi Mani, like last time, this time too, I am permitted to send you a letter every day during the fast and you too can write to me daily…Vallabhbhai is bearing it all very calmly and has promised to Mahadev that he will co-operate with me—maybe by keeping silent— without entering into any argument. I like this attitude of his. For a few days he carried his silence too far. Even the fountain of his humour seemed to have dried up. But it has welled up again. The fast was absolutely necessary. I have no doubt that this was the best time for it. I have thought about the matter from every point of view and am fully convinced of the correctness of my decision. The fast is not directed against anybody. I do not even know what event pained me and precipitated the fast. Many things had their felt or unfelt influence on me. The point is that if the workers doing Harijan work under my guidance are not perfectly sincere, the cause must be some impurity in me. Moreover, the monster of untouchability is more frightful than Ravana. The latter had only ten heads, but this one has hundreds of them. They cannot all be cast off by any number of organizations or any amount of money collected for the purpose. It is not enough to secure rights for Harijans. What is wanted is a change of heart among caste Hindus if they and Harijans are to embrace one another as blood-brothers. This great spiritual task can be accomplished only if we spend all the spiritual strength we possess. This is an ancient and well-trodden path. The wonder is that I did not think of it before. Remain calm both of you and contribute your share when the time comes. A fast in sympathy with me is out of question. Blessings to both from BAPU.'

During the Quit India in 1942 she was arrested and jailed yet again. While in jail she would start her day with prayers, spinning, reading, mending, and looking after the sick inmates. After independence, she was elected as a member of parliament in Lok Sabha and later in the Rajya Sabha. She went on a Satyagraha in 1975 against the arrest of Opposition leaders during the Emergency and was arrested in 1976 for shouting slogans for the release of leaders and removal of Emergency and Press Censorship. Manibehn was also the Vice-President of the Gujarat State Congress Committee from 1957 to 1964 and it's President from 1976 to 1977.

Manibehn Patel was honest and fiercely loyal to her father and the nation, she lived a disciplined life and died on 26 March 1990. She was 87. For almost three decades she was a member of parliament, she continued to travel in a rickshaw, led a simple but active public life, and was associated with many Gandhian institutions. She was a Trustee of Gujarat Vidyapith, Navjivan Trust, Mahadev Desai Memorial Trust, and Sardar Vallabhbhai Seva Trust. After her father died, the Birlas invited Manibehn to stay at the Birla House however she preferred to stay in her cousin's house in Ahmedabad. She was truly a nationalist and a Sardar's daughter.

CHAPTER FORTY-THREE
THE CREATIVE FREEDOM FIGHTER

Kamaladevi was born on April 3, 1903, in a Saraswat Chitarapur Brahmin family of Mangalore, the youngest daughter of Ananthaya and Girijamma Dhareshwar. Her father was in government service and later retired as a senior official. Girijamma was his second wife and she came from an aristocratic family. Kamaladevi admired her mother's invincible spirit which went on to shape her life.

The family was well-educated including the women and encouraged Kamaladevi to pursue her dreams and raise her voice for good. She was an exceptional student and had the determination and courage to fight against anything wrong. Girijamma was determined that Kamaladevi receive the best education and attend a regular school instead of being taught at home, as was the practice in families at the time. Thus Kamaladevi was enrolled at the local Saint Anne Convent. Encouraged by her progressive husband, Girijamma was herself very well versed in traditional art forms, dance, music, and studied ancient Sanskrit drama.

Kamaladevi's father died suddenly, without a will and everything was passed on to the elder son from his first marriage. Though the family home remained with her mother, the land attached to the home was taken away, and therefore there was no money left for a household that had several dependents. The property had been built by both her parents after their marriage, yet they inherited nothing. What they received was only by way of a family settlement. In fact during finalising the settlement her mother was put through a great amount of humiliation. This may have been the reason that Girijamma formalized the marriage of Kamaladevi, who was eleven, to one of the richest men of Mangalore. A very close family friend's son, Krishna Rao who was four years older than Kamaladevi.

Krishna Rao unfortunately died within a year of the marriage. Kamaladevi, who was still living with her mother after her marriage, continued with her studies at school. Her mother sheltered little Kamaladevi from the uncivilized customs, which were practiced toward the widows. Krishna Rao's family were equally supportive and did not demand that Kamaladevi live the lonely life of a child widow. Kamaladevi witnessed the evil social norms of society for the first time. In her book, Awakening of Indian Women, she writes of the plight of young widows-the two and a half crores of widows as "Souls in agony. They were, disfigured and relegated to a life of servility with scant regard for their feelings or needs. They are even regarded as objects of ill- omen." Remarriage was still looked at with disfavour despite the Widow Remarriage Act of 1856.

Kamaladevi moved with her mother to Madras in 1917. Girijamma may have moved away from Mangalore not only because of the failing health of her older daughter, but to take Kamaladevi away from the more conservative members of the community. She encouraged Kamaladevi to study and groomed her for active participation in the socio-political movements emerging across the country in the early 1900s. Kamaladevi would accompany her mother to Seva Sadan where she would see her mother speak to women on literacy and also read to them from the papers, magazines, and books written by social reformers and nationalists. She would see a change in the women's perspectives after the talks and meetings.

While studying at Queen Mary's College, in Madras Kamaladevi became friends with Suhasini Chattopadhyay, Sarojini Naidu's younger sister, who introduced Kamaladevi to their older brother Harindranath Chattopadhyay. Both had similar interests and got married in an unconventional registered civil marriage in 1919. Kamaladevi was sixteen and married to an individual, considered a genius in the intellectual world. A few months after their marriage, Harindranath travelled to Cambridge to study for a Ph.D. Kamaladevi remained in India and later in 1921, she joined her husband. In her autobiography, she mentions, 'to pursue the normal academic studies with the hope of continuing piano lessons!' It is believed that she sold her jewellery to manage her travel expenses. Kamaladevi's interest in social work led her to enrol in a Social Work Diploma Course at Bedford College, London, and she passed with a degree in Sociology. The course in sociology combined with practical training allowed Kamaladevi to visit the slums in London. She realized that to prepare herself for her life as a Satyagrahi, academic study would be less useful than a sociology course.

The couple returned to India in 1922. The marriage didn't last long and Kamaladevi was probably the first woman to be legally divorced through an Indian court of law. After this, she committed herself to fighting for India's independence. Her interactions with prominent freedom fighters such as Mahadev Govind Ranade, Gopal Krishna Gokhale, and Annie Besant strengthened her resolve to join the freedom movement. By now she was much more aware of the inequalities in society and was unable to accept what was happening in India at that time. Kamaladevi, joined the Indian National Congress (INC) in 1927. She was appointed the secretary of the All-India Women's Conference (AIWC) and took part in legislating equal rights for women, ensuring they were equal partners in both the socio-economic and political spheres. An outspoken supporter of Satyagraha, in her tours in America and some other parts of the world, during the Second World War, she requested support for self-governance in India. She proposed that civil rights, environmental justice, religious freedoms, and political independence were all interrelated issues. The British came to know of her activism and banned her from returning to India. However, she continued on her journey!

On 26 January 1930 at a meeting in Azad Maidan, Bombay where the Congress workers had gathered to take a pledge and hoist the Indian flag. A scuffle ensued in which an attempt was made to pull down the tricolor. Rushing forward to hold the flag Kamaladevi received injuries but was not conscious of anything except that she must save the flag. This incident has been written about and she came to be known as The Nation's feisty daughter. There are photographs of Kamaladevi along with other satyagrahis marching with the flag and a banner that read 'Up with the National Flag and Down with the Union Jack.'

At the Indian National Congress's Lahore session on 19 December 1929, Gandhi declared January 26, 1930, as Puran Swaraj Day, or complete self-rule day. He had planned the various phases of the movements, first by violating the salt tax. When Gandhi spoke of the Salt Satyagraha, not many including Kamaladevi, understood how a fistful of salt could be the beginning of a massive movement. But Gandhi knew that a common Indian identified the handful of salt as an essential ingredient in every home! Women were to be excluded from the long march, starting on 6 April 1930 from Sabarmati Ashram to the Dandi seashore. However, the women were not deterred. On the same day that Gandhi marched to Sabarmati, Kamaladevi led a group of women and marched to Chowpatty, Bombay! They started making salt from the seawater on makeshift chullhas. The police intervened followed by a lathi charge. Kamaladevi suffered burns, however she along with the other women continued, refusing to call off the protest or take medical aid. The crowds grew and several women leaders and housewives carrying pots and pans joined in! Later the salt collected was placed in small packets and sold outside the Bombay Stock Exchange. She was arrested, taken into a police lock-up with criminals, and sentenced to one-year imprisonment. Later she was sent to Yerwada Women's Prison, where shared the prison room with Sarojini Naidu.

In her book, Indian Women's Battle for Freedom, she describes the salt Satyagraha day and writes, 'A rough boot pushed me aside and I came down with my arm on the burning pole.' She adds, 'The salt satyagraha must stand out as not only unique but as an incredible form of revolution in human history. The very simplicity of this weapon was as appealing as intriguing. So far as women were concerned it was ideally tailor for them. As women naturally preside over culinary operations, salt is for them the most intimate and indispensable ingredient.' Kamaladevi organised volunteers for a variety of programs, including Prabhat pheris (early morning processions) and gathering salt at Chowpatty and Juhu beaches.

To defy the norms of the social world, she took to acting which was not a respectable career for women. "Let men learn to be equal to women first.'' Kamaladevi started her film career with the first silent film in the Kannada film industry, Mricchakatika (Vasantsena) in 1931. She acted in Films like Tansen starring K. L. Saigal and Khursheed, followed by Shankar Parvati in 1943, and Dhanna Bhagat in 1945. Later she gave up her acting career, however, continued her associations with the music and dance fraternity. While in Germany she was introduced to European experimental theatre and after she saw the plays of Bertolt Brecht, where he reminds the audience that the play was a representation of reality, she felt that India too could try new forms. In 1944 she set up the Indian National Theatre (INT), Bombay, and a theatre organization that took theatre to people.

Kamaladevi's interest in crafts was cultivated while she was a child, watching decorations being prepared during rituals. She would see jewellers working in her home, with simple tools to make jewellery with diamonds and precious stones, all under the attentive eyes of the women of the house! And with this creative mindset, she was most definitely the driving force behind the revival of Indian handicrafts and bringing them into the contemporary environment. She was not only building the crafts world, reviving the cultural traditions, in the areas of crafts, performing arts, and theatre but also improving the lives of people. Kamaladevi was the first chairperson of the All India Handicrafts Board which was set up in 1952. She was instrumental in setting up the Central Cottage Industries Emporium all over India, the World Craft Council, the

Craft Council of India and Delhi Craft Council and they became important agencies for governments to reach out to the master craftsmen. She opened several institutions for art and theatre, including the National School of Drama, Bharatiya Natya Sangha, Lady Irwin College, and Sangeet Natak Academy.

Kamaladevi continued to be engaged in politics and social work, particularly in promoting handicrafts. In a significant speech in 1962, she said, 'The continued existence of cottage industries meant to an appreciable extent the decentralization of social and economic power and the creation of an institutional plurality which effectively stood between the ordinary citizen and a powerful state. Besides providing ample employment to the rural folk, the cottage industries played an important role in the process of decentralization of economic power on the rural level. The ability of the village to fulfil its own manufacturing needs gave it a remarkable social cohesion, which could not be loosened in any significant way by even the most devastating war.'

'History may have happened in Pataliputra, Kannauj, Delhi, or Agra, but it was always against the backdrop of stability in village life. The cottage industries almost acted as a defensive economic wall against the ravages of time and man. And these industries were by no means primitive. Within their warp and weft, they displayed fine skill and varied techniques developed through generations of dignified toil. Through the centuries until the calculated destruction of the indigenous industries in British times, the products of India were famed in all the markets of the world. These brought wealth to the country, but it seldom concentrated on a few layers of society. It is true that the royalty displayed fabulous riches, but poverty was not so great and absolute as in more recent times. If the cottage industries taught the village independence in its ordinary life from the exactions of the capital, they also taught the people in the village interdependent.'

'Handicrafts are rightly described as the crafts of the people. In India it is not an industry, as the word is commonly understood; for the produce is also a creation symbolizing the inner desire and fulfillment of the community,' she added.

She founded the Indian Cooperative Union which helped to rehabilitate the refugees from the Northwest Frontier Provinces who were displaced during the Partition. The Government of India awarded Kamaladevi Chattopadhyay the Padma Bhushan in 1955. In 1966, the Ramon Magsaysay Award for Community Leadership, and in 1974, she was felicitated with the Sangeet Natak Akademi, Fellowship. She also received the Charles Eames' Award for contributing to the Quality of Life in India and in 1977, the UNESCO Award for the promotion of handicrafts. She was awarded the Padma Vibhushan in 1987. Her mother's love for music was shared by Kamaladevi and was a motivation for her later years. Many of her books on politics, society, women's rights, and the arts and crafts were inspired by her personal experiences. Her books questioned the atrocities on women, including her memoir, Inner Recesses, Outer Spaces which was published in 1986. Kamaladevi Chattopadhyay died in Mumbai on 29 October 1988, she was 85. Google doodle honoured her on her 115 birthday. She stood up for the rights of her people to live with dignity. She lives on, through the skills of people, the performing art institutions for which she created the foundation in contemporary India.

In her memoir, Kamaladevi Chattopadhyay's closing lines read, 'As I lean back and close my eyes to relax and let my memories run back the long aisles of time, to know what are the things I wanted most and discover, the same yearning remains most poignant in me still. It is the little things—an unhurried life of leisure to dream, to suck in the slow notes of music, to savour of the gifts of nature, the play of light and shadow so reminiscent of life with its joys and sorrows. For I am very human and it is very human to want the trifles that we usually brush and throw away. In the ultimate an individual is a lovely soul, away and apart holding on these little things of life while all else has faded away.'

CHAPTER FORTY-FOUR
TOFANI

Born on 26 July 1904 in Calcutta, Malati's father Barrister Kumudnath Sen, died when she was three and she was brought up by her mother Snehalata Sen who then took up a teaching job at Bethune College Calcutta. A bright student Malati studied at the Bethune School, passed her matriculation and wanted to study in a college managed by Indians. She applied to Rabindranath Tagore's Visva-Bharati, Santiniketan who agreed to admit her if her mother took charge of the hostel called Notun Bari (New House.) and her mother agreed. During the six years that Malati was in Santiniketan, she frequently interacted with Tagore and was influenced by his ideals. The classes were held in the open, under a tree with nine other girls. An extrovert, she would take part in dance dramas and music sessions.

In an article 'Reminiscences of Santiniketan,' her mother Snehalata Sen wrote, 'Malati was very happy and benefited much from her residence at Visva-Bharati as a student. The personal influence of Gurudev and his teachings, his patriotism, and idealism, have influenced and guided Malati throughout her life.'

Nabakrushna Choudhury a young student visited Santiniketan and met Malati during the visit. They married in July 1927 and moved from Santiniketan to a small village, Anakhia, in Orissa, where Nabakrushna had his ancestral farm and he started sugar cane cultivation. At the village, the couple began educating the villagers. During the Salt Satyagraha, Malati and her husband were arrested and imprisoned, and even while they were in jail, they encouraged other prisoners to take part in the freedom struggle. After their release they formed the Utkal Congress Samajvadi Karmi Sangh which later came to be known as the Orissa Provincial Branch of the All India Congress Socialist Party.

Malati Choudhury set up the Baji Rout Chhatrabas (Students' Hostel) for the children of freedom fighters and tribal people in 1946. The hostel was named after the young hero Baji Rout of the area who was shot dead by the British when he refused to take them in his boat across the river. Today most of the inmates of Baji Rout Chhatrabas are orphans, tribal and Dalit children. Along with veteran freedom fighters of Orissa she set up the Utkal Navajeevan Mandal in 1948 at Angul, Orissa. The Mandal was initiated for the protection of the children of political activists and to provide education to them as well as the marginalised castes and tribes. Today it is one of the few pioneering organizations, working among tribal people and Dalits. In fact, in 1978, the government established a State Resource Centre for Adult Education in Orissa with the help of Utkal Navajeevan Mandal. She remained its motivation till the end of her life. She also founded the Post Basic School at Champatimunda in 1954, located in a rural area in Angul, Orissa. The school consists of Grades from 9 to 10. Odia was and is the medium of instruction in this school.

Malati Choudhury along with her sister-in-law Ramadevi Choudhury accompanied Acharya Vinoba Bhave to the villages of Orissa during the Bhoodan Movement. She understood Bhave's mission that, 'everyone must have land to till and make one's living.'

She was selected as one of the 15 women members of the Constituent Assembly in 1946, however, resigned from the Assembly same year to continue working at the grassroots. She emphasized the role of education, especially adult education, in the rural reconstruction of India. Leading campaigns against the zamindars, dictatorial rulers in the princely states, and ensuring that Congress in Orissa has a democratic and socialist face.

Her husband, Nabakrushna Choudhury, was one of the founders of the Congress Socialist Party in India and was the President of the Utkal Pradesh Congress Committee in 1946. He later became the Chief

Minister of Orissa in 1952. After independence, she did not join politics, as per Gandhi's advice to Congress activists that all of them need not hanker for political posts, but should work for and with the people. During the communal riots, she accompanied Gandhi to the villages of Noakhali in 1947. Her pace of work earned her the nickname 'Tofani' (the storm) from Gandhi! Having been jailed several times during the freedom struggle, in 1921, 1930, 1936, and 1942, she had no issues battling for democracy even at an old age and fighting for the backward classes.

As President of the Orissa Civil Liberties Committee in 1968, she strongly condemned the killings of 'Naxalites' in false encounters. Her fight against injustice did not end with Indian independence, she continued to advocate for the rights of the tribal and the marginalized and liberate them from the exploitation and harassment by money lenders, landlords, and forest officials. Fiercely opposed the Emergency in 1975, and went underground to organize opposition to the dictatorial rule, which of course led to her imprisonment.

Baji Rout Chhatrabas became the home, for Malati Choudhury and her husband Nabakrushna Choudhury, where they lived after independence and from where they launched many struggles for justice. Consciously avoiding publicity and never yearning for power, she continued to work with the marginalized communities of Orissa. She was bestowed Deshikottam, the highest honour from her Alma mater, Visva- Bharati in 1998. She initially refused the Jamnalal Bajaj Award however the award was presented to her at her home and she accepted! Malati Choudhury died on 15 March 1998, at the age of 93 at her home in Baji Rout Chhatrabas. Gandhi had nicknamed her 'Tofani' because of her daring activities, the pace of work, and for being the first to reach out to the affected people. And Malati Choudhury was also fondly called Numa by her people, for whom she voiced her protest against repression by bureaucracy and landlords. Her politics was only to be of service to the people and certainly not from the status of political power but by being a part of them in their struggles.

CHAPTER FORTY-FIVE
THE WOMEN'S RIGHTS ACTIVIST

Growing up in a Brahmo family where customs derogatory to women's self-respect were rejected and independence encouraged, nudged Renuka Ray towards activism and a champion of women's rights. Born on 4 January 1904, in Calcutta, her father Satish Chandra Mukherjee was the son of Nibaran Chandra Mukherjee, a leader of the progressive Brahmos in Calcutta during the first schism of the Brahmo Samaj. Her mother Charulata was a social worker and the daughter of Sarla Roy a well-known social worker and founder of Gokhale Memorial Girls School, Calcutta. Her grandmother's vision was that 'Education meant the development of thought and culture- that education brought a wider outlook of life.'

Renuka studied at Loreto House and later the Diocesan College, Calcutta. She was sixteen when she met Gandhi. Influenced by his position on education and the need for Indians to study in schools and colleges run by Indians as well as learn the national language, she quit the Diocesan College which followed a British system of education. In British India, Macaulay's Education policy was introduced not for the development of people's intellect, but to create literates, whose hearts and minds were British! Whereas Gandhi's views on education was aimed at an all-around development, with an emphasis on physical, mental, social, and spiritual development in the child. His vision was that at the primary level, the medium of education must be the mother tongue of the learners.

In 1921, Renuka's parents requested Gandhi to ask her to study at the London School of Economics. She followed Gandhi's advice, that she should take full advantage of her education and come back well-equipped to serve the country. He further mentioned to her that the freedom movement required 'educated workers.' On her return from London, Renuka married Satyendra Nath Ray on 26 October 1925, who was in the civil services and his job postings invariably took him to rural India. These constant shifting from one district to another, brought Renuka in contact with village life.

She was convinced that the way to development was through the Gandhian constructive programs. After her return from London, Renuka was nominated as the representative of the All India Women's Conference (AIWC) to discuss legal changes in the laws related to women. Instead of complaining about the conditions of women she spoke of how to accomplish their dreams and worked for women and social reform. She became the President of AIWC in 1932 and again in 1953. In 1943 Renuka was nominated to the Central Legislative Assembly to address social legislation. Renuka played an important role as one of the fifteen members of the Constituent Assembly of India, and made several interventions in the Assembly including her debates on women's rights issues, minority rights, and bicameral legislature provision-questioning a system of government in which the legislators comprise two houses and felt that it was expensive to have two houses in the parliament when India was a poor country. A strong advocate for gender equality, she argued the need to formulate and implement a single personal law irrespective of gender, now referred to as the Uniform Civil Code. She said, "The women in this country have striven for their rights, for equality of status, for justice and fair play, and most of all, be able to take their part in responsible work in the service of their country. The social backwardness of women has been sought to be exploited in the same manner as the backwardness of so many sections in this country, by those who wanted to deny the country its freedom.' She was aware that changing times meant that women needed reservation of seats in politics and later dropped her opposition to the women's reservations bill.

Concerned with the condition of women workers in plantations and mines she carried an adjournment motion in the Central Assembly in

1944 against the British Government and succeeded in restoring the ban on restricting women from working in mines. She also represented India at the United Nations General Assembly in May 1949. Renuka was appointed as Minister of Relief & Rehabilitation, West Bengal in the years 1952-57. She was also a Lok Sabha member for the years 1957-1967 from the Malda Lok Sabha constituency. In 1959 she headed a committee on Social Welfare and Welfare of Backward Classes, which is popularly known as the Renuka Ray Committee. Here she recommended that a separate department should be created under the Ministry of Home Affairs for backward classes. She also served on the Planning Commission and at the governing body of Visva-Bharati, Santiniketan. She went on to establish the All Bengal Women's Union and an ardent supporter of consumer rights, she established the Consumer Action Forum.

Renuka Ray opposed the Emergency in 1975. She was awarded the Padma Bhushan in 1988. An outspoken politician, she is remembered as the voice for women. After her death, in the monsoon session of the Lok Sabha, the Speaker described Renuka Ray as, 'an active social and political worker, Smt. Ray vigorously worked for the welfare of the weaker sections of society particularly women. She was the President of All India Women's Conference during 1953-55. A widely travelled person, Smt. Ray was a delegate to the United Nations General Assembly in 1949. Smt. Renuka Ray passed away on 11 April, 1997 at Calcutta at the age of 94 years.'

In her memoir, 'My Reminiscences: Social Development During Gandhian Era and After, which was published in 1982, she writes, 'without education a nation would tread in the darkness of ignorance.' A Gandhian, women's rights activists and a politician, Renuka Ray's vision was to bring changes in the life of women of India.

CHAPTER FORTY-SIX
THE SOCIAL REFORMER

She was born on 28 May 1905 into an affluent family however believed her real contribution was to her country. Yashodhara's father K.H. Ramaiah was the registrar of the cooperative department in Maharaja Krishnaraja Wodeyar IV's kingdom Mysore and had a great deal of influence on her. Her mother Revamma was a home-maker. She studied at the London Mission High School, Bangalore, and graduated from Queen Mary's College, Madras. After her graduation Yashodhara returned to Bangalore and joined the Indian freedom struggle. Her father was the leader of the backward classes in the state and was the founder of the Vokkaligara Sangha. The Vokkaliga community, though a land-owning class had remained backward as they did not recognize the need for education. He took it upon himself and encouraged education amongst the community.

Yashodhara married H. C. Dasappa, a lawyer and later a minister under Jawaharlal Nehru. He supported Yashodhara in the activities of the National Congress and Gandhian movements. After meeting Gandhi in 1927, Yashodhara became his follower and took part in the various campaigns, organising boycotts, picketing and so on. She was against establishing liquor shops, wore and promoted Khadi, as well as spun the charkha. Her home was a meeting point for the satyagrahis. The British had become suspicious of her activities, hence positioned secret service police near her home! They even restricted her movements, keeping a surveillance on visitors, however Yashodhara who was by now an inspiration for the satyagrahis kept on with the movement objectives.

When her husband won elections for the Mysore assembly under the Praja Samyuktha Party, she remained in Congress. Later she influenced him to join the Congress Party and he became a prominent leader, frequently imprisonment, and of course, losing his legal practice. Yashodhara converted their residence in Mysore into a boarding home for girl students of surrounding villages. She also managed the Kasturba Kanya Vidyalaya a school for poor girls in the state. The right propaganda was required to spread the message of swadeshi and this could only be done through publishing articles on the movement. Hence along with the satyagrahis she secretly printed articles in a journal which they named 'Jwale.'

During different phases of the non-cooperation movement Congress leaders in the Mysore state were arrested, there was strict control over their activities and Yashodhara was put under house-arrest which at times made it difficult for her to move out of her home however she managed to connect with the satyagrahis and led the various movements secretly.

Yashodhara took part in what was called the Forest Satyagraha in 1930. The forest was a source of income for the people who lived around the vicinity and they would go to the forest, for grass, firewood and cattle grazing. The British government had passed the Forest Act, and under this act, the entry of animals into the forest for fodder was banned and there was a compulsion to keep animals at home. Unacceptable to the tribal, thousands joined the Satyagraha. While implementing the forest law the forest administration harassed the cattle owners and captured cattle. The forest satyagrahis protested and disobeyed the law by leaving the cattle for grazing in the forests. They cut grass and collected wood and leaves from the forests without permission from the forest authorities. They further boycotted the employees of the forest and revenue departments working for the British. Women played an active role in this movement.

Yashodhara visited the Wardha Ashram in 1941 along with her husband and stayed there for over six months. While at Wardha, she worked among the rural women. Later she established a training centre for women in Mysore, to ensure they are economically self-sufficient, the centre trained the women in tailoring, handcrafts, and midwifery. This centre was especially beneficial for the widows and women who were deserted by their families.

When Kasturba Gandhi died, Gandhi suggested to his followers that a trust be established in Ba's memory for the rural women. Yashodhara managed the Kasturba Gandhi Memorial Trust as a trustee in Mysore. She bought eighty acres of land in Arsikere, Karnataka, and with her money established an ashram. The Kasturba Gandhi Smarakh Grama, Arsikere, committed to the rural reconstruction of the area. Today it provides temporary shelter for deserted women and young widows and a school and boarding for girl students from poor families. Young girls are trained to become teachers, and midwives, they are taught tailoring, and other skills.

After independence Yashodhara Dasappa spent her time at Arsikere building the ashram centred on rural reconstruction. In 1964 she became the Minister of Social Welfare in Karnataka, and passed an order making it an offense not to allow Harijans to draw water from common wells and ordered the utilization of the grants given to Harijan children as scholarships as well as for welfare measures. She went ahead and ordered the government to open sarvajanik hostels for the students of all castes and communities, without caste bias. She was of the view that if students' stayed together they would develop mutual respect and gradually this would eliminate caste discrimination.

Gandhi had planned a complete prohibition of liquor sales in independent India as he was of the view that revenue from the sale of liquor was a sin. Later several states decided to abolish prohibition, Mysore too wanted to abolish prohibition as the sale of liquor was a big revenue generator. Yashodhara opposed this and argued against it however the government decided to go ahead and abolished prohibition in the state. She firmly believed that alcoholism was a burden on the poor, resulting in poverty, and destroying the social structure and families. She immediately resigned from the ministry in 1969! Her resignation from the ministry left her more time to take forward several constructive programs.

In 1955, Yashodhara, founded the Bharatiya Grameen Mahila Sangh, a National Association of Rural Women along with C. Sharada. She was awarded the Padma Bhushan in 1972. A Gandhian, social reformer and activist, Yashodhara Dasappa died in 1980.

Anna Chandy

R. Sivabhogam

Durgawati Devi

Sushila Mohan

Mahadevi Verma

Sucheta Kripalani

Aruna Asaf Ali

Tara Rani Srivastava

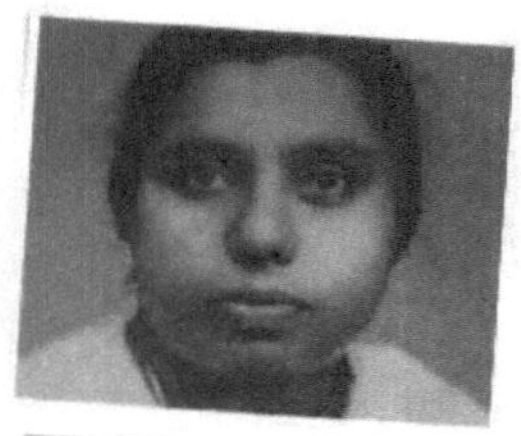

Accamma Cherian

Lalitambika
Antharjanam

CHAPTER FORTY-SEVEN
THE PURPOSEFUL JUSTICE

Born in 1905 in Travancore in a Syrian Christian family Anna Chandy was brought up in Trivandrum. Her father died soon after her birth and she and her sister were brought up by their mother. Fortunately, Anna belonged to a state with matrilineal traditions and she was brought up to be independent. Post completing her school in Kerala, Anna decided to study law after Maharani Sethu Lakshmi Bayi, the regent in the Travancore Dynasty opened admissions for women in the Government law college. Her mother was not very keen, but Anna went ahead and enrolled herself and was the first woman in Kerala to be a lawyer. She received her postgraduate degree in law with distinction in 1929, passed the bar exam the same year, and started fighting criminal law cases in a male-dominated field of India.

In 1930, as a first-generation feminist, she founded and edited a Malayali Magazine titled Shrimati, which served as a platform to voice women's rights. Through the magazine, she questioned child marriage and wage discrimination faced by women working on the farms, the right to widow remarriages, and so on. Anna hoped to see a change in the patriarchal system and realized that one would need to fight the system not only from the outside but from within as well. She decided to stand for elections in 1930, as a representative of the Travancore state. Her opposition and a few publications started a smear campaign against her and she lost the elections. However, she had become a public figure by now and also very popular. When she re-contested she won the assembly seat for a tenure of two years between 1932 and 1934.

Anna married PC Chandy, an inspector general of police who encouraged her to study and was instrumental in her becoming a criminal law expert in court. She was one of the first women in India to fight for women's reservations in government jobs, as women were still considered inferior to men. Due to her efforts the satute that prevented women from working in government jobs was abolished. She also inspired women to pursue law and hold an important key in the judiciary.

In 1937, Anna was appointed as the first female munsif (lower court judge) by Sir CP Ramaswami Iyer, the then prime minister of the state, and later she was appointed as the first female district court judge in 1948. On her appointment, she remarked, "I admit that I was not free from trepidation when I first stepped up to the Bench. However, what was foremost in my mind was a fierce determination to make a success of this experiment. I knew I was a test case... If I faltered or failed, I would not just be damaging my career, but would be doing a great disservice to the cause of women."

On 9 February 1959, Anna Chandy became the first female high court judge of India and held this position until 5 April 1967, after which she retired. Post-retirement, she served on the Law Commission of India. In 1996, Justice Anna Chandy died at the age of 91. In her autobiography 'Aatmakatha,' published in 1973, she writes about her life and her husband as her big support in her career. 'This is not written with a lot of thought or attention. I have never kept diaries or memoirs. I am just scribbling down whatever comes up in my memory without much order or elegance of language, in a very ordinary style. I have no idea of bookish language. This is my first attempt at literary writing. Therefore I beg the large-hearted readers to forgive whatever failings that may be found in the narration of the story of my life.'

CHAPTER FORTY-EIGHT
THE ACCOUNTANT

R. Sivabhogam was born on 23 July 1907 in Madras. She studied at the Lady Wellington School and graduated from The Queen Mary's College, Madras. After her graduation, she became a satyagrahi and a member of the Swadeshi League in Madras. She boycotted British goods and picketed liquor shops and was imprisoned for a year in Vellore jail. Post her release from prison, she contemplated either marriage, freedom struggle, or pursuing a career.

Influenced by Sister R S Subbalakshmi, an educator and activist, she went ahead and registered for the Government Diploma in Accountancy and later became the first Indian Woman Accountant in 1933. After her articles training, she wanted to start an independent practice but the British Government passed a law that did not allow anyone who had undergone a prison sentence from registering themselves as Accountants. Sivabhogam went ahead and filed a writ petition to revoke the Act and subsequently, the verdict went in her favour. She won the legal fight and started her independent practice in 1937.

After independence, Sivabhogam became a member of the Institute of Chartered Accountants of India (ICAI) which was formed in 1949. She created a record when she was elected as a member in the very first year of the formation of the Madras Regional Council of ICAI and was the Chairperson from 1955 to 1958. A very kind person, she provided pro bono services to people and organisations who could not afford audits.

R Sivabhogam was a Senate member of the University of Madras and a Committee member of the Society of Auditors. Active in the sphere of social service, she contributed to various charities and several scholarships. In 1956 she instituted an award for a woman who would successfully clear the ICAI finals in one sitting during her final examination! Sivabhogam was a nationalist, would wear only Khadi travel everywhere by bus and followed the Gandhian principle of leading a simple yet active life.

R. Sivabhogam died on 14 June 1966. The Southern India Regional Council of ICAI created an endowment in her name for scholarships for female students. Sivabhogam's prime goal was to champion women's education and it was because of her that as of 2020, ICAI had 82000 female Chartered Accountants.

CHAPTER FORTY-NINE
DURGA BHABI

Durgawati Devi was born on 7 October 1907, in Kaushambi, Allahabad. Her father Pandit Banke Bihari was a court official at the Allahabad Collectorate. Her mother died when Durgawati was young, after which her father took sannyasa, a life of renunciation leaving the young girl with his sister. She was married at eleven to Bhagwati Charan Vohra who was the Propaganda Secretary of the Naujawan Bharat Sabha (Youth Society of India,) Lahore, a leftist youth movement co-formed with Bhagat Singh. This was used as a recruiting ground for the Hindustan Socialist Republican Association (HSRA) an Indian revolutionary party, with the primary goal to achieve independence. Their mission was to liberate India from British colonial rule through a revolution that included armed rebellion. Durga Devi worked at a girls' college in Lahore and also carried out the HSRA activities in Lahore.

Her husband was an effective writer and would write small booklets and pamphlets addressed to Indian youth. One of his booklets titled 'Message of India' was popular among the youth of Punjab. Through this literature, he brought out the social and political philosophy behind the Indian revolutionary movement. One of the articles he wrote was titled, The Philosophy of Bomb, appealing to the youth to come forward and join the party, he concluded the article by writing, and 'There is no crime that Britain has not committed in India. Deliberate misrule has reduced us to paupers and has bled us white. As a race and a people, we stand dishonoured and outraged. Do people still expect us to forget and forgive? We shall have our revenge, a people's righteous revenge on the tyrant. Let cowards fall back and cringe for compromise and peace. We ask not for mercy and we give no quarter. Ours is a war to the end to Victory or Death.'

In early December 1928, Bhagwati Charan had to travel from Lahore to Calcutta to attend the annual meeting of the Indian National Congress. During the same time, Bhagat Singh along with Sukhdev Thapar and Shivaram Rajguru had planned to avenge the death of Lala Lajpat Rai. Their plan was to shoot the superintendent of police, James Scott in Lahore. However, in a mistaken identity, they killed a British officer John Saunders on 17 December 1928. The HSRA posters had boldly claimed responsibility and the news was everywhere in Lahore. Two days after the assassination, on 19 December, Sukhdev, Bhagat Singh, and Rajguru reached Durga Devi's home. Consistent with party protocol, Durga Devi did not ask them any questions and presumed that Rajguru, was a servant.

Since there was a lookout notice for Bhagat Singh, Durga Devi agreed to act as Bhagat Singh's wife to help him escape from Lahore. Taking her son with her and accompanied by Rajguru they boarded a first-class train departing from Lahore to Howrah station, Calcutta. While she presented herself as the wife of Bhagat Singh, Rajguru carried the luggage posing as their servant. Bhagat Singh bought three tickets, two first-class tickets for Devi and himself, and a third-class ticket for Rajguru. When the train stopped at Lucknow, Rajguru travelled separately to Benaras. From Lucknow, Bhagat Singh sent a telegram to Bhagwati Charan, informing him that he was reaching Calcutta with 'Durgawati.' Bhagwati was surprised in a very pleasant way, at his wife's role in helping Bhagat Singh and Shivaram Rajguru escape!

There was no communication regarding a plan to bomb the Legislative Assembly. It was just understood among them that Bhagat Singh was going to carry out a task and probably would not make it. Bhagat Singh went to the Assembly, on 8 April 1929 and along with Batukeshwar Dutt, another HSRA revolutionary, they activated two low-intensity bombs on vacant benches at the Central Legislative Assembly in Delhi. They hailed leaflets from the gallery on legislators assembled below, shouted slogans, and let the authorities arrest them.

After Bhagat Singh surrendered himself for the 1929 Assembly incident, several revolutionaries were arrested. An outraged Durga Devi attempted to assassinate the Punjab Governor Malcolm Hailey. Devi was, however, arrested after a failed attempt. After her release, she continued to support the families of revolutionaries in Lahore, and acted as a 'post box,' receiving mail for absconding revolutionaries and procuring weapons for the party as well. She sold her ornaments worth 3000 rupees to rescue Bhagat Singh and his comrades under trial. Moreover, during that time she had to engage a lawyer as the police wanted to seize the family home on the basis that her husband was an absconder in the Lahore Conspiracy Case.

Bhagwati Charan planned to carry out a bomb blast on the Delhi-Agra railway line on 23 December 1929. The bombs were placed under the train that Viceroy Irwin was travelling in. However, the Viceroy escaped unhurt. Later Durga Devi and her husband had planned to free Bhagat Singh from prison, unfortunately on 28 May 1930, while her husband was testing a bomb it exploded prematurely. He was severely wounded and could not be taken to the hospital, nor could any doctor be given his identity, so he died without medical attention.

Following her husband's death, Durga Devi was constantly on the move, and in hiding. A few months after her husband died, on 8 October 1930, she shot at a European couple standing outside the police station in Lamington Road, Bombay. A newspaper described it as 'the first instance in which a woman figured prominently in a terrorist outrage.' And the Times of India reported, 'the first outrage of its kind in Bombay in recent years, and is reminiscent of the anarchist outrages of Bengal. It turned out they happened to be a police sergeant and his wife and they had a miraculous escape!' Witnesses reported that they saw three assailants. A trace on the car's license plate quickly led the police to the driver, who after five days of intense questioning confessed that one of the assailants was a Gujarati woman disguised in male attire. The police began a search for a suspect described as a young, fair, good-looking woman, dressed in khaddar, who went by the name of Sharda Devi.

They were unable to track down Durga Devi. Hastily conceived to revenge the death sentence accorded to Bhagat Singh, Sukhdev Thapar, and Shivaram Rajguru the previous day, the initial target was the Governor of Punjab, Geoffrey de Montmorency. Since there was tight security around the house where he lived and a last-minute decision was taken to target a police station instead. According to Durga Devi, as the car moved past the pair, her counterpart cried shoot and together they leaned out of the windows and opened fire; she recalled firing three or four times!

There was insufficient evidence to convict Durga Devi in court and she was released. Durga Devi then escaped out of Bombay. On 23 March 1931 Bhagat Singh, Shivram Rajguru, and Sukhdev Thapar were executed and the headlines read, 'No last interview with relatives. Dead bodies secretly disposed of.' Durga Devi and a fellow revolutionary, Sampuran Singh Tandon, surrendered to the police. Her husband was dead and Bhagat Singh, Rajguru, and Sukhdev had been executed. Several revolutionaries were sent to The Cellular Jail, also known as Kālā Pānī, in the Andaman Islands, to serve long sentences. After her release, she led a quiet life. Durgawati Devi died on 15 October 1999, in Ghaziabad at the age of ninety-two, in anonymity after India's Independence in 1947.

CHAPTER FIFTY
THE DUTIFUL

Sushila Mohan was born in Dattochhuhar Punjab on 5 March 1905. Her father was a high-ranking army officer. Her mother died when Sushila was young and not much is documented of her early life. She studied at the Arya Women's College in Jullundur, At a Hindi literature convention, she met a few students from the Lahore National College and who introduced her to Bhagwati Charan Vohra and Durga Devi Vohra. Inspired by them, she joined the revolutionary group HSRA and would distribute revolutionary literature for the party as well as enlist members for the party. Initially, her father instructed her to stay away from politics or he may lose his job, however, he soon joined the Indian freedom movement.

Sushila was most upset with the news that the HSRA revolutionaries were convicted in the Kakori Conspiracy also known as The Kakori Train Robbery. This had taken place on 9 August 1925. The HSRA revolutionaries were accused of involvement and in subsequent court trials, the revolutionaries were convicted. She quickly without a thought handed over her gold bangles to the party to collect funds to fight their case. Four death sentences were carried out from 17 to 19 December 1927 which enraged the HSRA and they wanted to avenge the sentences.

From Jullundur Sushila Mohan moved to Calcutta in 1928, on the insistence of her college principal Shannodevi. Here she took up a job as a private tutor to the daughter of the philanthropist Chhaju Ram Lamba. After the assassination of Saunders in Lahore, Bhagat Singh and Durga Devi were to reach Calcutta. Sushila arranged their stay at Chhaju Ram's home.

After Bhagat Singh and the other revolutionaries in the Delhi Assembly bomb case were arrested, the HSRA revolutionaries planned to assassinate Viceroy Irwin. The British were watching all revolutionary activities therefore Sushila was given the directive to collect details about the train and schedule of the Viceroy. Impersonating a British woman in European attire she was able to collect all the details of his journey. However, the Viceroy escaped unhurt. After Bhagat Singh was arrested, the HSRA revolutionaries planned to free him from jail. Hence Sushila resigned from her job in Calcutta and travelled to Lahore and she lived there in disguise as a Sikh boy. Other revolutionaries were assigned to collect weapons and materials to carry out the jailbreak.

Bhagwati Charan Vohra however died while testing a bomb at the banks of river Ravi, following which the plan had to be shelved. The police started to search for all revolutionaries and issued arrest warrants against Sushila Mohan and Durgawati Devi. The duo immediately went into hiding. Sushila had written a letter to Bhagat Singh which was published in a nationalist newspaper Swatantra Bharat for which the police had a second warrant on her. The editor of the paper was charged, with sedition, fined 10000 rupees and six years of imprisonment.

After the hanging of Bhagat Singh, Sukhdev, and Rajguru on 23 March 1931, the HSRA was without direction. Sushila Mohan then took command of HSRA activities in Delhi and Lahore and planned the assassination of Henry Kirk, the secretary of the Punjab government, holding him responsible for the hanging of the three revolutionaries. Known in the inner revolutionary circle as the Lahore Kirk plan, the revolutionaries assembled in Lahore however the police came to know of the plan. She was arrested and imprisoned in the Parliament Street police station. The Delhi police were unable to produce a case against her and therefore she was released and ordered to leave Delhi within 24 hours. While attending a banned Congress Session in Delhi in 1932 she was arrested yet again, and imprisoned for six months. The following year she married a Congress activist and lawyer Shyam

Mohan and moved to Delhi.

Although she joined the Indian National Congress in Delhi but did not discontinue her revolutionary duties. In 1937, when the Kakori revolutionaries who were lodged in the Andaman Jail were released, Sushila Devi and Durga Devi planned a huge political rally to honour them in Delhi. Gandhi forbid this as both were Congress members, but they still went ahead. During the Quit India movement of 1942, she was arrested once again and imprisoned.

After independence Sushila Mohan started a handicraft school for women in the Ballimaran neighbourhood of old Delhi, working in Harijan colonies, and training the women. She was nominated as Aldermen in the Delhi Pradesh Congress Committee. Sushila Mohan died on 13 January 1963. 'Sushila Mohan Marg' in Khari Baoli, Chandni Chowk, is named after her. Sushila Devi was addressed as Sushila Didi by her fellow revolutionaries.

CHAPTER FIFTY-ONE
I TOO AM A RIDDLE

Mahadevi Verma was born on 26 March 1907 in Farrukhabad. It is said that her father Govind Prasad Varma prayed to Durga for a daughter since there were no daughters born in their family for years. Govind Prasad was a western educated scholar and a professor of English at a college in Bhagalpur. Her mother Hem Rani Devi was a religious woman with an interest in music from Jabalpur. She could recite the Ramayana Gita and Vinaya Patrika, hymns composed by the 16th-century Indian poet, Goswami Tulsidas, for many hours. Born in a forward-thinking family she was encouraged to study Urdu and Persian at a time when women's education was given very little importance.

Tutored at home, Mahadevi's grandfather wanted her to become a scholar. However, her mother inspired her to write poems and read literature and introduced the young girl to Sanskrit and Hindi. She taught her the Panchatantra tales, the ancient Indian collection of interrelated animal fables in Sanskrit verse and prose, arranged within a frame story, and introduced her to the poetry of the bhakti saint and Hindu mystic poet Mirabai. Later Mahadevi was dubbed the 'Modern Mira.' It is said that she walked out of a class when she saw the Buddhist guru, hiding his face with a palm leaf while teaching. She said that someone who could not trust himself had nothing to teach her!

At nine Mahadevi was engaged to Swarup Narain Verma, a young boy from Bareilly. They were to marry after her college degree from Crosthwaite Girls College in Allahabad. Though Mahadevi mostly stayed away from her husband, meeting him occasionally. After college Mahadevi completed her masters in Sanskrit from Allahabad University.

While studying in college she would secretly write poems, which were discovered by her roommate and friend, Subhadra Kumari Chauhan. Both were friends from the time they studied at Crosthwaite. Subhadra was also her senior and a prominent Hindi author and poet. She encouraged Mahadevi to write in Khari Boli, the dialect spoken in the Western United Provinces. They would send their poems to weekly magazines and attend poetry seminars, where they interacted with established poets.

In 1932, Mahadevi applied for a scholarship to Oxford University, she was keen to study English. A bit confused, she asked Mahatma Gandhi for his advice. He remarked 'our fight against the British is going on, and you will go abroad to study English? Be proud of your mother tongue. Teach other sisters in our mother tongue.' Mahadevi then started teaching students Hindi. She was the first residential principal of Prayag Mahila Vidyapeeth in 1933, and later continued to serve as the chancellor of the institute

In the mid-twentieth century the Chhayavad movement, (1914-1938) was considered to be a period of romanticism in Modern Hindi poetry and a departure from the earlier Hindi and Urdu poetic traditions. Chhaya which translates to 'a reflection, an image in a mirror,' developed as a break away from Khari Boli poetry, which had replaced Braj poetry by the beginning of the twentieth century. Khadi Boli had experienced an accepted progression and emerged out of Hindu revivalism and reflected patriotism and nationalism. In contrast Chhayavad poetry dealt with expressing emotions as gently as imaginable. Verma is known as the foundational and leading poet of the Chhayavad movement in Hindi literature. Her writing was steeped with emotion and both her poems and essays often centred on the experience of being a woman.

Verma's collections of poems, such as Nihar which was written in 1930, Rashmi in 1932, Neerja in 1934, Yama in 1939, and Deepshikha in 1942 won many accolades. They were characterized by a sense of personal experience and self-expression and she used her works to express the innumerable barriers in her own life and a fresh impetus at each impediment to carrying on.

A self-aware poet, her poetry and essays therefore often centred on the experience of being a woman. As modern Hindi became more acceptable in the literary circle, she started to publish her work in Hindi. Her works were known for both romanticism as well as sorrow. Her collection of short stories, Sketches From My Past, portrays the women she encountered while she was the principal of Prayag Mahila Vidyapeeth. Verma consistently wrote on women's rights, their issues, and solutions and edited several journals, in particular, the women's magazine Chand Patrika, which was well known for taking up social issues during the freedom struggle.

A much-respected writer Verma was well known in political circles. In the year 1934, she received the Sekseriya Puraskar from the Hindi Sahitya Sammelan for her work, Neerja. She established the Literary Sansad in the year 1955. Here writers were given a platform to showcase their work, as well as new writers had the opportunity to interact with senior writers. In 1979, she was the first woman to be made a fellow of the Sahitya Akademi. Varma also received the Jnanpith Award in 1982 for her contribution to Indian literature and for 'Yama,' her anthology of poems, published in 1936. She was honoured with the Padma Bhushan in 1956, and the Padma Vibhushan posthumously in 1988.

Google Doodle paid tribute to Mahadevi Verma with an image of her seated under a tree in the countryside, busy writing. She translated numerous works from Sanskrit to Hindi and also drew illustrations for her poetic works. In her poem 'Priye, Main Hoon Ek Paheli Bhi' (Dear One, I too, am a Riddle,) she cites the reason for both her courage and frailty and her delight and unhappiness. She pens:

'However much nectar, however much sweet laughter,

However much intoxication in your glance.

However much weeping, however much sadness.

However much poison in the trembling of the universe.

Drinking it all, I have an ancient thirst for sadness.

But also the merriment of the river of joy.

Ceaselessly, from all pores of my being.

Flows the torrent and the fire.

I love detachment and desire.

Awakening in my breath.

Dear one, I was cradled in the lap of limitation,

But I have also played with the limitless!'

Mahadevi Verma founded the Sahitya Sahakar Trust in 1985. She wished to establish a library and start publishing, but this wish could not be actualized as she died two years after its establishment on 11 September 1987 in Allahabad. She was eighty. A women's rights activist, educator, and freedom fighter, she wrote on real issues, politics, and social reform. Many of her works have been included in the Hindi school curriculum of India.

CHAPTER FIFTY-TWO
THE LIMITLESS

'There is no limit to what we, as women, can accomplish,' remarked Sucheta Kripalani, member of the Constituent Assembly and first lady Chief Minister. Born on 25 June 1908 in Ambala, Punjab, in a Bengali Brahmo family, her mother Prembala was a homemaker and her father Dr. Surendra Nath Mazumdar was a medical officer in the Punjab Medical Service. He was often transferred to different states, as a result, she and her sister Sulekha, studied in several schools. Later Sucheta completed her master's in history from St. Stephen's College, Delhi University.

Growing up when India was struggling to be free from colonial rule, both the sisters were equally passionate nationalists. As students of Kinnaird College in Lahore, the Bible class teacher made derogatory remarks on Hinduism. Enraged, the sisters learnt a few lines from the scriptures and the next day in class, recited from the Bhagavad Gita!

In her book, An Unfinished Autobiography, Sucheta writes about Prince of Wales's visit to Delhi. The students from her school were asked to stand at the Qudsia Bagh, a large garden complex on the fringes of Old Delhi, close to Kashmere Gate to welcome the Prince. He was certainly not on the welcome list of the sisters! Both sisters reluctantly stood with the other students to welcome the Prince, since they could not refuse the teachers, only to be infuriated later at their gutlessness! She further states, how she felt as a ten-year-old after the Jallianwala Bagh massacre. 'I could understand enough to feel great anger against the British. We vented out anger on some of the Anglo- Indian children who played with us, calling them all kinds of names.'

Sucheta's father and sister Sulekha died in 1929 and the responsibility of looking after a large family came to Sucheta. She was unable to join the freedom movement and began her career as a teacher of constitutional history at Banaras Hindu University. She taught at the university until 1939. At times when students took out demonstrations, Sucheta would not take classes, however, lecture them on the importance of India being free. Sucheta met Acharya Kripalani who would visit the university looking for volunteers to participate in the freedom struggle. They build a good rapport during the Bihar earthquake relief operations and got married in 1936. Kripalani was 20 years older than Sucheta and many were opposed to the marriage including Gandhi as he was concerned that he would lose his 'right arm JB Kripalani! He asked Sucheta to marry someone else and she responded that it would be 'immoral and dishonest.' Kripalani a liberal thinker asked Sucheta to do any work of her choice, not necessarily politics. In her autobiography, she writes, 'Early in life his advice to me was 'Apna daman saf rakhna.'

In August 1942, when the fight for Independence was at its peak, Gandhi was brought to the Aga Khan Palace Detention Camp, Poona, and kept under house arrest for 21 months. He was fasting and critical. There were warrants issued against many freedom fighters including Sucheta Kripalani, which forced her to work underground. She decided to visit Gandhi as his health had deteriorated considerably. "I am Mrs. Kripalani, and I want to see Gandhiji now at his place. And you must allow me to go and see him; you can arrest me when I am on my way out, this much you have to do for me," she said to the Home Secretary in Mumbai. She was allowed to meet Gandhi, and advised to leave the city in 24 hours! And she was not arrested.

She was imprisoned for a year in 1944. "I was keen to start political work. I used to feel small before the veteran jail-goers, as I had not graduated through jail life.' She became the secretary of the Kasturba Gandhi Memorial Trust in 1946, formed with an objective to support women and children with education, health, and housing.

Sucheta was among the fifteen women elected to the Constituent Assembly to the Draft Constitution of India and led the rehabilitation efforts during the Partition. On the eve of India's independence, before Nehru's speech, 'Tryst with Destiny,' Sucheta Kripalani was officially invited to sing Vande Mataram, while all members were requested to stand.

She followed her husband out of the Congress party, in 1950, but re-joined the party in 1957 and was general secretary of its national executive from 1959 to 1960. She held an important post as Minister for Labour Development and Small Industries in the State of Uttar Pradesh in 1963 and went on to become the first woman Chief Minister of Uttar Pradesh, the largest state of India from 1963 to 1967. As a Chief Minister, Sucheta had a big task in hand as the state economy was not good. When the Congress split in 1969, she left with the Morarji Desai faction to form the Indian National Congress (Organisation) also known as Congress (O). After Sucheta lost as Congress (O) candidate from Faizabad, Lok Sabha constituency she retired from politics in 1971

A brilliant and decisive Sucheta Kripalani died on 1 December 1974 of a heart attack at 67. Her memoir, An Unfinished Autobiography was published four years later in 1978. 'I learned that it is not enough to help people by giving them things from above. What we should try to do is generate strength in people to help themselves,' she wrote and navigated her own independent journey.

CHAPTER FIFTY-THREE
THE GALLANT TARA

There is little documented on Tara Rani Srivastava, except that she continued to be part of the freedom struggle after her husband was shot by the British troops. She was a motivation for women in Siwan, Bihar. Her exemplary courage to continue to march onwards with the national flag in her hands with composure despite witnessing her husband falling to police bullets must mean she held her country as top priority.

Tara Rani Srivastava was born into a poor family in Saran, Bihar. Married at 13, a young Tara and her husband Phulendu Babu were very passionate satyagrahis, participating in protests, campaigning, and staunch followers of Gandhian principles.

During the August movement, on 12 August 1942, Mahatma Gandhi, had called for flag hoisting in Siwan. Hoisting of nationalist flags over private and public buildings had become a nationalist act of disobedience. Termed Flag Satyagraha, in defiance of the British restricting civil freedom and also the legitimacy of British rule in India, Indians were encouraged to violate the law and hoist the flag without resisting arrest or retaliating against police.

Tara and her husband led a Flag Satyagraha to the Siwan police station which was the administrative headquarters of the Siwan district. The police lathi-charged the protesters and when they were unable to control them, the police opened fire. Her husband, Phulendu, was shot and wounded. Tara Rani bandaged her husband's wounds with strips of cloth torn from her sari. Then she left him at a safe place and continued her march to the police station, to hoist the flag. By the time she returned to her husband, he had died of his injuries. Since there is no other documentation available on Tara Rani, the fearless and passionate patriot, her story is among the lesser-known freedom fighters who vanished from the pages of history.

CHAPTER FIFTY-FOUR
THE JHANSI RANI OF TRAVANCORE

She would often hear people tell her friends, 'you are a girl.' Her father would dismiss any jibes and remark 'they are not liabilities, they are assets.' No wonder Accamma Cherian grew up to be a decisive woman. Born on 14 February 1909 in Kanjirapally in Kottayam, Travancore her parents Thomman Cherian and Annamma Karippaparambil brought up their children as equals. Their home was a meeting place, especially on Sundays when friends and neighbours would convene to discuss the happenings of the First World War!

Travancore had an impressive system of government-run schools and Accamma studied at the Government Girls High School, Kanjirapally, and later at St Joseph's High School, a boarding school in Changanasserry. Her father was able to educate all his children and send the girls to boarding schools and colleges. Accamma completed her college degree in History from St. Teresa's College, Ernakulam, and a teaching course as well. In 1933 after turning down a teaching post in Burma which she had accepted initially, she started to teach at St. Mary's English Medium School, Edakkara, and later went on to become the headmistress of the school. She gave up her teaching after six years to join the Travancore State Congress which was formed in 1938.

Travancore in the late 1930s was troubled with conflict and the State Congress was declared illegal. On 26 August 1938, C. P Ramaswamy Aiyar, the Dewan of Travancore, banned the State Congress. The British government arrested eleven Presidents of the State Congress including the political activist and editor of Swadeshabhimani (The Patriot) newspaper. As per law, the British authorities were permitted to arrest any office bearer, members, and any associations, without a warrant. The State Congress leaders were forbidden from participating in public and the Congress working committee was dissolved. A Strikers' Union was formed instead. The State Congress consisted mainly of Syrian Christians and Accamma Cherian knew many aspiring leaders, hence when President Pattom A. Thanu Pillai was given dictatorial powers to choose a successor, just before his imprisonment, he nominated Accamma Cherian as President of the newly organized Strikers' Union.

The Maharaja of Travancore's birthday used to be a grand event and the roads would fill up with processions. The State Congress Committee assigned Accamma to lead a procession to the Kowdiar Palace on Maharaja's birthday and submit a memorandum of rights to reverse the State Congress ban as well as dismiss the Dewan. The Strikers Union asked the Congress volunteers to meet on 23 October 1938. It was a Sunday, thousands gathered wearing white khadi with Gandhi caps and marched to Thampanoor railway station, the busiest railway station in the state. Accamma addressed the people in an open jeep and then moved along with the crowd towards the Maharaja's Palace to present him with the memorandum of rights. There were several attempts on the way to stop the march and when the police chief asked his officers to open fire, Accamma dared them, 'I am the leader, shoot me first before you kill others.' The protest continued till the government agreed to release the imprisoned Congress leaders. Gandhi got to know of the daring Accamma Cherian and called her, 'The Jhansi Rani of Travancore.'

This was a significant move staged in Travancore before India's independence. In her autobiography 'Jeevitham: Oru Samaram'- Life: A Protest, dedicated to her mother, she penned, 'I was aware of the seriousness of the assignment and knew what the consequences could be, yet I volunteered to do the job.' Accamma was twenty-nine at the time!

In her speech to the crowd before the march, she had said, 'The massive revolt that is happening in Travancore to establish responsible government has compelled me to leave the academic atmosphere and to take up a responsible rank in the revolt. There is an attempt to reduce this revolt to a mere struggle for the rights of citizens. But, let me say that, dismissing all such undesirable technical interpretations that are being uttered around and the legal complexities involved, the assumption that the State Congress would be satisfied with just the grant of citizenship rights after going through all these hardships and sacrifices is mere foolery. The rights of the citizens can be ensured only in a democratic society. Hence, I find it my duty that I shall take part in this strike till the very end.'

'Thus, I consider this revolt to be part of not just the Indian Freedom struggle, but as part of the revolt taking place in the whole world between the imperial and democratic powers. Viewed from this perspective, this strike has more than just provincial importance. Hence, I am proud of devoting my energies to the inception of justice, freedom, and democracy.' When the Congress prisoners were released, she handed back the President's title to Pattom Thanu Pillai. She became an active member of the Congress, traveling to various Congress centres and engaging with women, requesting them to join the newly formed Desa Sevika Sangh (Female Volunteer Group) and many women volunteered to be part of the local bodies of the State Congress.

On 24 December 1939, Accamma was arrested and sentenced to a year in prison along with her sister Rosamma Punnoose for taking part in the first annual conference of the state Congress. After her release, she worked full-time in the State Congress and was also the acting President in 1942. Accamma was in and out of prisons between 1939 and 1947 for questioning the Dewan of Travancore, C. P Ramaswamy Aiyar, and for fighting for an independent Travancore. She had by now become an important leader in the State Congress. In Travancore's first elections held in February 1948, she won unopposed and was one of three women elected to the 120-member assembly.

In 1951, Accamma Cherian married V. V Varkey Mannamplackal, a member of the Travancore Cochin Legislative Assembly and also a nationalist. She resigned from the Congress party, after being denied a Lok Sabha ticket and contested as an independent candidate from the Muvattupuzha constituency. Her sister Rosamma married a leading Communist member, P. T. Punnoose. The State Congress now had an excuse to keep her out of the new government and removed her from key positions.

When Pattom Thanu Pillai, became the Chief Minister of Kerala in 1960, he offered Accamma a ministry but later pulled back. In 1967, she contested the Assembly election from Kanjirappally as a Congress candidate but was defeated by the Communist Party's candidate. She then served as a member of the Freedom Fighters Pension Advisory Board. In her autobiography, Life: A Protest, she writes of occasions when she was almost offered the position of a minister in independent India. But by then, many freedom fighters had started fighting for positions and titles and women who stood at the forefront of the struggle were sidelined. She blamed the subsequent failure of her political career not so much on the fact that she was a woman as on her fierce independence. 'I did not belong to any group. I did what I thought was right.'

In the beginning of her autobiography Accamma Cherian's writes, 'Shakespeare has said that the world is a stage and that all the men and women merely players; but to me, this life is a long protest – protest against conservatism, meaningless rituals, societal injustice, gender discrimination, against anything that is dishonest, unjust…when I see anything like this, I turn blind, I even forget who I am fighting…'

The Joan of Arc of Kerala, the Iron Lady of Kerala, and the Jhansi Rani of Travancore, Accamma Cherian died on 5 May 1982. When Syrian Christian women lived an extremely orthodox life, she challenged the traditional status quo. In her unpublished book, 1114 nte Katha (The Story of 1114,) a critique on patriarchy, she analyses the active male dominance and merit of a man's expertise over a woman's.

Accamma Cherian's statue stands tall in Vellayambalam, Thiruvananthapuram. She had said, 'society has always been quite guarded in their attitude towards women who had shown a certain amount of awareness regarding their status as free individuals… the reason for this might be the potential fear of the damage such women are capable of inflicting on the patriarchal structure.'

CHAPTER FIFTY-FIVE
THE GRAND OLD LADY

Aruna Asaf Ali nee Ganguly was born on 16 July 1909 in a Bengali family in Kalka, Punjab. Her parents Upendranath Ganguly and Ambalika Devi were Brahmo Samajists and were originally from Barisal in East Bengal. Educated at the Sacred Heart Convent in Lahore and All Saints College, Nainital, she was an intelligent and focused student. After completing her studies Aruna taught at the Gokhale Memorial School in Calcutta. At nineteen, she had made up her mind to marry a prominent Congressman, barrister Asaf Ali. They shared similar beliefs and an age difference of twenty-three years and family opposition on religious grounds did not matter. Since her husband was in politics she too became an active member of the Congress Party after marriage.

Aruna was arrested during the Salt Satyagraha in 1930 while she was addressing public meetings and leading processions, on charges of being a vagrant. After Gandhi's release in January 1931, the Gandhi-Irwin Pact was signed on 5 March 1931. One of the conditions in the pact was that the authorities would release prisoners arrested for participating in the civil disobedience movement and despite a signed political agreement with the British government, Aruna was not released. The other women prisoners arrested with her refused to leave unless the authorities released Aruna. This was followed by a big public agitation in her favour forcing the British government to release her. She was arrested again in 1932 and sent to Tihar Jail where she went on a hunger strike against the harsh treatment of political prisoners. She was subsequently moved to solitary confinement in Ambala Jail. After her release, she dropped out of the national movement for ten years. She raised the tricolour at the Gowalia Tank in Bombay and activated the Quit India Movement after Gandhi called for the British to leave India in August 1942.

When nearly 100000 Indians, including prominent leaders, were arrested and imprisoned during the movement, she went underground to evade arrest. The district magistrate of Delhi declared her an offender and a month later properties registered in her name were seized. On 26 January 1944, the police raided her house in Karol Bagh, Delhi and recovered a number of copies of Congress Party's monthly newspaper called Inquilab, as well as a hand press and some of her letters. The British went ahead and announced a reward of 5000 rupees for her 'capture!'

While underground, Aruna Asaf Ali fell ill and Gandhi wrote to her, 'I have sent you messages that you should not die underground. You are reduced to a skeleton. Do come out and surrender yourself and win the prize offered for your arrest. Reserve the prize money for the Harijan cause. If you surrender yourself you would do so to raise yourself and the country with you. The surrendering won't be out of your weakness but out of your strength.' However, only when the warrants against her were cancelled on 26 January 1946 did Aruna Asaf Ali surrender.

Within 3 weeks of her surrendering, on 18 February 1946, she played an important role in the Royal Indian Navy (RIN) revolt. On 17 February 1946, the sailors or 'ratings' protested against racial discrimination and demanded decent food. The British officers taunted them that 'beggars cannot be choosers.' The next morning, 1,500 sailors or 'ratings' walked out of the mess hall in protest. By 4.30 pm, the ratings had rejected the appeals of their officers and the Rear Admiral. They wanted to take over the RIN and place it in the command of national leaders. A formal list of demands was handed over which included the release of all Indian political prisoners including INA POWs and naval detainees, withdrawal of Indian troops from Indonesia and Egypt, equal status of pay and allowances and decent Indian food. They formally asked the British to quit India. By the morning of 20 February, the strike had spread to Calcutta, Karachi, Madras, Jamnagar, Visakhapatnam, Cochin, and other navy stations. The military police fired at the strikers in Karachi. Around eighty ships, four flotillas, twenty shore establishments, and more than 20,000 sailors or 'ratings' joined the mutiny. In two days, British India had lost control of its navy and in five days, the ratings had delivered a deep blow to the entire structure of the British Raj. The ratings then marched at Colaba and Flora Fountain, with slogans of 'Hindu Muslim Ek ho' and 'Inquilab Zindabad,' while the people of Bombay cheered, the British shot down 250 people.

The strikers demanded the intervention of Aruna Asaf Ali who responded favourably but was overruled by more senior nationalist leaders, from both the Congress and the Muslim League. She informed Jawaharlal Nehru, of the situation that was 'climaxing to a grim close' and asked for support. Gandhi, disapproved of the indiscipline and violence and said that in case the sailors found their service conditions humiliating they should have resigned, instead of revolting. The revolt was called off after a meeting between Congress and the President of the Naval Central Strike Committee (NCSC.) Under great compulsion, the strikers gave way. Many arrests, were followed by courts-martial and the dismissal of 476 sailors from the Royal Indian Navy. And those dismissed were never reinstated in the navy after independence. The mutineers were betrayed because of the lack of support and later again as the government refused to rehabilitate the mutineers. The Royal Indian Navy (RIN) revolt contributed to the British decision to leave India, the next year! BC Dutt, a young rating at the HMIS Talwar, the training school in Colaba, who protested over the bad food was arrested for the mutiny and was never allowed back into the navy, contrary to assurances given by Congress leaders. In his memoir he penned, 'The barrack walls were no longer high enough to contain the tide of nationalism.'

Swaminathan Anklesaria Aiyar had written a column in the economic times where he mentioned that in 1967 he had attended a seminar when India was celebrating its 20th Independence year. This was attended by the then British High Commissioner, John Freeman, who declared, 'the British were petrified of a repeat of the 1857 Mutiny, since this time they feared they would be slaughtered to the last man.' He further mentioned that during the 1857 revolt, the Indian troops were limited in number but in 1946 they had increased, to over 2.5 million soldiers, inducted during World War II. As well as a vague impact of Subhas Chandra Bose's Indian National Army (INA.)

Aruna Asaf Ali in a press conference said, if following Gandhi's advice the naval ratings resigned there would be hundreds, with unemployment all-round, to take their place; and they would be subjected to the same discriminatory treatment. Moreover, she felt that it did not look proper for Congressmen, who themselves went into the legislatures, to ask the ratings to give up their means of livelihood. She stressed the solidity of the unity between the Hindus and the Muslims at the barricades rather than political patch-ups.

In September 1946 Aruna Asaf Ali was elected as the president of the Central Public Works Department Union formed in Delhi and was the Vice- President of the All India Trade Union Congress. At the time of independence, she was a member of the Congress Socialist Party, which until then had been part of the Congress framework. A year later, however, the socialists, including Aruna Asaf Ali formed a separate Left Specialist Party. The party went through various changes, and she exited. Aruna travelled to London and later to Moscow and after some reflection joined the Communist Party of India (CPI) in 1950, where she formed the National Federation of Indian Women, the Women's Wing of the CPI. In 1956, she moved out of the Communist Party and was elected as Delhi's first mayor in 1958 and in the same year she launched a daily newspaper, Patriot, and a weekly called Link. Supported by the Soviet Union and Eastern Europe, the Link was successful. However she exited the newspaper in the late 1970s,

She was Awarded the Lenin Peace Prize' in 1964, the Jawaharlal Nehru International Goodwill Award in 1991, and the Padma Vibhushan. As well as the Indira Gandhi Award for National Integration in 1992. The Grand Old Lady, Aruna Asaf Ali died on 29 July 1996. She was 87. She was posthumously awarded the Bharat Ratna and a postage stamp was issued in her memory the next year. Aruna Asaf Ali Marg in New Delhi is named in her honour. She had said, 'He who is not courageous enough to take risks will accomplish nothing in life,' and she endorsed this in her lifetime!

CHAPTER FIFTY-SIX
THE DEFIANT SHORT STORYTELLER

Born on 30 March 1909 at Kottavattom, Kollam district, Kerala, in a conservative Malayali Brahmin family, the Nambūdiris. Considered traditionally the most elite in the Indian state of Kerala and also known for extreme orthodoxy. Wealthy landowners who were the 'keepers' of Hindu scriptures and in a family where women and girls led a very restricted life. The only Malayali women in purdah, with no freedom of movement, no ownership of property, and very little education.

Lalitambika's parents Kottavattathu Illathu Damodaran Namboothiri and Changarappilli Manaykkal Aryadevi Anthyrjanam were progressive and educated their daughter in Malayalam, Sanskrit, and English at home. Her father was a member of the Kshema Sabha, a socio-cultural organization of the Nambūdiri community and her mother was a passionate reader who imparted the same habit to her daughter. Growing up in a home where discussions on politics and social issues were usual and women participated as well, the young Lalitambika was inspired by the Gandhian ideology.

She took lessons on religion, nationalism, and literature. Perhaps it was these lessons coupled with the reform movements in Kerala, which compelled Lalithambika to think differently. Aware that men held power in most spheres of life, social, cultural, or personal, she was looking to change this status quo. After her marriage to a farmer, Narayanan Nambūdiri all contact with the outside world ended. An oppressive routine of physical work in the kitchen, walled courtyards, along with domestic discontent of other confined women. She further observed with shock the tenacity of the women in the house who endured the everyday suffering despite deplorable circumstances. Her only channel to express herself was to write. After putting her children to sleep, she would lock the door and write under a flickering lamp. Continuous exposure to smoke and poor lighting damaged her eyes, and it is said that when the pain was unbearable, she would close her eyes and keep writing. Knowing she had to be up at dawn and face the same drudgery of life.

In the Nambūdiri custom, only the eldest son could marry within the caste, the other sons contracted sambandhams, an informal mode of marriage. This was done to ensure that there was no inheritance dispute, as the children of sambandhams did not have the right to inherit. Resulting in many of the Nambūdiri women never marrying and any deviation amounted to harsh imprisonment. So much so that the women could not let the sun's rays touch their bodies.

The other very alarming practice was, Smārthavichāram (inquiry into the conduct.) The trial was mainly conducted by the smārthans. They could remove a woman from her social position and leave her out to starve. This was both financially and mentally suffocating for the women and to begin with, they were never allowed to look out of the windows! Lalithambika Antharajanam was moved by these atrocities against women and she poured out her grievances through her stories. Soon social reforms began in Kerala and this inspired her. These reforms aimed at addressing the social inequities, particularly the intersectional oppression of various groups preserved through centuries, by the structure of caste, religion, and patriarchy. Naturally, the women were discouraged from participating in these reforms!

Between the late 1930s and 1970s, Lalithambika wrote over a hundred short stories, her favourite medium of expression. According to her, this art form was best suited to interpret thoughts and emotions. Most of her works highlight the harsh treatment of Nambūdiri women in Kerala. Her engaging stories forced the readers to think about society and the treatment of women and the marginalized. Lalithambika sensed that through her stories she could bring a change in society no matter how small the change was, it could still be a change. She writes, 'I believe that even as the artist, man or woman, pulls down the girders of a narrow, decaying society, he or she must also forge the tools to build a cultured and wholesome new structure in its place.'

Her stories emphasized the dangerous patriarchy which controlled the women and therefore their exploitation. Her initial stories are critical of the patriarchal practices of the Nambūdiri community and why there was a need to both educate and enable women. In the forty years that she wrote, changes started and her short stories throw light on an altered India, especially its women. In the four decades, she published nine volumes of short stories and wrote a collection of six poems and two books for children. Her autobiography Aathmakadhakkoru Aamukham (An Introduction to Autobiography) is critically acclaimed as an important piece of literature, she writes about the life, customs, and culture of the Nambūdiri community, along with their struggle and yearning for their freedom. A film was made on the novel with the same title in 1977.

In her stories, Lalitambika wrote with a feminine consciousness and through her work disapproved the treatment of women in a male-centric society and questioned their supremacy. Having been through and experienced the atrocities hence the voice in her writings is credible. Through her stories, she brings up a wide context of politics and caste conflicts. She highlights the plight of young girls, married to men old enough or older than their grandfathers. She writes of restrictions within the four walls of a kitchen once girls reached puberty. Not allowed education, the women had to practice backbreaking rituals. Isolation of widows, most of whom were very young. Widows were forbidden to remarry and expelled from the community if they were audacious to challenge or refuse any of the conditions.

On very isolated occasions, when Antharjanams (The women of Nambūdiri Brahmins are called Antharjanam) left the house, they had to cover themselves in a thick cloak and carry an umbrella made of a leaf with the canopy reaching to their waists, thus, they only saw their own feet while walking. In comparison, the lower caste women were required by law not to wear blouses when in the presence of higher caste men, and if they did not, they could be punished. Several social reformers and missionaries in the early twentieth century, in Kerala, encouraged the lower caste women and forced them to cover themselves with blouses, and by the 1930s, most royal households allowed their women to wear blouses, but the custom took longer to influence or reach the poorer women.

In most of her stories, she highlights the difficulties women faced in isolation, for instance in her story Revenge Herself (The Inner Courtyard) she highlights the moral choices faced by upper-caste Nambūdiri women secluded in their homes. In her story, Mulappalinte Manam, Lalithambika puts a spotlight on woman's role as the central inseparable force in society, and she supports birth control, so long as it does not counter the fundamental attributes of women. Her short stories Prathikaradevatha (The Goddess of Revenge) and Kuttasammatham (Admission of Guilt) condemn the repressive caste system and expose the shunning of women for the same things that men do, that too openly and without fear of being shamed. Her stories fiercely voice the muted sobs of women in her community and represent women who are vulnerable to a system that discredits their status or pays any significance to their existence or their emotions.

Lalithambika's stories do not only point at the conditions of women in Kerala but also across the nation. Her short stories Kodumkaattilpetta Orila (A Leaf in the Whirlwind) and Dhirendu Majumdarinde Amma (The Mother of Dhirendu Majumdar), depict the devastating consequences of the partition of Punjab and Bengal and how this affected the women of each of the communities. Soon, Lalithambika's stories had a significant impact on women, they became aware of the mistreatment meted out to them and realized they did deserve better. And then the protests against the repression started! In time the changes envisioned by Lalithambika materialised.

Drawn to Gandhi and Vivekananda, however, Tagore's depiction of women in the traditional Bengali society and his book, Ghaire Baire (At Home and The World) appealed to her and she would refer to

Tagore as 'God in the early phase of my literary career.' Lalithambika was also inspired by Sree Narayana Guru known for his ideology, oru jathi, oru matham, oru daivam, (one caste, one religion, one god,) and Kumaran Asan who connected gender oppression to caste oppression. His poem Duravastha, revolves around a high caste Nambūdiri woman who falls in love with a lower caste Pulaya man in the raging backdrop of the Mappila rebellion.

Her novel Agnisakshi which was published in 1976 won her the Vayalar award and Kerala Sahitya Akademi Award in 1977. Lalithambika Antharjanam died on 6 February 1987. She played a critical role in shaping feminist literature and with her stories, she exposed the duplicity, inequality, and cruelty with which women were treated in the Nambūdiri society. An author of many prolific literary works and a social reformer, she was known for her literary works in the Malayalam language, fighting against the mistreatment of women and the marginalized and not afraid to expose the inherent hypocrisy in her community. Her writings reflect a women's role in society, and the woman as an individual.

Durgabai Deshmukh

Bina Das

Amalprova Das

Pritilata Waddedar

Kalpana Datta

Lakshmi Swaminathan Sahgal

Putalimaya Devi Poddar

Rani Gaidinliu

Suniti Choudhury

Indumati Patankar

CHAPTER FIFTY-SEVEN
THE DARING DURGABAI

In her memoirs she writes, 'When I was young, the social conditions in India were feudalistic. Child marriages were in great vogue. And I was a victim of this primitive social custom. The only mistake my father had committed was to marry me off when I was eight years of age, to an adopted son of a zamindar who had estates yielding, a large income. Later my father regretted this. He died in 1929 at the early age of thirty-six.' Born on 15 July 1909 in Rajahmundry, a coastal district in Andhra, Durgabai Deshmukh's father B. V. N. Rama Rao was a social worker. She was married at eight to a relative, Subba Rao, a rich zamindar and by fifteen, she decided she wanted to separate from him to pursue her education and her father supported her decision.

'When I grew up to the age of fifteen I realized the significance of marriage. I told my father that I could not treat the man to whom I had been married as a husband. I also told him that I would tell Subba Rao (that was his name) that I could not accept him as a husband, and that I would be prepared to give him in writing to that effect. I also told him that he could marry any girl he liked. This was before the marriage was consummated.''

When Durgabai's father died, her mother, Krishnavenamma, faced a tonsure in keeping with the customs. However, as a daughter, she protested and her mother was spared the ritual. She writes, 'The relations and the kith and kin who came to offer their condolences to my mother insisted that her head be shaved. I protested against this and told them that if they persisted in their demand they had better get out of the house. My mother had lovely, long hair. She was good-looking. I requested her to resist the demand, and finally, she did not yield to the pressure. Since then I found her example being emulated in several families in the neighbourhood.'

Durgabai grew up in Kakinada, and from an early age, she was aware of social inequity and was observant of the ill-treatment and cruelty toward women. She left her school because they taught in English. In 1921, when she was all of twelve, she was told that Gandhi would be visiting Kakinada, to address a town hall. She quickly made arrangements for him to address the Devadasis, and Muslim women and enlighten them with his talk. The local hosts conveyed to her that if she met their condition of collecting five thousand rupees for a purse to be presented to Gandhi they would allow the address. Durgabai with the help of the Devadasis managed to collect the money. Not many would let out their place for an event that Gandhi was attending as his meetings often meant that the owners could be arrested! Durgabai then organised a venue for the address, a school compound where 1000 womengathered to listen to Gandhi and she translated Gandhi's speech from Hindi to Telegu. She writes, 'Gandhiji started to address them. Five minutes passed, ten minutes passed, half an hour passed, and still, he went on speaking. I translated his speech from Hindustani into Telugu. The half-a-dozen hosts who were with him to take him to the Town Hall were very angry with me. I told them that it was not my fault and that they could ask Gandhiji to conclude his speech, but they dared not.' After Gandhi's visit, her mother, brother, and she decided to wearonly Khadi.

In 1930, during the Salt Satyagraha, Durgabai took a lead in Madras and was imprisoned for two years and a year of solitary confinement. Durgabai recalls her years in imprisonment where she had to share cells with women wrongfully convicted and women convicted of various crimes and writes in her memoir Chintaman and I, a reference to her husband, Chintaman Deshmukh, 'I was released in 1933 from my third spell of imprisonment, after undergoing solitary confinement for nearly one year in Madurai Jail. After this I did not take an active part in politics, one reason being that my mental health was completely shattered. As I was locked up in Madurai jail in a cell next to the death cells and gallows, I used to hear the agonizing cries of the prisoners to be hanged early the next morning. This greatly upset me and I began to get fits of hysteria. Also, the food in the jail was of bad quality and it was suspected that there was an attempt to subject me to slow poisoning.'

After her release in 1933, Durgabai decided to leave politics and continue with her education. She had decided to become a lawyer and extend pro bono legal advice to people. Also empower deserted and widowed women with education. She started a condensed course for women who had discontinued school and through this intensive coaching, they could then finish their secondary school.

She writes, 'There was at the time in Kakinada practically no one who learned Hindi. Therefore, the classes which I started with help and encouragement were given by my father and mother, who allowed me to use a couple of rooms in our own house, attracting hundreds of women. The number grew with every passing day. This was the beginning of the Balika Hindi Pathasala. When Sri Jamnalal Bajaj found at the Balika Hindi Pathasala a few hundred women learning Hindi, spinning on the charkha, weaving cloth, and singing national songs, he wanted to know who the head of the institution was. Bulusu Sambamurti, who accompanied him, introduced me as the principal and head of the institution. As I was a young girl in my early teens, he could not at first believe this. But when he did bring himself to do so, he asked me whether he could offer some money to help me run the school. I told him politely that I did not require money at the time and that if and when I did, I myself would ask him.' In six months, she learned Hindi and began running teaching centres with the help of her mother to spread the nationalist cause.

Durgabai launched the Andhra Mahila Sabha in 1937, which later evolved as a key institution of education and social welfare for women and by 1946, grew into a full-fledged institution. In 1942, Andhra Mahila, a monthly magazine was started by Durgabai's brother Narayana Rao, the idea was to bring together members from different places to be in touch with each other and share the work done by Andhra Mahila Sabha for the women and children. The journal shared news and stories about the struggle for Independence.

She writes in her autobiography, 'Since I had been rated in the first class in my M.A. degree, I got the Tata Scholarship to pursue my studies at the London School of Economics and also a seat in the Inner Temple to study Law. But I could not avail myself of these opportunities, as the Second World War broke out by that time. I, therefore, joined the Law College in Madras. I took the degree of Bachelor of Laws in 1941, and I was called to the Bar in December 1942.' By 1946, Durgabai was one of the leading criminal lawyers in Madras.

Towards the close of 1946, she was elected to the Constituent Assembly as a Congress candidate among the fifteen women elected to draft the Constitution of India. As a member of the Steering Committee, she took an active interest in the Constituent Assembly debates. With a law background, Durgabai contributed to all judicial matters arising during the debates. She probably moved over 750 amendments, many on her own and some in collaboration. 'I made it a point to attend every sitting of the Constituent Assembly and also of the Congress Assembly Party which was held almost every alternate day in the Constitution House,' she writes in her autobiography. She also led the amendment to the draft constitution to lower the age from 35 to 30 for a seat in the council of states. In the Constituent Assembly debates, it was not Hindi she championed, but Hindustani, 'The national language of India should not be and cannot be any other than Hindustani which is Hindi plus Urdu.'

In 1950, when Durgabai was planning to return to her legal practice, Jawaharlal Nehru appointed her to the Planning Commission as leader of social services. Nehru then invited Chintaman Deshmukh to help him draft the resolution for setting up a Planning Commission. At that time, Deshmukh was then Governor of the Reserve Bank of India. When she joined the Planning Commission, the first thing she did was to study the conditions of the existing institutions, the sources of their funds, and the problems they confronted. She opined that there was no use just talking about bringing up the weaker sections of society and a better status for women, unless there was a budgetary provision to help them and to save the institutions working for their welfare from being closed down. This was accepted by the Planning Commission.

Chintaman Deshmukh proposed marriage and Durgabai accepted. She did mention to him that it would not look good for both to continue in the Planning Commission after marriage and offered to resign. She carried a letter of her resignation to Nehru when they went to announce the news. However, he ridiculed the idea, saying that Chintaman had not appointed her to the Planning Commission! And they got married on 22 January 1953 with Jawaharlal Nehru as a witness to the civil marriage.

Durgabai became the first Chairman of the Central Social Welfare Board, in 1953. Steps were taken to establish thirty thousand rural welfare centres covering one-and-a-half lakh villages with one centre for five villages. A Grama Sevika (village woman welfare worker) was posted in each centre, along with a craft teacher and an auxiliary nurse midwife. The scheme became very popular and several women came forward to equip themselves through education and training. Another scheme she launched was for the economic development of families this scheme sought to provide housewives with part-time or 'own-time' work in industries such as the beedi and the match box industries and organize industrial cooperatives for the sale of products. She was also the Chairperson of the National Small Savings Committee, she created a separate section on Women's education in the First Five Year Plan, and in 1959, she was appointed as Chairman of the National Committee on Girls and Women's Education.

'I firmly believe that millions and billions of rupees cannot create what sincere, honest, and devoted workers can. Millions and billions come running after a devoted worker. That is why I believe that dedicated workers are the backbone of an institution or a country,' she wrote in her memoir. 'I never imagined that I would be offered membership of the Planning Commission, or chairmanship of the Central Social

Welfare Board. When, however, offices that we considered worthwhile came our way, we tried to do our very best. We knew well that the important thing is not coming to occupy a particular office but how you go out of office with your reputation unsullied.'

Having spent time in prison she was aware of the conditions of the jails. She looked at reforms of jails and the rehabilitation of criminals and requested the Director of the Delhi School of Social Work, to examine the conditions of offenders and the problems of their rehabilitation.

She advocated the establishment of family courts in India. She said, 'I thought that for a country of India's size, establishment of family courts as part of its judicial system would be of immense help in many ways. It would not only reduce the workload of the High Courts and the Supreme Court but also provide a good forum for preventing familybreak-ups and restoring happiness to men, women, and children, making it possible for them to remain united.' Three years after she died, family courts were finally established in India in 1984, under the Family Courts Act.

Durgabai Deshmukh received the Paul G Hoffman Award and was honoured with Padma Vibhushan. She was also felicitated with the UNESCO World Peace Award for her work in promoting literacy and the Nehru Literacy Award. 'Life is uncertain and the lifespan is limited. Why, then, wait to do a good thing?' Durgabai Deshmukh died on May 9, 1981. She concludes her autobiography with, 'Chintaman and I feel happy and contented that we have lived a life which has been satisfying to ourselves and of some service to the community. We have tried to live according to certain principles which we value, and life has given us ample rewards.'

CHAPTER FIFTY-EIGHT
THE YOUNG REVOLUTIONARY

Bina Das was born in 1911 in Krishnagar, Nadia District, Bengal. Her father Benimadhav Das, was a scholar and a well-known Brahmo Samaj teacher. He was also the teacher and influencer of Netaji Subhas Chandra Bose at Ravenshaw Collegiate School. She was inspired by her father, who was very affectionate towards his daughters. Her mother Sarla Devi was a social worker, and an educated and rational- minded woman. She ran a women's hostel named Punya Ashram in Calcutta which was also a storage space for weapons used by the revolutionaries. Bina had a strong emotional bond with her mother and got her courage and political aspirations from her.

Bina studied at the local Diocesan School and went to Calcutta in 1928 to study English Literature at Bethune College. While in college, she joined a revolutionary group and along with her fellow students organized their first protest. They held a demonstration at the college against the Simon Commission, which was set up to examine the administration in Colonial India. It consisted of seven members and met a hostile reception in India because it had no Indian members. It recommended giving greater autonomy to Indian provincial governments but maintaining a veto for the Viceroy. It also rejected parliamentary government for India as a whole. The Principal of the College threatened the demonstrators with dire consequences unless they tendered their apologies.

During an examination, she did not think twice before writing an essay on 'Pather Dabi' (The Right of Way.) The book depicts a secret society named Pather Dabi whose goal is to free India from British rule. The book was banned by the British government when it first appeared in book form on 31 August 1926, and the author, Saratchandra

Chattopadhyay, was prosecuted on charges of sedition. The book sold 5,000 copies within a week of its publication. Bina then joined the Chhatri Sangha, which taught women all the skills they needed to assist the country in the independence movement. Essentially a semi-revolutionary organization for women it had members like her courageous elder sister, Kalyani Das Bhattacharjee. Apart from being trained in physical strength, they studied international politics and current affairs. Bina also served as a Congress volunteer during the Calcutta session of the Congress in 1928 and extensively contributed to the journals, Mandira edited by Kamaka Dasgupta, and Jayasree edited by the founder of Dipali Sangha, Leela Nag Roy.

Bina was to receive her graduate degree in 1932, she learned that the Governor of Bengal, Stanley Jackson, would attend the convocation ceremony at Calcutta University. During the convocation ceremony, on 6 February 1932, the Governor arrived and reached the podium. While he was addressing the assembled students, Bina fired five shots at the Governor, at close range, but was disarmed by the Vice-Chancellor of Calcutta University. She was imprisoned. Newspapers in England reported, 'Calcutta Outrage; Stanley Jackson's Narrow Escape.' The Glasgow Herald mentioned, 'A girl graduate of Calcutta University fired five shots from close range at Sir Stanley Jackson, Governor of Bengal, while he was addressing the Convocation of the University on Saturday. The governor who was not injured owed his escape to his own marvellous coolness and the fact that the Vice-Chancellor of the University promptly grappled with the assailant.'

Another newspaper reported that, 'Bina Das, Indian girl student who was accused of attempting to shoot Sir Stanley Jackson. The British governor, on 6 February was sentenced today to nine years imprisonment at hard labour by A Special Tribunal. The girl pleaded guilty to a charge of attempted murder.' She was arrested, imprisoned for nine years of hard labour. While being deported she was secretly given a paper to write a letter to her parents to let them know of her location.

In her trial statement she said that she had nothing personal against Governor Stanley Jackson and received the sentence calmly.

She documents her prison experience in her memoir. 'I fired on the governor, impelled by love for my country which is repressed," she said. I sought only a way to death by offering myself at my country's feet and thus end my suffering. I invite the attention of all to the situation created by the measures of the government. This can upset even frail women like myself, brought up in all best traditions of Indian womanhood. I can assure all that I have no personal feeling against the governor of Bengal he represents a system which has kept enslaved 300,000,000 men and women of my country.'

According to her it was morally correct and aligned with her principles 'even if people do not expect violence from a woman of her nature.' In her memoir, she states, that it 'would be a great occasion to register (her) protest against the empire.' Her father while meeting his daughter in prison had remarked that both his daughters had inherited their dare from their mother. Her elder sister, Kalyani Das Bhattacharjee, was already in prison. While studying at Calcutta University, Kalyani became a member of the Chattri Sangha in 1926, a semi-revolutionary association of women students, to carry out rebellious activities. Around the same time that Bina tried to shoot the Governor, her sister had led a protest of female students against the Governor of Bengal and she was arrested.

Bina Das remembers her childhood and writes in her memoir, 'My childhood centred on my home, protected by the abundance of affection from my parents… I loved to listen to the stories sitting on my mother's lap. It seemed more interesting to me than playing with friends my age. I maintained the practice of reporting all my activities like a vivid story to my mother even after attaining maturity. I have never had such an attentive listener as my mother.' She celebrates her scholarly father, and writes, 'The greatest gift from our father was unfathomable love, affection, and boundless freedom with parental concern. I realized the difference when we compared ourselves with other girls of our age

…I do not know if our parents spoiled us but there is no doubt that without such adoration in the very beginning of my life, I could not have won the strength to challenge the hurdles in the later days.'

When new political prisoners arrived in jail, they were greeted with 'Bande Mataram,' a way of communication between the prisoners with a similar purpose. The brutal and erratic environment of the state-run prisons with inedible food and the bathrooms located outside their cells were harsh conditions that all Indians were put through in prison. The intelligence officer told her father that a revolver could release his daughter and she need not go through torture. Bina Das reacted by telling him that her father had not taught her to be a traitor.

Bina Das mentions in her memoir, that the prison gave her time for reading, writing, meditating, and teaching, which led to deeper insights into herself. The prisoners were forced to look within and she wrote that those years in prison ensured her an identity. While in prison she tutored many young girls who cleared their examinations while they were in prison. She went on a hunger strike and was admitted to the prison hospital. The male prisoners of Rajshahi jail sent her soap, biscuits, oil, and cream to extend their solidarity. Bina Das was released after nine years of rigorous imprisonment in 1939, after which she joined Congress. She then participated in the Quit India movement and was again imprisoned for three years till 1945. After independence, she became a member of the Bengal Legislative Assembly from 1946 to 1951 and secretary of the South Calcutta Congress Committee. She worked diligently during the rehabilitation of refugees from East Bengal after independence. In 1947, she married a fellow revolutionary, Jatish Chandra Bhaumik, a member of the Jugantar party and like Bina, he too was imprisoned for more than 15 years in jail.

Pritilata Waddedar and Bina Das were both not given their graduation certificates by the British Government because of their revolutionary activities. However, in 2012, they were conferred the Graduation Certificates posthumously by Calcutta University.

In 1960, the Government of India awarded her the Padma Shri for her contributions to social work. She authored two autobiographical books, Shrinkhal Jhankar and Pitridhan. Shrinkhal Jhankar (Sounds of Chain,) the first political autobiography to have been written by a Bengali woman. When Bina Das's husband died in 1986, she moved to Rishikesh. And some reports mention she died the same year in December 1986. She was called Agnikanya (daughter of fire) not without reason!

Bina Das's statement before the special tribunal of Calcutta High Court embodies her unwavering courage, her deep love for her country, and clarity in her aspirations. This statement necessitates its inclusion in her story, as she represents countless Indians who had to go through humiliation under tyrannical colonial rule.

'I confess that I fired at the Governor on the last Convocation Day at the Senate House. I hold myself entirely responsible for it. My object was to die and if I had to die, I wanted to do it nobly, fighting against this despotic system of government which has kept my country in perpetual subjection to its infinite shame and endless sufferings, and all the while fighting in a way which cannot but tell. I fired at the Governor impelled by my love for my country which is being repressed and what I attempted to do for the sake of my country was a great violence on my own nature too. It was a severe injury to the family to which I belong and the Institution where I was having my education — an institution which loved me dearly and exercised the highest influence on my life and character, and which I looked upon with all regard due to a mother; but the love for my country was always supreme in my mind, and I felt very deeply in my heart at the miserable condition of my country. All the ordinances, all the measures to put down the noble aspirations for freedom in my countrymen, came as a challenge to our national manhood and as indignities hurled at it. This hardened even the tender feminine nature like mine into one of a hero's mould. I had been thinking — is life worth living in an India so much subjected to wrongs and continually groaning under the tyranny of a foreign

iovernment or is it not better to make one supreme protest against it by
ffering one's life away? Would not the immolation of a daughter of India
nd of a son of England awaken India to the sin of its acquiescence to its
ontinued state of subjection and England to the iniquities of its
roceedings? This was one question that kept thundering at the gates of my
rain like incessant hammer blows which would neither be stilled nor
uffled. My sense of religion and morality is not inconsistent with my
ense of political freedom. I believe that a person who is a slave politically
annot realise God who is the embodiment of the spirit of freedom and has
ade His sons and daughters free to share in the joy that is in Him. I have
eld, therefore, that political freedom is organically connected with
ligion and morality; and there ought to be no conflict between them. In
ict, I feel in my heart of hearts that the best and the divine in humanity
ies out in revolt against all forms of tyranny in this world. Political
eedom, religion and moral ideals should, therefore, be blended together
ito one harmonious whole and the subject races inhabiting this globe
hould be politically free. It was for the purpose of bringing this fact home I
lected as my field of action, the Convocation Hall of my sacred alma
ater.

I studied in Diocesan College for my B.A. degree and passed with
onours in English and my father sent me to that College for an additional
ourse of study for a B.T. Degree, in order to bring me into closer touch
ith truly Christian souls and to give opportunities to see the best side of
ritish character. I gratefully acknowledge that I have immensely profited
y my study under the Sisters of my dear College. But at the same time,
ith the comparative knowledge of things, I felt with deep anguish that the
ue Christian spirit was not much in evidence in the administration of a
hristian Government. The series of ordinances savouring of Martial Law,
) my mind, showed nothing but a spirit of vindictiveness and were only
easures to crush all aspirations for freedom. The outrages perpetrated in
e name of the Government at Midnapore, Hijli, and Chittagong (my own
istrict), the refusal to publish the Official Enquiry Reports, and many more
f such instances, were things I could never drive away from my mind.

The outrage on Amba Debi of Contai and Niharbala of Chittagong literally upset my whole being. I used to help the wife of a detenu in her studies as a work of love. Every day I saw with my own eyes the sufferings of the poor girl who was leading the life of a widow during the life- time of her husband as also the demented parents of the detenu, slowly sinking into their graves, without their having the faintest notion of the supposed guilt of their son. I attended the Court proceedings during the trial of my sister Kalyani. She was punished to serve a term of rigorous imprisonment for having allegedly attended a meeting which could not be held and for being a member of an unlawful society only on the basis of the evidence of her having a proscribed leaflet in her possession. This was, to my mind, grossly unjust. Though she is an Honours Graduate who had earlier lived in all the comforts of a middle-class family, yet ignominy was hurled on her during her prison-life. What with the jail- dress and jail-diet of ordinary convicts classified as third class prisoners, and the sleepless nights amongst such criminals, militated against my whole being. I saw all these with my own eye and also witnessed the bitter tears welling out of the eyes of my dearest parents. I thought that such must be the sufferings of innumerable others. All these and many other incidents worked on my feelings which worked themselves into a frenzy. The pain became unbearable till such time I felt that I would go mad if I could not find relief in death. I only sought the way to death by offering myself at the feet of my country and inviting the attention of all by my death, as a mark of the most immaculate form of protest against the situations created by the repressive measures of the government, which can unsex even a frail woman like myself, brought up in all the best traditions of Indian womanhood. I can assure all that I could never have any personal grudge against any person or anything on earth; I have no sort of personal feelings against Sir Stanley Jackson, the man and Lady Jackson, the woman. But the Governor of Bengal represents the system of repression which has kept enslaved 300 millions of my countrymen and country women.

Now I stand alone before the judgment seat of God and open myself before Him and pray for His all-forgiving love to wash me clean, so that I maybe a worthy offering to Him. May I see the benign countenance of the Mother Divine and feel Her loving embrace for me at this most solemn moment of my life. If it be Her will that I should die, then let it be so. If She wills that I live, let me consecrate my life to the service of suffering humanity, which is the fondest longing of my heart, if She out of Her infinite mercy spares it to be used by Her as Her instrument. May God fulfil Himself through my death or my life, if it so pleases Him. Thy will be done. Oh Lord.'

This statement reflects the mindset of several other women who were imprisoned for years and were not given a fair hearing because they participated in the fight for freedom for their motherland!

CHAPTER FIFTY-NINE
THE GANDHIAN

Citing patriotic reasons she turned down a teaching job at the Cotton College Guwahati, as they had earlier denied her admission. Amalprova Das was born on 12 November 1911, in Dibrugarh, Assam. Her parents Dr. Harekrishna Das and Hema Prabha Das were staunch Gandhi followers. After Amalprova was denied admission at the British-run Cotton College, she was forced to move to Calcutta to study. She studied at the Bethune School and later at the Scottish Church College where she graduated in chemistry and followed it up with a master's degree in applied chemistry. This was the first time that an Assamese woman received a master's degree in science. After this, she completed a diploma in clinical pathology.

Das had an opportunity to meet with Gandhi when he visited Guwahati in 1934 for the Harijan Yatra. He stayed at her parent's residence. Constructive Programs were part of Gandhi's social work initiatives, he realised that he had to mobilise people and strengthen the work at the grassroots through initiatives he had outlined. These programs included the construction of new institutions, organising and implementing the programs based on Khadi, spinning, working with Harijans, skill education for women, and activities relevant to the grassroots. Many women leaders worked on promoting these initiatives and setting up enterprises during the freedom movement. Amalprova was one of the women who spent her entire life developing institutions and taking Gandhi's plan and vision forward.

In 1939, Amalprova, along with her mother Hema Prabha Das, visited the Maganwadi Centre of Self Development at Wardha. They stayed there for three months to understand the activities and the village reform movement of Gandhi. Encouraged by what they saw, on their return to Guwahati, they set up an indigenous cottage industry on the Sarania Hills and called it the Maitri Ashram. A self-help group for women and their economic independence, Maitri Ashram was set up as a cottage industry for women to be trained to make soap, handmade paper, extracting oil, etc. A special priority was given to weaving and common crafts. Soon it became a centre of excellence for the north-east states, promoting the Gandhian concept of gramodyog and a pivot of Gandhian activities in the state.

When the Congress women wing was set up in September 1940 Amalprova Das was made joint secretary. In keeping with Mahatma Gandhi's vision for the Kasturba Gandhi Memorial Trust, after Kasturba Gandhi's demise in 1944, the Ashram was renamed Kasturba Ashram. Gandhi wanted to expand the work of the Trust in the entire country. To head the Trust in the Northeast States, Gandhi selected Amalprova. Her mother had died by now and her father donated their entire property in the Sarania Hills to the Kasturba Gandhi Trust.

The people trained at Kasturba Ashram were ever ready to work during natural calamities, communal clashes, or border disputes. The volunteers helped during the 1950 earthquake, which devastated Assam. Later Kasturba Kalyan Kendra was established in north Lakhimpur, Assam under the fold of Kasturba Ashram for widows and orphans who had lost their homes during the earthquake. Another initiative of the ashram was setting up the Guwahati Katai Mandal. The Mandal aimed at strengthening the concept of self-help and gramodyog.

The Kasturba Kalyan Kendra, Guwahati Katai Mandal, Gram Sevika Vidyalaya, and Assam Go Seva Samiti were all founded by Amalprova and continue even today. In 1952 she established the Guwahati Yubak Sevadal, a non-governmental organization working for the social development of Harijans and rehabilitation of Harijans. She also established the Harijan Colony at Solabeel area in the heart of the town. Amalprova participated in the year-and-half- long padyatra in Assam during the last leg of Vinoba Bhave's Bhoodan movement.

Many institutions and schools have been built in the memory of Amalprova Das and her legacy continues. An area in Guwahati is named after Amalprova, where a hostel for girls has been established by the local people. She received the Padma Shree in 1954, when the Padma Awards was first instituted and the Jamnalal Bajaj Award in 1981 for her Outstanding Contribution in Constructive Work. She declined the Padma Vibhushan. In 2013, the Government of Assam Social Welfare Department instituted the Amalprova Das Award in her honour for commitment and excellence in social service.

CHAPTER SIXTY
THE DETERMINED

She had no clear idea in her school days about the future. At times dreamt of becoming a great scientist, another time imagined herself as the Rani of Jhansi and at times to be a fearless revolutionary. Growing up in a family where only swadeshi goods were bought, Pritilata Waddedar was born on 13 May 1911 in Dhalghat, Chittagong, Bengal. Her father, Jagabandhu Waddedar, was a clerk in the civil administration of Chittagong, and her mother, Pratibha Waddedar, was a home-maker.

An intelligent student, Pritilata studied at the local Dr. Khastagir Government Girls' School, where she passed in first class in 1927. She was very keen to study at Calcutta University however s h e was unable to get a scholarship and thus completed her intermediate arts at the local Eden College, which was an hour from where she lived. She passed with a first class here as well. While studying at Eden College, Pritilata joined Shree Sangha, an all-male revolutionary group. This was founded by Anil Roy and his wife Leela Nag Roy. Leela had also established a female student group called Dipali Sangha (Torchbearer's Association) in 1923. The goal was to create awareness among women on both political and social fronts. Both groups were allies and supported each other. While Leela Nag's initial focus was women's education however, the organization soon became the centre for diverse activities with branches in different parts of Bengal. The members were taught the art of physical training, such as drill, parade, national awareness, sword fighting as well as stick combat.

Pritilata later moved to Calcutta and studied philosophy at Bethune College and passed with distinction. In Calcutta too she joined the

Chhatri Sangha. This was another woman-led, semi-revolutionary group and recruiting ground for female revolutionaries. Like its counterpart Dipali Sangha, Chhatri Sangha coordinated study workshops and lessons in physical combat. Soon Pritilata was an active member, balancing her revolutionary activities with her studies. She graduated from Bethune College in 1931, with distinction in philosophy. Pritilata's father would tell her, 'My hopes are bound up with you.' After her graduation, she returned to Chittagong. Her father had lost his job and now Pritilata had to look after the family financially. She took up a teaching job and later became the head teacher of Nandankanan Aparna Charan English Medium Secondary School, Chittagong.

However, her passion was elsewhere, to be a revolutionist and therefore she resigned from the school. She soon met Purnendu Dastidar, a member of the Chittagong Jugantar Party, together with Surya Sen popularly known as Master Da. She asked him to include her as a member of the Party. Surya Sen was not in favour of women's direct participation, as the job required to use firearms, however, women could be assigned to send secret messages, shelter the revolutionaries, and conceal proscribed books. Surya Sen changed his decision after he met Pritilata and she was inducted as a member of the Party.

Surya Sen had led the Chittagong armoury raid, also known as the Chittagong uprising. This was a planned attempt on 18 April 1930 to raid the armoury of police and auxiliary forces, with a slogan-'Gandhi's Raj has come.' This was followed by a series of events like the battle of Jalalabad where young revolutionaries in the age group 14 to 19 fought against well-trained and mechanized British arms and the British had to retreat after three hours of continuous struggle!

Since Pritilata was living in Calcutta, Surya Sen assigned her the task of regularly meeting Ramkrishna Biswas serving a death sentence at Alipore Central Jail. Biswas an active member of the revolutionary group assigned to assassinate the Chittagong Inspector General of

Police, Officer Craig on 1 December 1930. However, he mistakenly killed a rail inspector, Tarini Mukherjee. Biswas was arrested the next day. His family did not have money to travel from Chittagong. Hence, Pritilata was given the responsibility to visit him in jail. She introduced herself as a cousin of Biswas and met him forty times. She diarised every visit, recording her inner emotions during the meetings. The police got to know of her visit much later after they discovered a note she had scribbled regarding her meeting with Biswas. On 4 August 1931, Ramkrishna Biswas was executed at the Alipore Central Jail which was a shock to Pritilata.

In May 1932, Pritilata went to meet Surya Sen who was in hiding at a shelter in Dhalghat. The police got to know of this and at dusk, a police force led by Captain Cameron surrounded the house. Cameron opened fire and during the encounter, Pritilata who had never been in action before sized up the situation and began firing back. Cameron was killed and Nirmal Sen, another revolutionary was fatally wounded. On receiving an order to escape, Pritilata had to get away. She quietly returned home. Her parent did not suspect their daughters' involvement in political activities. The police had found her clothes at the Dhalghat Shelter. The DIB reached her home and searched her house but did not find anything except a photograph of hers and some scribbled notes. They confined her at her home as a suspect. The confinement was intolerable and when she received instructions from Surya Sen to go underground, Pritilata absconded on 5 July 1932. The British authorities declared a reward of five hundred rupees for her arrest. In the three months that she went underground, Pritilata was trained to handle revolvers, pistols, and bombs.

On 24 September 1932, Surya Sen planned to attack the Pahartali European Club which had a signboard that read, 'Dogs and Indians not allowed,' a signboard at many clubs during the colonial rule. The reason was to restrict the natives from entering the clubs and an attempt by the British to justify their superiority over Indians. Surya Sen entrusted Pritilata to lead and raid the Pahartali European Club along with eight other revolutionaries. Their plan was not to attack individual Europeans but the Club where they gathered in large numbers during the evenings. Pritilata and her team of eight assembled near the Club on 24 September 1932 at 9 pm. Pritilata was dressed as a soldier and the others were dressed as coachmen resembling the coachman of the club's members. All of them were armed. They were helped by a cook who was angry with club members for mistreating the club staff. The revolutionaries stood at the doors and windows of the club, while the Europeans inside the club panicked, as all the exits were blocked. Pritilata was wounded during the attack and she ordered her team, who were unhurt to leave the club. Instead of surrendering to the British, she chose to swallow cyanide.

Priitilata's fellow revolutionary and friend Kalpana Datta describes what happened at the club that day, in her book, Chittagong Armoury Raiders: Reminiscences. She writes, 'The Pahartali Railways Officers' Club is near the railway station. British officers and their wives used, to come for drinks and dancing every Saturday night. 24th September 1932, was one such Saturday. The music, laughter and revelry came to a dead stop suddenly at about 9 o'clock in the night. Instead, there was the sound of bombs exploding and shots being fired. Those inside tried to get out by the windows, but then rushed back again in panic. Within a quarter of an hour, it was all over there was silence. Only the wounded groaned in pain and fear. Eight boys made the attack under Preeti's leadership. All the boys went back unhurt but Preeti never came back. She took potassium cyanide and collapsed dead about 10 yards from the clubhouse. A splinter wound on her breast had soaked her shirt in blood. Plenty of men had mounted the gallows, had been killed in action in the struggle of the terrorist revolutionaries. But Preeti was the first woman known to have been in action and to have died in action. In 1930, some girls had joined the movement but were not then known to have gone into serious action. From Preeti's actions, people were convinced for the first time that Indian women can do what our men have done. They can give their lives for their country as easily as men can. Whatever criticism there may be of the methods of the terrorists, all Chittagong remembers Preeti as their brave daughter. They say with deep reverence 'She did not give herself to the Police.'

'Sometimes, Masterda used to say she might have thought of suicide because of the death of these two very dear comrades of hers. Masterda used to say, "I don't believe in suicide. But she took potassium cyanide out of me when she came to bid her last farewell. She was so eager and argued so well about its need in case she was trapped. I could not hold out. I gave it to her.' Kalpana also describes the person Pritilata was, in the book, 'A tiny incident not big in itself brings out Preeti's extremely gentle character. During the Puja holidays in 1930, she had asked me to go to their place for a feast. We were discussing whether either of us could slaughter a goat for the mutton. I said, 'Of course, I can! There is nothing much in it,' Preeti said, 'There is nothing frightening in it, of course, but I won't be able to slaughter a poor inoffensive creature in cold blood.' Somebody asked at once, 'What? Do you want to fight for the country's freedom too non-violently or what?' I remember her straight reply, 'When I am ready to give my own life for the country's freedom I won't hesitate a bit in taking somebody's life too if necessary. But I shall not be able to kill a poor harmless creature just like that." Within two years, she proved by her own death that she believed in what she said then.'

Regarding Pritilata's family, she writes, 'Preeti's family were never well off. Her father was a clerk in the Municipal offices and was barely able to balance the family budget. He handed over his monthly salary to Preeti and she had the key to the cash box. One afternoon, we were discussing the problem, of funds, sitting at her place. Masterda needed Rs. 500 urgently on that very day. Rs. 450 had been collected, the balance of Rs. 50 was wanted. She had not been asked to give anything because we all knew their family finances were bad. Preeti quietly walked out of the room while the discussion was going on and slipped back with Rs. 50. When she was asked where she got it from, she answered 'Yesterday Father got his salary. All the cash is kept with me, so I am giving the whole amount.' We protested for two reasons: firstly, she would be left with no ready cash at all if we took it. Secondly, she would be causing misunderstanding and panic in the house when anybody asked for the cash and got nothing. Preeti would not agree. She said, 'I run this household, I shall manage on my own. Please don't waste your time worrying about it.' She added, "And of course, there will be no problem at all about my having the cash. Father has implicit faith in me. Besides, I will tell him myself that I have spent the money he will know I cannot spend it on any but a good cause which makes our sacrifice more than worthwhile." But when nobody would agree to take the money she almost burst into tears "you won't take our money just because we are poor? Won't you give me the chance to prove our devotion to the cause even?'

Kalpana Datta further writes, 'Preeti was not only good at her studies. She could write very well too. People used to quote what she wrote in her underground days. Her father gave her a good education even though he could not afford it, because of her striking intelligence. He used to tell her, 'My hopes are bound up with you.' She too adored her father. Her face would light up when she spoke of him. He lost his job just before she went up for her B.A, exams. So she had to maintain the family out of her own earnings. She became a teacher in a high school and was a tutor to some girls. In this way, she maintained her father, mother and four little brothers and sisters. She knew what a shock her death would be to so many who loved her so much. But she gave her life for the hundreds and thousands of mothers and fathers of our country who need a daughter. She was daughter to them all.'

Kalpana Datta concludes in her book Chittagong Armoury Raiders: Reminiscences, that Pritilata's father nearly lost his reason to live over her death. But her mother used to say proudly, 'My girl has given her life for the country.' They had a very, difficult time after she went away. But the mother took up midwifery and managed to balance the family budget somehow. 'They are still carrying on somehow, Preeti's father has not been able to forget his sorrow. He is reminded of her whenever he sees me. He took a keen interest in relief work during the famine and used to say, 'My girl would have helped us to do so much more.' The people of Chittagong have not forgotten Preeti or her great sacrifice. They point out her father to any stranger and say, 'He is the father of the first girl who gave her life for our country.'

Thus ended the brief but determined and courageous life of Pritilata Waddedar on 24 September 1932. Very little has been documented on her life, therefore the references and story of Pritilata have been taken from Kalpana Datta's memoir *Chittagong Armoury Raiders: Reminiscences*.

CHAPTER SIXTY-ONE
THE REVOLUTIONIST

Kalpana Datta was born on 27 July 1913 at Sripur, Chittagong. Her father Binod Behari Dattagupta worked with the government. After completing her school in 1929 from Chittagong, she moved to Calcutta to study science at Bethune College. While in Calcutta she joined the Chhatri Sangha (Women Students Association), a semi-revolutionary organization.

Kalpana Datta met Surya Sen in June 1931 in Chittagong and became a member of the armed independence movement led by him. Pritilata was already part of the group. Many of the leaders of the Chittagong Armoury Raid had been arrested and were awaiting trial. Kalpana was given the responsibility of carrying explosive materials from Calcutta. She also prepared guncotton which is a mild explosive, used in printing ink bases, leather finishing, and celluloid. The plan was to plant these explosives under the court building and inside the jail to free the revolutionary leaders, who were being tried in a special Tribunal for the Armoury Raid. However, the British authorities came to know of the plan, and restrictions were imposed on Kalpana's movements. She would meet Surya Sen and others at midnight to discuss the strategy to free fellow revolutionaries.

In her memoir, Chittagong Armoury Raiders: Reminiscences, she pens, 'In June 1931 Masterda sent word that I was to meet him. It was a dark night with a slight drizzle. I was quietly waiting under a mosquito net in the front room of a house deep in the interior. Someone came and said "hullo', then came another. I could not see much in the flickering light of an oil lamp. The two strangers were, talking to each other under their breath, so I could, not make out who was Masterda. Then I came to know he was Masterda. He was a smallish, short man, very reserved.'

'Nobody would guess that this quiet man was the darling 'King of Chittagong.' There was nothing remarkable about his appearance. He asked me how I had done my Intermediate Science examination which I had just sat for. I said, 'Not very well. 'He asked again, 'Why, were you given too much political work?' I got the impression from his tone that he did not like slackness in studies. I was overwhelmed by this first meeting with Masterda. I felt a sense of joy, deep respect, wonder, a touch of fear. I felt as if I could do whatever he wanted me to do at a moment's notice. I was bursting to tell anyone I met after that I have talked to Surya Sen! I used to tell my comrade Preeti Waddadar, who had not seen Masterda: 'Do you know, I think our Masterda is greater even than Doctorda,' ('Doctorda' was the famous terrorist character in Sarat Chandra's Father Dabi). Preeti used to say, 'Yes, I too think so.'

In September 1931 Surya Sen assigned Kalpana Datta and Pritilata Waddedar the task to attack the Pahartali European Club at Chittagong. Kalpana was arrested a week before the attack while she had gone to the club to survey it, dressed in male attire. She was still in jail when she was told about the events of 24 September at the Pahartali Club and Pritilata's death. While on bail after spending two months in the prison, she went underground on Surya Sen's instructions. After over two months in hiding in the early hours of 17 February 1933, the police surrounded the hideout where she along with other revolutionaries and Surya Sen were hiding. The police arrested Surya Sen, however, Kalpana, escaped. After two months in hiding, on 19 May 1933 the police caught up with Kalpana and she was sentenced to life and sent to the Hijli Detention Camp, Midnapore. During the non-cooperation movement, those who participated in armed struggles, could not be accommodated in ordinary jails. Hence the British established a few detention camps like the Hijli Detention Camp. She met plenty of old acquaintances, Bina Das had been sentenced to nine years for the attempt on Bengal Governor Stanley Jackson's life in the Calcutta University Convocation.

Surya Sen was hanged on midnight of 13 January 1934. Kaplana Datta came to know of this much later when she was moved from

Rajshahi Central Jail, another jail constructed by the British. His relatives were not given charge of the body. Kaplana Datta mentions in her memoir, 'He left his torch behind for us to carry forward. I just could not believe that Masterda was no more. But I had taken a vow: We shall carry forward your heritage! In May 1939, I had just come out of jail. A hawker said, 'The day they hanged Surya Sen, the sun did not dawn.'

After her release in 1939, she graduated from Calcutta University in 1940. She saw an extensive change around her in the six years that she was in prison. She asked herself, where she would now fit in the new environment and went back to Chittagong to join the Communist Party. She was of the view that freedom could be achieved only through Communist ideology. Kalpana married Puran Chand Joshi, then General Secretary of the Communist Party of India in 1943.

Kalpana in her memoirs writes, 'I had been arrested a week before Preeti went into action. The police were at their wit's end, they could not make out why I was seen going towards Pahartali dressed in male attire. They were highly suspicious over the 'circumstances' of my arrest, but could not bring any definite charge against me. On the morning of the 25th of September, the D.I.B. Inspector came to see me. He started off at once, 'God, we saved you in the nick of time!' A little later, another official came and said, 'It is our great good fortune to have saved a girl like you from death.' What were they driving at? The suspense made me crazy with impatience. The D.I.B. Inspector came out with it finally. 'Preeti died yesterday,' he said, 'She raided Pahartali Club and then took potassium cyanide. Thank God, we arrested you or you would have gone the same way. Preeti was dressed exactly as you were.' He went on talking and seemed to be well-meaning in his own way. But I could not stand his chatter anymore, I came to my cell. Preeti was a very dear friend of mine. Of the four girls who had joined Surya Sen's party only two of us had been left. The rest had gone. The night before my arrest, I got the news that we were to go into action together. I was asked to come away from home for action so that I don't have to go back home again. Preeti had been absconding for a month and a half, this was our first meeting after she went under-ground. We went to the sea beach and did some target practice. Then we sang songs and came away, our leader, told me that I would have to return home once more before going into action. He said the finishing touches to preparations for the raid would take some time yet, there would be suspicious if I did not return. There was still a restraint order on me. Preeti backed him and I got annoyed with her. I was sure I would get caught and not be able to go into action if I went home. For some time the D.I.B. Inspector had been coming daily to our house to keep watch. He would have noticed my disappearance already and was bound to run me in for breaking the restraint order. It was decided in the end that if I noticed any danger, I was to come back at once. I was also given a revolver, just in case they tried to arrest me, I could shoot my way out. Preeti saw me off with a patronising, 'Now don't be childish' advice. She was only two years older than I and we were both very young then. I was furious with her for trying to play the big sister,' adds Kalpana.

'On the morning of the 17th of September, I saw the police on our verandah as soon as I sighted our house. I turned back at once but was caught trying to get to Preeti's shelter that very night. I was mad with Preeti. She was my best friend. If she had put in a word, maybe I would not have got trapped like this. For seven days I was brooding over my bad luck and just could not forgive Preeti for letting me down. And now the sudden, impossible news that she was dead If only I were by her side, in action together, I would never have let her commit suicide. Later, Masterda (Surya Sen) told me that she had died in order to show our people that women too can fight and die for their country like their men-folk. But I was convinced that she could have done much more by coming back alive.'

Kalpana writes with a lot of fondness for Pritilata, 'I got to know her when both of us were very young. We went to school together. She was only a class ahead of me in the same school. We got to know each other on the badminton courts. The rules were that you got the right to play on the badminton courts and to take books out of the library as soon as you reached class V. But we had to give up the courts to girls from the senior classes when they wanted it! That is why I used to play in the burning sun, during the tiffin recess. And Preeti was the only one who would play at that hour. So we became best friends. When we got to the senior classes both of us joined the Girl Guides.'

In 1946, Kalpana contested the elections for the Bengal Legislative Assembly as a Communist Party of India candidate from Chittagong but did not win. After 1947 she stayed back in India however resigned from active politics. She then joined the Indian Statistical Institute where she worked until her retirement. Kalpana Datta died in Calcutta on 8 February 1995. 'We used to tell each other that it was our duty to learn all the methods of the 'other side,' (the British). It would be useful to us for building up our own strength. We wanted to get the pledge: 'To be loyal to God and the King-Emperor' changed into: 'To be loyal to God and Country.' She proved it as well!

CHAPTER SIXTY-TWO
THE CAPTAIN OF THE SHIP

Lakshmi Swaminathan Sahgal was born on 24 October 1914 in Madras. Her father S. Swaminathan was a leading criminal lawyer in the Madras High Court and her mother Ammu Swaminathan a freedom fighter. As a child, she was inspired by her mother's social work and wanted to be of service to her country. Lakshmi completed her MBBS from the Madras Medical College in 1938 and received her diploma in gynaecology and obstetrics in 1939. The Second World War had broken out and there was a move to recruit all doctors into the British Indian Army. Lakshmi did not want to join and decided to move to Singapore where she had close relatives. She soon started her private medical practice and became a prominent gynecologist in the city. In March 1942, Rashbehari Bose, the revolutionary leader, established the India Independence League in Singapore and appealed to the Indians to join the League. Lakshmi found this as a great support as then they got their ration cards, and Indian real estate was not treated as enemy property. She joined the League to do welfare work and underground broadcasts only. A month earlier the Indian National Army (INA) was formed by Captain Mohan Singh however disbanded a little later. When Subhas Chandra Bose arrived in Singapore in early July 1943, Rashbehari Bose handed over the leadership of the India Independence League to him. Subhas Chandra Bose wanted to reorganize INA into a revolutionary establishment. The very next day he announced to the world the existence of the INA and its aim: to March to Delhi (Dilli Chalo.) He asked volunteers to join to fight to free India and soon the strength of the INA doubled from 30,000 to 60,000.

In the second meeting, at the Padang rally speech on 9 July, 1943 Bose said, 'I want a unit of brave Indian women to form a death-defying

Regiment who will wield the sword which Rani of Jhansi wielded in India's First War of Independence in 1857.' And the Rani of Jhansi Regiment was announced on 12 July. After the first meeting with Bose, Lakshmi said, 'His utter, absolute sincerity struck me most and I felt this man would never take a wrong step and that one could trust him completely and have the utmost confidence in him.' And Lakshmi volunteered and from there on Dr. Lakshmi Swaminathan became Captain Lakshmi.

She helped recruit a regiment of 1500 women and 200 nursing staff, from several eastern countries like Thailand, Malaya, Singapore, and Burma, with no formal education. Many were mothers, with children as young as 12 years old. Leaving their family members behind to free a nation they had never visited! The training for the Rani of Jhansi Regiment in Singapore and Rangoon started on 23 October 1943. Two days earlier, Bose had formed the Provisional Government of Azad Hind. Lakshmi Swaminathan was appointed as the Minister of Women's Affairs within the Azad Hind government. An Indian government-in-exile, with 11 ministers and eight representatives from the INA. Subh Sukh Chain was the national anthem and the government soon had its own currency, court, and civil code. Captain Lakshmi took charge of the regiment's fighting and nursing units. That way she was active both militarily and on the medical front. They were trained rigorously for three months and the only weapons they had were rifles and hand grenades, with no automatic weapons. The women underwent not only physical training but also were taught to read the map and military strategy. Bose would help in political classes. They were given khaki uniforms: caps, shirts, jodhpurs, breeches, and boots. Most of them cut their hair short as the intent was that the women dress as soldiers if they were to be taken seriously. Captain Lakshmi was happy to have a haircut as she had hair below her knees! The recruits were mainly South Indians, thus Hindi classes were given and within three months they had all learnt the language.

After the three month training, the first batch moved to Burma, and in May 1944, small batches of the regiment moved from Rangoon on the way to Imphal. The regiment took part mostly in guerilla attacks. However, the regiment was able to proceed only up to the middle of Burma as the attack on Imphal by the INA, was met by a full strength of the British regiment. They suffered heavy casualties and Bose asked them to withdraw. The Rani of Jhansi Regiment was then disbanded.

Lakshmi volunteered to work in an INA hospital situated in the thick jungles, which had been set up for the wounded. After Bose visited the hospital in June 1945, the hospital was bombed and destroyed and most of the patients were killed and while evacuating the remaining survivors they were caught on the road to Rangoon by the British forces. In the crossfire, she was separated from the INA personnel and the British forces arrested her and send her to Rangoon for interrogation. Here she was under house arrest. Released on 4 March 1946, she was sent back to India. The British had realised that keeping her a prisoner would prove counter-productive.

In March 1947 Captain Lakshmi married Colonel Prem Kumar Sahgal in Lahore. A leading member of the INA, Colonel Prem Kumar Sahgal was among those released from the Red Fort by the British. After their marriage, they settled in Kanpur where Captain Lakshmi returned to her medical practice and took care of the refugees who were arriving in large numbers following the Partition of India. She decided not to join any party. In 1969, her daughter, Subhasini, returned from America and joined the CPI (M.) In 1971, during the Bangladesh War, refugee camps were set up in border areas of West Bengal for the Bangladeshis. Lakshmi wanted to volunteer in the relief work and saw the then Chief Minister Jyoti Basu's appeal for support for the People's Relief Committee. Lakshmi volunteered and worked in the border areas for about six weeks, organising relief camps and medical help for Bangladesh refugees who streamed into India. When she was returning to Calcutta, the politburo of the CPI (M) was meeting and she decided to go and meet the leaders. It was then she decided to join the Party and represented the CPI (M) in the Rajya Sabha.

'My way of thinking was already communist, and I never wanted to earn a lot of money or acquire a lot of property or wealth,' she said and believed that 'Freedom comes in three forms, the first is political emancipation from the conqueror, the second is economic (emancipation) and the third is social. India has only achieved the first.'

She was the founding member of the All India Democratic Women's Association (AIDWA), formed in 1981. An independent left-oriented women's organization committed to achieving democracy, equality, and women's emancipation. She was instrumental in many of their activities. Later she became its leader. When the Bhopal gas tragedy took place in December 1984, Lakshmi Sahgal led the medical team. She wrote a report on the long-term effects of the gas on pregnant women. During the anti-Sikh riots that followed post-Indira Gandhi's assassination in 1984, she confronted anti-Sikh mobs and ensured that no Sikh or Sikh establishment near her clinic was attacked.

In 1998, she was awarded the Padma Vibhushan. In 2002 Lakshmi Sahgal was nominated the CPI (M) candidate in the presidential elections 2002. She was the sole counter-candidate to A.P.J. Abdul Kalam. She campaigned across the country, though admitting that she did not stand a chance of winning. Captain Dr. Lakshmi Sahgal died on 23 July 2012. An officer in the Indian National Army (INA), Minister of Women's affairs in the Azad Hind Government, and a qualified doctor by profession who participated in the Indian Independence in the true sense of the word.

CHAPTER SIXTY-THREE
THE RANI OF THE NAGAS

Manipur or the Kangleipak Kingdom became a British protectorate in 1824. The royal family was from the Meitei community, the Vaishnavism, and there were the Nāga tribes living in the hills of Manipur. Rani Gaidinliu, a Kabui Naga from the Rongmei tribe, was born on 26 January 1915 in Tamenglong district, Manipur. When she was only thirteen, she remarked, 'We are free people, the white man should not rule over us,' and went on to join a movement launched by a local Naga leader.

Unrest in the 1920s in the Nāga tribes in the region and an increase in the activities of the missionaries along the hill communities were disturbing the customary way of life followed by the Nāgas. Looking at reviving the Nāga Tribal religion and resisting conversions of the Nāgas to Christianity, Rani Gaidinliu's cousin Haipou Jadonang launched a movement referred to as the Heraka (Pure) Movement. It was not only a reformist religious movement but a political movement to set up self-rule by the Nāga and against British rule.

In 1931, the British arrested Rani Gaidinliu's cousin and hanged him after a mock trial, prompting the seventeen-year-old Gaidinliu to lead the movement. She altered the religious movement into a struggle for freedom. Described the Heraka Movement as a movement to reform old religious practices to strengthen the movement for ousting the British. The British forces launched a manhunt for her, which forced her to go underground. She moved across villages of Assam, Nagaland, and Manipur, evading the British and continuously shifting from one village to another. She also mobilized the Zeliangrong tribe, a large indigenous Nāga community living in the tri-junction of Assam, Manipur, and Nagaland, to resist paying taxes to the British administration and refuse aid to the British. A threat to the British because of her growing popularity, her anti-British stance, and strong defiance, they declared monetary rewards for any valuable information about her, including a ten-year tax break to the informant!

In 1932, her forces engaged in a rebellion against the British in Cachar Hills and the Hangrum village, Assam. The British sent the special Assam Rifles contingent to arrest and capture Gaidinliu. On receiving an intelligence report that Gaidinliu and her followers were in the village of Pulomi, they deceived them by sending the troops in the opposite direction, tricking Gaidinliu into a false sense of security. The British forces then launched a surprise attack on the village and arrested Gaidinliu and her followers. Captured, handcuffed, and taken to the capital of Nagaland, Kohima, on foot, they were later sent to Imphal, the capital of Manipur, for an inquiry. They convicted her on charges of murder, and abetment of murder and sentenced her to life imprisonment. She was shifted constantly from one jail to another, imprisoned, in Guwahati, Shillong, Aizawl, and Tura jails. Most of Gaidinliu's associates were either imprisoned or executed, which led to a decline in the movement. Jawaharlal Nehru who met her in the Shillong Jail in 1937, described her as a 'daughter of the hills' and called her the Rani of the Nāgas. He promised to pursue her release. After which he wrote to the British Member of Parliament in the House of Commons, Lady Astor to help release Rani Gaidinliu but the then Secretary of State for India, Lawrence Dundas rejected this request stating that there would be chaos if she was released.

After meeting Gaidinliu, Nehru in a statement in the Hindustan Times said, 'and now she lies in some prison in Assam, wasting her bright young womanhood in dark cells and solitude. Six years she has been there. What suppression of spirit they have brought to her who, in the pride of her youth, dared to challenge the Empire. And India does not even know of this brave child of her hills. But her people remember her as their Rani Gaidinliu and a day will come when India will also remember her.' Gaidinliu was released in 1947 on the orders of

Prime Minister Jawaharlal Nehru. After her release, she lived with her younger brother, Marang, in Nagaland and five years later moved back to Manipur. She went underground in 1960 for six years, organizing a private army of 1000 men to fight the Nāga National Council (NCC,) who advocated separation from India and demanded a state of their own. She campaigned for a separate Zeliangrong territory within the Union of India. However, after six long years of living underground, she came out from her hiding to work to improve the living conditions of her people peacefully. The government conferred her with the Tamrapatra Freedom Fighter Award in 1972, and ten years later the Padma Bhushan in 1982. Followed by the Vivekananda Seva Award in 1983, and the Birsa Munda Award posthumously. Rani Gaidinliu died in Longkao Manipur on 17 February 1993. A postal stamp was issued in her honour in 1996 and 2015, as well as a commemorative coin. The Indian Coast Guard commissioned its inshore patrol vessel and named it Rani Gaidinliu.

Remembered for her unconquerable spirit, connecting the Naga movement to a wider movement for an independent India and for the liberty she fought for fearlessly, 'The Daughter of the Hills' Rani Gaidinliu, was truly a 'Rani.'

CHAPTER SIXTY-FOUR
LADY MAA

She was born on 22 May 1917 in a family of freedom fighters and brought up in the environment of Swadeshi. Suniti Choudhury studied at the Faizunnissa Balika Vidyalaya in Comilla, Chittagong. Both her elder brothers were active in the freedom movement. In school, her seniors Santi Ghosh and Prafullanandini Brahma who was a member of the Jugantar Party were her mentors. Suniti Choudhury soon joined the Jugantar Party and was made the head of the District Volunteer Corps. When Subhas Chandra Bose visited Comilla to address the student organization she led the parade of girls. She also joined the Chhatri Sangha and was in charge of training female members in lathi, sword, and dagger play. She was known by the alias of Meera Devi and was selected as the custodian of firearms!

When some of the members were reluctant for the women to take up arms Suniti remarked, 'What good is our current dagger-and-stick play if we shy away from real action? During the practical training, she would skip school, reach Mainamati Hills which was eight kilometers away and practice firing. Soon Suniti was selected along with her colleague Santi Ghose the co-founder of the Chhatri Sangha for direct action. The plan was to assassinate Charles Geoffrey Buckland Stevens, the District Magistrate of Comilla.

Stevens was an arrogant and cruel man. Bengal was emerging as a centre for freedom struggle, with open revolts, which led to several arrests. There were too many atrocities being committed by the British police officers who would arrest and brutally beat up the satyagrahis. During this time an ordinance was passed against free speech and the British district magistrates and officers started to misbehave with the Indians, especially those who were arrested. Bhagat Singh, Rajguru, and Sukhdev had been hanged on 23 March 1931, and this further shocked the nation.

At 10 am on 14 December 1931, two teenage girls reached Charles Geoffrey Buckland Stevens the District Magistrate's bungalow. Dressed in saris with a shawl they asked to meet with him, stating that they were arranging a swimming competition in school. Since they were school girls, they were not physically searched and allowed to meet with the Magistrate. Under the shawls, Suniti and Santi carried pistols. The Magistrate came out, along with the Sub-divisional Officer (SDO.) Stevens looked at the letter which had the names and signatures of Illa Sen, and Meera Devi. Illa also introduced herself as the daughter of a police officer and requested Stevens to sign the letter as a reference. He took the letter to his office and returned with it duly signed. Suniti and Santi shot at Stevens, killing him on the spot. The girls were overpowered and arrested. Since the first bullet was fired by Suniti which caused Stevens's death she was given a harsher punishment than Santi! Suniti was imprisoned in Hijli Detention Camp as a third-class prisoner and Santi with the other revolutionaries. Mercilessly beaten but maintaining calm at all times expecting to die a martyr's death.

During the trials, a local newspaper reported, 'Their smiles faltered only when the verdict was out. The audience saw a different side of them, two depressed faces over the sheer disappointment. It was lifetime imprisonment, which meant they missed their window of martyrdom. They were heard on the way, fuming, 'This should've been a hanging! Hanging would be so much better! When the trial began, the courtroom was taken aback, both the women were smiling and had their backs to the judge and court members since they were denied the basic courtesy of chairs to sit on. They had no fear and sang patriotic songs while they sat in the police van to the courtroom and back. The assassination of Stevens was reported by the western media, 'as a sign of Indians outrage against an ordinance by the Earl of Willingdon that suppressed the civil rights of Indians, including that of free speech.' Indian newspapers reported the assassination as a response to the 'misbehaviors of the British district magistrates who had abused their positions of power.'

The British stopped the pension of Suniti's father, detained her two brothers without trial, and tortured them. Her younger brother became a hawker in Calcutta and died of starvation. This news reached Suniti but it did not break her resolve to carry on. With no human rights and inedible food, she went on with her daily jail work.

After seven years of imprisonment, Suniti was released, along with Santi Ghose in 1939 as per the amnesty negotiations between Gandhi and the British. In Calcutta, she did not have a place to stay but was determined to become a doctor. Kalyani Das, the elder sister of Bina Das, ran a destitute home in Tiljala, Calcutta and Suniti went on to live there. Six months after her release, she cleared her tenth examination, with first division, and took admission at the Asutosh College in Calcutta. She had to walk from Tiljala to her college, she passed with a first division here as well. At the destitute home, there was no one to guide a science student, her brother was friends with Pradyot Kumar Ghose and his family invited Suniti to their home. Pradyot's aunt taught Suniti English and Pradyot taught her science and math. After passing her exams, she studied medicine at the Campbell Medical School, and in 1944 she enrolled at the Calcutta Medical College and completed her medical degree. Suniti later married Pradyot.

Suniti was now a qualified doctor and worked at the Chandannagar Hospital for a few years, at that time Chandannagar was a French colony. Later she took voluntary retirement and set up her own nursing home. In the first general elections held in 1951, both Congress and the Communist party offered Suniti a party ticket to contest for elections, however, she was never interested in politics. She refused to accept the pension for freedom fighters as well. Dr. Suniti Choudhury died on 12 January 1988, Lady Maa was the youngest female revolutionary in India.

CHAPTER SIXTY-FIVE
THE RESPECTED MATAJI

A proud Gorkha and a champion of the nationalist movement of India, she challenged not only the British but also the patriarchal and conservative social order. Putalimaya Devi Poddar was born on 14th January 1920 in Kurseong, Darjeeling, and was the eldest daughter of Man Bahadur Tamang, who worked in the Kurseong Sub-divisional office as a watchman. Putalimaya was fifteen when she met Saryu Prasad Poddar, a Congress leader who had come from Bihar to Kurseong for party work. The British administration had declared that any association with the congress would be illegal, but this did not dissuade Putalimaya. Very inspired by the work he was doing she expressed her desire to take part in the freedom movement. Saryu Prasad Poddar asked her how old she was and, considering Putalimaya's age, asked her to return to school!

Putalimaya continued to follow the activities of the Congress and when Congress was establishing the Congress Saka Karyalai, a branch office in Kurseong in 1936, she was in the forefront in helping set up the branch. She became a member of the Congress party when she was in class nine. Her father was warned and pressurized by the British to ensure his daughter does not take part in any of the congress activities and he discouraged the young Putalimaya. So much so that a nursing job in the Kurseong hospital was offered to her so that she was away from politics. However Putalimaya was interested in playing an active role in the freedom struggle, and much against her father's wishes she went ahead. The reason was not only to fight the British but she was also against the conservative social order in society. Soon Putalimaya started a Harijan Samaj in Kurseong and a school for the Harijans so that the community was educated and motivated enough to take part in the freedom movement.

Gandhi had listed thirteen issues of importance in the constructive programs he wanted to take forward in the country. Ranging from social and economic interventions, like the removal of untouchability, prohibition, khadi and village industries, basic education, and the promotion of economic equality. Conscious that women needed a platform to take part in constructive work, Putalimaya went ahead and established a Mahila Samiti (Women's Association) in Kurseong in 1941. Here the women were taught to stitch khadi clothing, given basic education, and taught relevant skills. The local communities considered the Harijan Samaj and the Mahila Samiti as important initiatives, as a consequence a very conservative society now opened its school doors to girls and women who earlier had no exposure to learning. The same year, the Hindukanya Pathshala, a girl school, and the first Gorkha library, Pratham Grokhajan Pustakalaya in Kurseong were established. Although the Loreto Convent and the St. Paul's School were functioning, they were schools for the British residents and the elite. Opening up a local girls' school was a bold step toward social reforms in a region which was extremely orthodox. Her activities unnerved the British administration, they would call her to the police station several times a week and warn her of serious repercussions. However, Putalimaya was not intimidated and went ahead without fear. On 8 August 1942, when Gandhi launched the Quit India Movement, many nationalist leaders, including Gandhi and Nehru were arrested and this led to mass demonstrations in the country. A few days later at the Jan Sabha, a public meeting was organized and Saryu Prasad was arrested. The following day Putalimaya organized a procession in Kurseong along with other party members, in protest against the arrests of their leaders. The British police promptly arrested all of them which led to demonstrations outside the police station with the locals demanding that they be arrested too! The police authorities had to whisk the arrested leaders from the backdoor toward the Darjeeling jail, where Putalimaya and the others were instructed to sign a letter that they would not associate with the freedom movement. Of course, they refused, which led to shifting them to cells with criminals. While in jail, Putalimaya kept herself busy reading the Gita and spinning khadi!

Released sixteen months later, in January 1944, her health had deteriorated. Her parents now insisted she decides between the freedom movement and the family. Putalimaya Devi chose the former! The party workers suggested that Putalimaya and Saryu Prasad Poddar get married. It is said that a mob surrounded the wedding venue, a library with Khukuris (Nepali daggers). The bridegroom was not Nepali which went against their traditions and the people of Kurseong were not willing to consider this marriage, shouting, 'Herui Tyo Madisele Kasari Hamro Nepali Chelilai Biye Gardo Rahecha,' (let us see how this Bihari marries our Nepali daughter). One of the guests who were in favour of the marriage stood outside the wedding venue, holding a Khukuri in her hand, and shouted, 'Harau Katiko Babuko Chora Rahecha, Mopani Gorkha Hui,'(let us see who has so much courage to stop the marriage, I am also a Gorkha.) And the wedding took place!

After marriage, the couple continued participating in the freedom movement. There were days they went without food as there was no source of income, but so committed were they to be part of a free independent India that they never stopped working toward it. After independence, Putalimaya continued her work as a Samaj Sevika and a member of the Congress party. She died on 1 December 1984 in Siliguri. A courageous woman, Putalimaya Devi Poddar, widely known as 'Mataji,' was recognized especially by the Gorkhas for her commitment to their community. She challenged the caste structure by marrying a Bihari during an orthodox social order and participating in the nationalist movement against her father's wishes.

CHAPTER SIXTY-SIX
THE SUPPORTING TAI

Indumati Patankar was born in 1925, in Indoli, Karad a subdivision of Satara. Her father Dinkarrao Nikam was a freedom fighter, and thus at a very young age, Indumati would participate in Congress rallies, help the local families, and read political literature. At sixteen she joined the Rashtra Seva Dal distributing party literature, organizing meetings, and encouraging women to participate in the freedom struggle. She would also transmit coded messages between imprisoned activists and their associates on the outside. Soon she was working with the parallel government or Prati Sarkar. The atrocities on Indians by the British led to the emergence of an alternative way of life and institution to fight injustice, called the Prati Sarkar. A militant anti-colonial movement it centred on peasant Dalits, caste-oppressed communities, and women. The activities of Prati Sarkar included peoples' courts or nyayadan mandals to combat discrimination and settle land disputes as well as different types of armed activities and constructive programs. What made it distinctive was the thousands of volunteers who were ready to remove the British from the country. Indutai soon became a leading face of this movement.

In 1946 Indumati married Krantivir Babuji Patankar the son of a landless migrant labourer who also was part of Prati Sarkar. Functioning in 150 villages in the Satara-Sangli region, they were organized into various groups and decision-making centres. The representatives of the groups would meet from time to time at the district level. Every group was assigned a specific job or department, like one group would collect arms and ammunition from private individuals by attacking police at railway stations and another would carry out effective propaganda campaigns and impress the masses by singing. And thus Prati Sarkar was successful among the rural masses and became the symbol of the freedom struggle during the Quit India movement. The villagers would lead protests, hoist the national flag, and move from village to village, carrying guns or other weapons. They were always ready to confront the police if necessary. The Prati Sarkar members carried out Gandhi's constructive programs as well as military and administrative work. At the village level, there were volunteer squads and panch committees chosen or elected by the villagers.

It was necessary to educate the locals on relevant issues, hence Indumati along with her husband established the Kasegaon Education Society and the first high school in Kasegaon called Azad Vidyalaya. Indumati not only became one of the first woman students to study in the school but later taught in the school apart from helping her in-laws in the fields. Their school provided the students with comprehensive schooling. After independence, the couple continued to work with the masses and their grassroots politics. The duo joined the Socialist Party and when Aruna Asif Ali launched the Socialist Party Marxist–Leninist in 1949, they followed however after three years they joined the Communist party. In 1952, Babuji Patankar was taken away by armed men while he was ploughing the fields and never found again. Indumati was twenty-seven, with an infant, single-handedly looking after her elderly in-laws and raising her infant son. She continued to participate in Communist party activities, working in women's organizations, including the agricultural labour movements. In September 1986 she established the Stree Mukti Sangharsh, Kasegaon with a demand that the state support deserted women and allow the women to retain their independence. Through this organisation, she advocated for separate ration cards which would not only provide increased food grains but also an independent social identity, housing, free legal aid to fight maintenance cases, and support to run plant nurseries for social forestry in the villages of the region collectively. As well as demanding that single mothers' signatures should be considered valid in government offices. This carries on to date in Satara, Sangli and Kolhapur districts. Indutai died on 14 July 2014, her entire life was focused on equal opportunities for women at the grassroots and qualitatively improving their livelihoods.

SECTION THREE
VOICES

TRADITION TO TRAILBLAZERS

In the last seventy-five years, women played and play an important role in building a new India. Aware that education and freedom of expression were critical in the journey toward women's empowerment, the Indian government encouraged the political and economic participation of women. Gender equality was no longer a women's issue, as it had become a development issue.

Today, women hold powerful positions, in the government, corporations, and as entrepreneurs. In this section, I share my conversations with a few women about their childhood influences, aspirations, and challenges. And how they navigate their lives in the twenty-first century. The women were candid and witty and in their stories, I have tried to capture their magical moments and bring attention to the extensive roles they play, their interests, and their journey.

Ameena Ahmed Ahuja

Vani Ganapthy

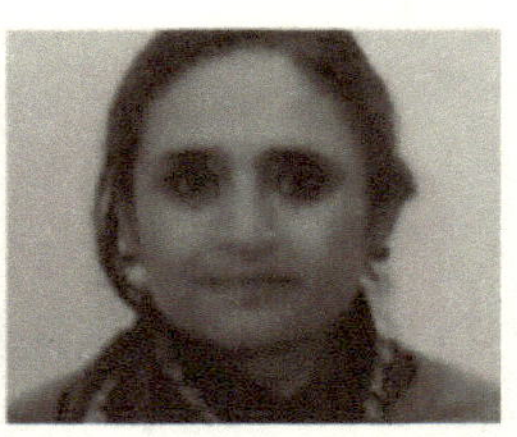

Aarati Saxena

Rekha Mody

Gitanjali Prasad

Suhasini Maniratnam

Anita Dongre

Elahe Hiptoola

Dr. Hena Singh

CHAPTER SIXTY-SEVEN
THE STYLISH CALLIGRAPHER

Ameena Ahmed Ahuja was born in Bombay. Brought up in her father's cultural-loving family, which lived in the heart of Old Delhi. As a family, we took great pride in our Mughal culture. My father, Nuruddin Ahmed, was an eminent barrister. I learned a range of calligraphic styles from my scholarly father. Acknowledged for Sanskrit literature and was also a three-time mayor of Delhi. He was a recipient of the civilian honour Padma Bhushan, in 1964.

The appreciation of nature and art I learned from my British mother. My mother was eighteen when she married my father and I have two brothers, Farid and Feroz. I grew up in Delhi, studied at the Queen Mary School, and in 1947 we moved to England post-partition. My mother was British and probably the reason we moved and also we knew England well.

Since I was interested in art, I joined the Slade School of Art, London, and did my BA in Russian from the University of London and broadcast from the Urdu Section of the BBC. I also taught Russian verbs at Queen's College, New York. As I studied and worked at various western art schools, my work, therefore, is a mixture and a blend of oriental sensibility with my stylized western training. I use a range of calligraphic styles, such as Kojic, Nastaliq, Shikaste, and Cyrillic. My calligraphy draws inspiration from my Indian heritage, and I mainly draw forms of animals and birds to reveal a combination of 'art and verse' in all of my calligraphy art.

As a young girl, I learned to write on a takhti with a kalam or reed pen of varying thickness, which I think gave my work a special accent. I used a set of special pens in all my artwork. Of course, black and white were my favourite colours. Like in the Japanese concept, I found the varying gradations and shades in black and white to be intimate. And the Sanskrit shloka which my father taught me 'dvanam pashet, rangam shunaya tam,' meaning we must see sound, and we hear colours. I further use touches of bronze, silver, and gold to highlight my Khate-Rehani (a twisted script, named after a little herb, Rehan- used for flavouring food).

Ameena Ahuja returned to India in 1955 and joined the External Services of AIR. I have a flair for languages, such as Russian, Persian, French, Hindi, and English, and also taught a few of them at different colleges, hence I was appointed as Associate Professor to teach the Russian language at Jawaharlal Nehru University, New Delhi. I am very proud that my Urdu is impeccable.

Since she was proficient in languages and a linguist in eight languages, Pandit JawaharlalNehru appointed her as the government of India's official interpreter during Khrushchev and Bulganin's visit to India. I also served as the official translator during the visits of Soviet dignitaries to India. I then became the official translator during the visits of Soviet dignitaries, including Alexei Kosygin, Nikolai Bulganin, Nikita Khrushchev, and Leonid Brezhnev to India. Scholars like Khwaja Ahmad Abbas have acknowledged my translations into Russian.

That same year, in 1955, she married Vishnu Ahuja of the IFS and went to live in Moscow. He was the ambassador to Japan, Iran, and New Zealand, and counsel-general in New York. His last posting was as India's ambassador to the Soviet Union. Early in his diplomatic career, he served two stints in the Soviet Union, from 1942 to 1952, and again from 1956 to 1959. We travelled and lived in many countries. My exposure to different countries helped me as an Indian painter, calligrapher, writer, and linguist, and I am known for my Urdu poetry-inspired artworks.

We lived in Moscow for three years; it was a big learning for me. I completed my Doctorate in Comparative Philology from Moscow

University. I translated Chekov into Urdu and wrote on Ghalib and Iqbal and Ghalib Academy, who revered me with an award for painting the verses of Ghalib. After my mother passed away in 1969, I devoted my time to my art as a diversion.

I learned a range of calligraphic styles which were incorporated into the calligraphic forms of animals and birds. My work draws on sources as diverse as the classical poetry of the East in Arabic, Persian, and Urdu, as well as poems by the Great Russian writers such as Pushkin, Tyutchev Anna Akhmatova, and Mayakovsky. My calligraphies of birds and animals are a synthesis of Art and Poetry, especially the poetry of the great masters of Urdu poetry such as Ghalib and Iqbal, Sufi masters such as Attar and Rumi, and the great Persian poets such as Hafiz and Saadi. And I use the poetry of these great masters and, through their couplets and verses, convert it into universal forms of colour and characteristic strokes of black and white.

My childhood learning of using reed pens of varied thicknesses still accompanies my work. I use special pens in my paintings which give them a distinct accent. I have tried and synthesized my lessons in my art of poetry and converted them into calligraphic forms of animals and birds.

I prefer working with black and white as I find their varied gradations and shades very intimate, as reflected in most of my works. I preserved the effectiveness of my calligraphic paintings with the use of varied elements such as Indian ink, Sumi ink, handmade papers from India, rice paper from Japan, and papers from Sanganer. I remember with great humility, during the opening of my exhibition in Moscow, the renowned poet Ms. Bella Almedina dedicated a poem to my work called The Day of Raphael. And so grateful for the presence of Faiz Ahmed Faiz, who recited a verse during the opening. I authored and published my book, Calligraphy in Islam, a text in Urdu, in 2009. My artworks have been exhibited widely in Moscow, Tokyo, Venezuela, Columbia, New York, and India. Ameena Ahmad Ahuja has donated 33 paintings, all black and white calligraphies of ink on paper to Jamia

Millia Islamia University.

I am grateful to the government of India for honouring me with the Padma Shri in 2009 for my contributions to the Arts.

CHAPTER SIXTY-EIGHT
THE VERSATILE DANCER

Vani Ganapathy was born in 1952 in Chennai. When I was five months we moved to Nagpur where my father had a corporate job. My sister Meera who is a year and a half younger than me was born in Nagpur. When I was two years old, my father's job brought us to Calcutta. I studied in Modern High School, a Birla School, right from its preschool. I clearly remember the school bus dropping both of us off at the corner of the street where we lived. My youngest sister, Padmini, was born in Calcutta. We have a nine-and-half-year age difference between us. I have almost mothered Pammi and still share a close bond.

My mother was the only child and my father wanted my grandparents to move in with us and a year later they too followed. As we grew up, so did the school and the authorities established the Rani Birla College in the school compound. My mother wanted to be a classical dancer, but I guess there were constraints in those days from her maternal grandparents. Hence she learnt proper Bharatanatyam only after we moved to Calcutta. As a student, she was artistic, and loved music, theatre, and dance, probably in her genes! When I was four my mother decided that I should learn dancing. I clearly remember, after getting back from school, I would finish lunch, take a snooze, and at 4 pm, we would set off for our classes. She was in the senior batch and I was with the toddlers! We had the same dance guru, his name was T.A. Rajalakshmi, and I still remember him since he was my first dance teacher. My parents were on the committees of almost every important cultural organization in Calcutta. Hence, from a very early age, I got exposed to the performing arts. From watching dance and drama to listening to fabulous Carnatic and Hindustani music. I have had the opportunity as an audience to see some of the best dancers.

It was my mother's love for the art that made me pursue Bharatanatyam and my debut performance, Arengetram took place in December 1959. I still remember the auditorium, the Rabindra Sadan, Calcutta, the magnificent stage, the audience, and the chief guest Raja of Santosh. There was absolutely no stage fright, probably it was my age. And I recollect that at the end of my performance I wanted to give a speech. I had mentioned it to my father the previous day and he said, 'you write your speech and I will do the corrections of your notes later.' But that day, at the end of the performance, since I did not carry any notes, I very confidently held the mic and said, "Ladies and gentlemen, thank you for coming to my performance today. Please forgive me if I have made any mistakes. I will correct myself and do better the next time." I am certain that at the age of seven and a half I must have had the audience's attention!

Three years later, my sister Meera performed her Arengetram when she was nine, on 17 January 1963. I still have that brochure with Baby Vani and Baby Meera printed on it. After this performance, everyone knew us as the dancing duo Vani and Meera. We performed together till 1985. My mother sang for all my dance performances, from my debut Arengetram till a year before she passed away. She also sang for all my students when they performed as well. Most of the vocalists for my later performances were all artists suggested by my mother. I guess she knew that she was not going to be with me forever. I miss her and her music hugely. She was my best friend and the backbone of my dance. I argued a lot with her, not on any unpleasant or personal matters but only during our rehearsals. I have never had an unpleasant moment with my mother. She was always a friend with whom I could discuss anything, even the first moment when Kamal held my hand. I could discuss anything with her without the fear of being judged. Without her, I would have been a big zero. She always had something positive to say about everyone. The sweetest, however, when it came to Meera and my dance practice, she turned into an absolute tigress. We just couldn't escape practice, not even for a single day.

My father was my biggest critic and also an enormous source of strength and support. He treated all three of his daughters like sons. When I look back, we are strong women because of him. He had excellent taste in interior decoration and probably my interest in interiors and designing clothes came from him. He even selected my wedding sarees. Till the day I got married he would select my dance costumes. A strict disciplinarian and principled man with modern thinking, my father and I would have serious debates on many subjects. We both had strong viewpoints and neither of us would give up in an argument. I would turn around and tell him, 'Just because you're my Dad, it doesn't mean you're always correct.' Of course, over time we changed and in the later years, we were very close till he passed away. It was very sudden and took me three months to get back to my dance. When my mother passed away, most people thought I would take a longer time to deal with the grief considering that she was the soul of my dance. However, I had promised her that I would take no break.

In 1963, we moved to Bombay. My father was working with Teddington Chemical Factory. Meera and I enrolled at St. Teresa's Convent School in Santa Cruz. My mother was clear that she wanted us to continue with our dancing lessons in Bombay too. We started learning dance from Sri Rajarajeshwari Bharatha Natya Kala Mandir in Matunga under Guru Mahalingam Pillai. After a couple of years, my father's company promoted him to the head office, Tata Fisons in the south of Bombay. We had to move our home and therefore change our school too. We enrolled at the Cumballa Hill High School, at Nepean Sea. I was made the Head Girl at the school and while I studied, I also choreographed dances and both Meera and I took part in a lot of sports and cultural activities.

Since we lived in south Bombay, we had to travel to the other side for our dance classes, thus my grandfather would accompany us to the dance school. The dance instructor Guru Mahalingam Pillai suggested that we join his younger brother K. Kalyanasundaram (Masterji) who was next door to the building where we lived. Masterji was and still is a perfectionist- a choreographer par excellence. He and his wife Mythili Maami have been more than parents to me.

I took Science as a subject in college because I wanted to do medicine, and it was my father's dream too that I become a Doctor. I was very comfortable with the biology lab and had no qualms about dissecting animals, insects, etc. However, during the first-year exams, I had an accident in the chemistry laboratory. When I tried to open an acid bottle, sulphuric acid spurted into my right eye and it burnt a portion of my inner eye. I could not appear for my physics lab exam the next day and that was probably a turning point in my life. Though I was keen to peruse medicine, dance happened by default! The following year, I shifted to Arts. Meera and I performed at the inauguration of the Bhabha Auditorium in Sophia College.

I had the opportunity to watch several dance performances at the Shanmukhananda Auditorium in Bombay. Two artists I admired then and whose dance I loved watching, were Vyjayanthimala Bali and Padma Subrahmanyam. Besides being beautiful both on stage and off it, Vyjayanthimala Bali performed authentic and traditional Bharatanatyam. She did not allow her cinema fame to dilute her dance. Paddu akka's (Padma Subrahmanyam) dance kept me mesmerized, her dance (Abhinaya) was so simple to understand that anyone could understand her expressions. I remember after every performance of hers, I would cry, and say, 'I hope at least in my next birth, I can emote like Paddu Akka.' She has been a tremendous influence on my dance performance.

My mother's side of the family is very artistic. They are creative writers, dancers, musicians, painters, and poets, while they also pursued careers in medicine, engineering, and so on. I did not think that dance would give me my livelihood and that it would be my identity. My success and who I am today are because of dance. Nor did I dream that someday day I would start my own Dance School, in 1994, and call it Sanchari School of Dance. I teach young children to dance.

In 1970, I got a call from the magazine Femina. The assistant editor of the magazine wanted to talk to me. A few months before that, Femina had done an article on 'Three Generations' from diverse fields. They had selected my family for the Arts. We were on the cover of Femina, my grandmother, my mother, and myself. The assistant editor wanted me to take part in the Miss India contest. I said I would think about it. My parents were not keen as they felt I may lose my focus from dance, however they agreed. It may sound a bit ridiculous today, but I had never been to a beauty salon and that was the truth. The next day, I went to the Femina office for the qualification round of the Miss India contest. The moment I saw Zeenat Aman there, I asked myself, "What am I doing here?" She was already a top model. Anyway, a week later, the contest was to take place at the Shanmukhananda Hall, Mumbai. My parents did not attend as they did not take the contest very seriously. My grandfather, Pammi, and my rakhi brother accompanied me. While the contest was on, I was not aware that there would be three winners in the final round. Zeenat Aman was declared Miss India Femina, and I was crowned the Teen Princess of India. I represented India at the International Teen Princess contest in Berlin and won the runner-up prize for the most well-groomed teenager with intelligence and poise.

In 1974, I met Kamal Hasan at a music recording studio in Madras. I had gone there along with my mother. He was a charmer from the word go and within a week of our meeting, he proposed marriage. We were engaged in 1976 and two years later, on 5 May 1978, we were married. It was a beautiful and happy marriage, full of fun and laughter. I designed costumes for Kamal's characters for many of his films. I designed costumes for his female co-stars as well.

With marriage, I inherited a loving and caring family. My brother-in-law Charu Hassan is fondly addressed as Anna (brother) and his wife is affectionately called Manni (sister-in-law). I still consider them my parents. Their three daughters, Nandini, Hasini (Suhasini Maniratnam), and Bhashini have given me a lot of love and both Anna and Manni consider me as one of their daughters, 'we have four daughters' they say and that makes me so proud. The four of us are buddies. We discuss anything and everything without the fear of being judged. It is because of the love and affection shown by Kamal's family that I have never festered any grudges towards anyone. My most beautiful times were the years between 1978 when I got married till 1985.

I have an exceptional bonding with Hasini (Haas as I call her) probably because she was the first person I met when Kamal took me to his home to meet his mother for the first time. Hasini is a multi-talented and multi-faceted woman and excels in anything she does. I have been with her during all important moments in her life, including when her husband Mani Ratnam proposed to her. Most of the time when she visits Bangalore she stays with me and I do the same when I am in Chennai.

While in Chennai, I learnt Abhinaya (expressional- dance) pieces from Kalanidhi Narayan, who I call Maami. She taught me how to think, emote from the heart and bring it to my facial expressions before any choreography.

From Madras when I moved to Bangalore in 1987, I felt welcomed in Bangalore. The city does not judge. When I moved to my home, where I continue to live, I remember I had two aluminum foldable chairs. As a single woman, I couldn't have come this far without my friends who have become my family over the years. Here I started my creative journey in interiors. The passion for Dance came from my mother and probably the love for Interiors came from my father! I did not go out looking for interior assignments, they just came to me and I realized how much I enjoyed my work. Whatever I designed for my own home, the colours, the furniture, the artifacts etc. I would do it for other homes as well. I dreamt of colours and designs!

My grandparents lived with me in Bangalore before they passed away. The night before my performance my grandfather would ask, 'Vani what shall I wear for your performance, my bandgala or my white dhoti and kurta?' He would be the first person to get ready and would watch all my rehearsals. He had a great sense of humour, and was an excellent singer and a connoisseur of the performing arts. I have had a very rewarding journey in dance and for that, I have to thank my amazing musicians and technicians of Bangalore. The artist fraternity of Bangalore is the most supportive and the audiences here are the most appreciative.

The prefix to my name, "Guru" could not have happened but for all my students. The word Guru is too big a word for a teacher. But if there was an alternative word in the Indian language I probably would have been more comfortable. I knew little about teaching dance. My students taught me to teach and they taught me patience and tolerance. I was a very strict teacher, however, over the years I have mellowed down. My support system, my staff at home and office without whom this journey would never have happened.

For me, the two people, who give me much love and affection are my Sai Baba. And my grandson Kabir, who is the Krishna in my life. His mischiefs bring out the creativity in my dance choreography! He is four and we have fascinating and funny conversations. He addresses me as Vani Paati and I hold him closest to my heart. And my Sai Satguru, who is my friend, guide, protector, and the eternal loving Boatman who has been ferrying me through the river of life. I have experienced the most beautiful surprises on both the banks of this river and with gratitude. I know with his blessings the journey moving forward will be full of beautiful surprises. I have never made any plans, but with his grace, my dance journey continues.

CHAPTER SIXTY-NINE
THE EDUCATIONIST

Dr. Aarati Saxena was born in Delhi on 1 September 1953. All I know about my biological father Naresh Chandra was that during the 1947 partition he was trapped in his home, in Lahore. He heard people calling him, which then alerted him, and he knew his life was in danger. Without a thought, he dug a tunnel underneath his home and escaped through the back lane! My father reached Delhi and made his way to the Lal Quila, where every person who had escaped the horrors of partition had assembled. The authorities were announcing names on loudspeakers, and my father heard his name being called out and was united with his elder brother.

I never saw my father or heard his voice, as he died young. All I have with me is my father's matriculation certificate from DAV College Lahore and 2 photographs of his. My mother, Prabha Asthana, a young widow, was married off to my father's cousin soon after my father's death, and the young married couple left me with my father's elder brother and my aunt.

I was brought up by my father's elder brother, Girish Asthana, who was an author and was in the army. After he graduated from Lahore, he joined the Royal Indian Army and went to the Middle East during Second World War. He often said we youngsters were misled to fight 'fascist forces.' He has written several novels, short stories and children's book and was felicitated with the Premchand Award. He used to attend literary gatherings in Lucknow and would take me along with him. At these gatherings, I would hear Amritlal Nagar, Bhagwati Charan Verma, Yashpal, and many stalwarts of Hindi literature speak on diverse subjects, which really fascinated me.

In Calcutta, he would take me to watch Bengali movies and plays and I remember going to the Hooghly River to watch the high and low tides. His incessant reading and prolific writing were inspiring. He wanted me to be a teacher and teach in a college, as he believed teaching was the best and noble profession. My father decided not to disclose to me that he was not my biological father and it still remains a feeling of angst as I know nothing about my real father. During family functions and weddings, when people would enquire about me, they would be taken aside, a story would be told, and the matter ended. However, it always remained at the back of my mind. During my growing years, there was a longing for my mother's love and it was only when I was in college I got to know about my parents.

On 1 September 1993, early morning, I was sitting in the courtyard gazing at the full moon when I received a call a little later that my father passed away, it was my birthday. Since then looking at a full moon makes me sad. After my father's death, my aunt, in a fit of anger, sold off all of my father's books and photo albums and all my childhood pictures went into oblivion. During my growing-up years, my biological mother and stepfather would visit us in Calcutta and Lucknow, however I did not know she was my biological mother. Though there was some connection I felt on seeing her and always had a longing for her.

I got married in 1976 to Anil Saxena. He was a journalist with the Times of India Delhi Bureau. We had a wonderful marriage. Anil passed away in 1998, leaving me and my two children completely shattered. By God's grace, my inner voice said that all will be well. Keep going, be strong! My early education was in Calcutta and I remember how culturally vibrant Calcutta was in the 50s and 60s. From Calcutta, I went to Lucknow for schooling and completed my final year in Delhi.

In pursuit of studying science, I graduated with honours in Botany, from Miranda House, followed by a Master's in Botany, and thereafter completed my Ph.D. My doctorate was on Triticale a lab-made cereal.

This was an ICAR (Indian Council for Agriculture Research) Project and studies involved working in the DU Botany Department Labs, Indian agriculture Research institute, and Delhi IIT for scanning electron microscopy. The academic ecosystem in the Department of Botany, University of Delhi and the illustrious professors, including my research guides Prof B. M. Johri and Prof S.P. Bhatnagar, have been mylife support. Delhi University gave me both, a means of sustenance and satisfaction. From studying at the Delhi University in 1970, later joining the Sri Venkateswara College, a constituent college of Delhi University where I was an Associate Professor in 1980 and then retiring in 2018, it's been a wonderful journey.

A woman, a single parent at forty-five, I was completely on my own. I could move on in life because of my education and the University- Botany Department ecosystem. My father's reading and writing habits further gave me the conviction and courage to carry on with my teaching profession. I enjoyed my teaching and gave it my 100%. I would ask my students to do mundane things like making a list of books purchased by the department. Engage them to jot down the author's name, classify the books, and also get them to interact with the museum curator and prepare specimens. I realized, that studentslook forward to taking part in projects unrelated to the curriculum. Like at one time, they were creating questionnaires to collect data fromstreet vendors working in 'istri' (ironing) stalls in Delhi. They helped researchers with data collection for their doctorates. I remember a bunch of students visiting Ranthambore to study the livelihood of the villagers living close to the forests. Our Visits to the Plant Molecular Biology Lab, University of Delhi South Campus, TERI (The Energy Research Institute) WWF, and Development Alternatives libraries were very enriching. Participation of the students in the debates on climate change negotiations, inspired many students in this area of specialization.

After my biological mother passed away, I visited Varanasi in 1999 at 47! My uncle insisted I must visit my maternal grandfather's home. When we reached Varanasi, it was in the middle of the night. I saw this very thick fog and we couldn't find anyone at the station to receive us. I walked towards a telephone booth to call up the family, to let them know we were waiting at the railway station. My children were waiting at the platform and my uncle crossed them, looking around for us many a time, but could not recognize them!

I took study leave and worked at Jamia Hamdard on Projects like Shankh Pushpi, museum renovation, and preparing a repertory of medicinal plants. During this time, CCRUM (Central Council of Research in Unani Medicine) offered me a consultant role. And I visited CCRUM Hyderabad, Srinagar, and Osmania University Museum to understand the history of medicine and botanicals. This paved the way for teaching a fresh paper on Ethno Botany and Medicinal Botany.

I feel walking the extra mile always yielded rich dividends. On excursions, we would fix a meal with the villagers in the mountains. Students would help prepare a meal, and learn about the staple food of the villagers and the flavours. We would invite Alumni and scientific officers from the Department of biotechnology as speakers. This helped us with summer training opportunities for the entire class in the top institutes of the country.

NCWEB (Non-Collegiate Women's Education Board), University of Delhi offered me the post of officiating Director on Deputation and as NSS Coordinator DU and I joined NCWEB and NSS in 2011. I always felt that NCWEB girls remain invisible during their stay at Delhi University and their footfalls are unheard of. This low-profile NCWEB Director posting changed my mindset completely. 15,000 girl students were studying in thirteen Delhi University Colleges on weekends. It was a purely administrative post but a challenging opportunity. I could do something for these girls who were determined to do well in life. The majority of the girls belonged to low-income families with a single parent, ailing father, daily wagers, and security guards. They knew that the phase of life from 18 to 25 years was crucial for them, either to make or break their lives. During this phase, they had to educate themselves, get a job, marriage, all rolled into this decisive seven years. In this scenario, I thought they deserve the best. Certificate courses on human rights and proficiency in the English language were launched much to their delight.

The prime concern was to prepare a robust curriculum that suited the needs of women's employment. An ICT lab and an interactive website were launched, this was needed to develop effective communication skills, written and spoken English language. To provide a background in liberal arts and to foster a sense of appreciation of our rich cultural heritage. Students were taken on an excursion in Delhi by some experts in archaeology and Mr. K K Mohammad of the archaeological survey of India was invited to deliver lectures on how the restoration of temples in the dacoit-infested areas in Madhya Pradesh was completed. We also revived the NCWEB magazine 'Pratibimb' this issue was dedicated to the Nirbhaya case. There were thousands of pages submitted by girls pained with the incident and harsh realities. We had to sift out a few of the articles and poems for the magazine of 120 pages. In the editorial, girls wrote that society is supreme and it cannot be punished but it can be made to repent. None of the articles received, expressed any fear or weakness which gave us a picture of a new mindset of today's women.

As a member of the Gandhi Bhawan Management Committee, we organised Gandhi Darshan Yatras so that students get an opportunity to visit Gandhi ashram and Sewa Gram. 100 students turned up for the interview and we could select only thirty. Gandhiji's books were distributed on the train. They would attend morning prayers at 4:45 am, bhajans and dhyan which were followed up with discussions and shram daan. What fascinated them the most was the practice of keeping 'maun' or silence. One of the students has written in her memoirs that the nine days were too short!

I had an open-door policy, which meant anyone could walk into my office for solutions or even barge into my room to give me a piece of their mind! They could scream at me for not getting any help. Their parents were always invisible, both at the time of admission or after. These girls often had gap years and part-time jobs. We would organize job melas for them. Some girls were scriptwriters, anchors, paratroopers, and who thought a bachelor's degree was relevant always. The NCWEB was awarded the commendation position in the 'Awards of Good Practice,' during the Antardhwani festival of Delhi University. About seventy colleges had participated in the competition.

There was an interesting program in November 2013. The University of Delhi hosted a 100 strong youth delegation from China accompanied by their minister. The ministry of Youth Affairs and Sports had invited them to the campus for two hours. As the NSS coordinator I had to organize and conduct the program. As I was halfway through my presentation of our volunteering activities, the Chinese got so enthused and they started explaining their volunteering efforts. Followed by an impromptu ballet. Two things we noted they came at 3.15 pm and left at 5.15 pm maintaining a pin-drop silence. While leaving the volunteers had to be quick to hand them a spinach brown bread sandwich and a diet coke! The Ministry hosted a cultural program followed by dinner, none of the Chinese touched the food. I was intrigued to know and they showed me their watches, it was probably very late, 8 pm!

After her superannuation, the University of Delhi, appointed Aarati as an advisor to NCWEB. Post retirement, she is associated with the greening of Ratnagiri hills, Dabhala in Barsana Mathura. At times I write course curricula for Ecology and Environment papers. I enjoy connecting with like-minded people and am also part of some veterans, think tanks, and my retired group of colleagues.

I feel the divine power seeks you and lifts your spirits even though I have sometimes felt during my odyssey of life that I am walking constantly and at low ebb times stepping at the same spot as on a stepper. Now that I have retired from my day-to-day teaching, I have more time to spend with family. My daughter Ketaki has a doctorate in teacher's education: professional identity and status, and she also has expertise in early school education and is a child activist. Kautuk my son is an author, filmmaker, and actor. After my husband Anil's passed away, we came in close contact with Sri Sri Ravi Shankar. It was a time we needed maximum strength and support. I strongly believe that there is a divine plan for us.

CHAPTER- SEVENTY
THE MULTI-FACETED PERSONALITY

Rekha Mody was born in 1955 into the illustrious industrialist family of Modis. In Modinagar, Uttar Pradesh, Rekha Mody, in her own right, is a woman who wears more than one hat. She is a connoisseur of art, a well-known publisher, a social worker, and a woman campaigner. Educated in a school where the children of labourers studied in Modinagar. The interactions brought her close to the plight of the less privileged people. She completed her high school in Gwalior, where she studied with tribal girls. These influences imbued her with a value system of social responsibility and accountability for fulfilling her role toward the welfare of society. She received her Bachelor of Arts degree from Meerut University in the first division.

I believe," Our talent we get from our father, but our souls from our mother," Anton Chekhov said. 'My journey of life is quite amazing. I plunged into new projects without any hesitation. As an owner of a bookshop in Kolkata, which I later converted into an art gallery, home to some of the best artworks. I brought Sotheby's first art auction house to India, twenty-eight years ago. As a literary agent, I was instrumental in translating and publishing Indian literature. I started the first FM radio station in Kolkata and went on to establish three charities, one for communities, the second an art foundation, and the third a society for women empowerment.'

All these endeavours have resulted in interesting interactions and positive experiences. 'I consider all these initiatives and decisions to launch new ideas, as and when required, as an act of art! A wise person said, ''knowing when to walk away is wisdom.   Being able to be courageous. Doing it with your head held high is dignity. 'In 1984, at twenty-nine Rekha, answered an inner call and set out for a cultural revolution, with a strong emphasis on social development. She started her journey by founding four prestigious institutions working in diverse fields.

Settled in Kolkata, Rekha is the founder of Divya Chaya Trust- a public charity that, along with an associate UK trust, Save A Child, works to restore hope and provide opportunities to deprived children. She is the founder of the publishing house, Garutman Pvt Ltd, which promotes quality Indian literature translated from Indian regional languages to English and promotes them internationally. She founded Habiart Foundation in 1989 to promote contemporary art and traditional craft.

Close to her heart is to bring clarity to women's issues, and she founded Stree Shakti–The Parallel Force, a networking women's forum with a few eminent women. She mentions that during the 1990s; they gave only an award or two to recognize women for their work and accomplishments. Rekha established the Stree Shakti Awards in 1998 and since then, 'we have introduced many prestigious awards for women in India' and this is a feather in the cap of her organization.

Rekha lost her husband Padam Mody in 2014 and single-handedly sorted over a hundred court cases. These cases were earlier handled by her husband. She has two wonderful daughters and son-in-laws. Both her daughters Aditi and Isha are qualified and independent women, like their mother, Rekha.

Committed to Women Empowerment. She feels that women all over the world are interconnected on various underlying gender issues. She edited 'A Quest for Roots', a book of more than 300 posthumous biographies of women from India significant in South-Asian history. The Hindi edition was released in 2018 by Vardha University and Rajkamal publisher. She has also edited 'Innovative Practices for the care of Elderly Women in India an initiative of Stree Shakti -The Parallel Force supported by UNFPA. Rekha raised women's issues at GCFWIN Conference in Geneva in United Nations on 16 May 2022.

Rekha Mody has also served on the Board of United Way, New Delhi. She is lobbying for a 33 percent reservation of women in state assemblies. Three Conclaves on this issue have been held in 2022. 'She Leads' is a political training online initiative launched in 2021. Rekha believes 'Strong women aren't simply born. They are made by the storms they walk through.' I think Rabindranath Tagore elegantly wrote, 'I have no trace of wings in the air, but I am glad I had my flight.'

CHAPTER SEVENTY-ONE
THE CREATIVE THINK TANK

Gitanjali Prasad grew up with an elegant, intelligent, loving mother who was undoubtedly a major influence. 'I am told that at four, when an uncle took us, children, to the club and asked us what we would like to drink, while all the other children asked for a lemonade or a coca-cola, I decorously asked for "a sherry, please". No prizes for guessing who I was trying to imitate!

On a more serious note, my father was a forceful personality. When I was just about a year old, he was appointed the Commandant of the Kumaon Regimental Centre, and so wielded a great deal of power as well. Many women would have settled for a subservient position in the relationship, but though my mother was a truly loving wife, and an excellent homemaker, she was equal in every respect. She knew when to hold her ground, and when to yield. One uncle called my mother, 'a lion tamer.' I learned a great deal from observing her and the dynamics of their relationship. I realized that while women were equal to men; they were not the same as men. Nor did they need to be. In a marriage, one could be most effective in equal but complementary roles.

I am and have always been interested in a wide variety of things. As a child, I loved books, writing, and growing up in the hills. Nature enchanted me. The spectacular sunrise, the flowers, the rustle of the wind as it went through pine trees. I loved cooking, though, in my childhood, my repertoire was limited to making chocolate fudge and apricot jam! I also loved children, dogs, and horses, and enjoyed horse riding very much. When I grew older, swimming became a passion, and I still find it an excellent way to clear my head when things are hectic.

After graduating in English Honours from Lady Shri Ram College, I was unsure about what to do next. I knew I did not want to do a Master's and go into academia. I wanted to do something that included writing and the media but was lively, and contemporary. A friend mentioned the Indian Institute of Mass Communication and Eureka! I had found my calling. I loved just about every aspect of mass communication. I loved the adrenaline-pumping pace of radio journalism, and being able to be a part of the very exciting times, we were going through as part of a daily newspaper, but in those days journalism paid poorly, and I wanted to be economically independent.

I knew that ideally, I would like to get married and have children, but I also wanted to marry only if I met the right man. With this aim in mind, I chose Public Relations and Advertising, as this one area in the media paid the best salaries. I am now often asked to give talks to young people and I emphasize the importance of being pragmatic. One is likely to be most fulfilled if one's career choice fits into one's larger ambitions about what one would like from life. For instance, at the start of one's career in media, one could go into TV journalism, a daily newspaper, or a monthly magazine. Each would work as well, but then some years down the line, if one wishes to marry and have children, the monthly magazine with its more relaxed deadlines, and greater ability to work independently, would offer a much better balance. Of course, the pandemic has turned everything on its head, but a vision of life that accommodates interests, other commitments, and also financial obligations is likely to result in greater peace and fulfilment.

Having found equilibrium in my career and family life and my own life, I was very keen that other women had better options to manage their lives. I must admit, despite making some smart choices early in my career, I was still unprepared for how difficult it was to have any career at all once I became a mother. Nothing prepared me for the trauma a mother experiences in having to leave a young child at home and resume work.

At twenty-three, I was the Creative Chief of an advertising agency. At thirty-two, when my younger child was two years old, I was unable to take on even a part-time job. It was 1983, and I defined my dream job as 3 hours a day, 3 days a week, and 3000 rupees a month. I applied to 13 advertising agencies, and while 10 turned me down, 3 were keen to hire me, and one was conveniently fairly close to my house. After the interview, the job was offered to me, with timings from 10 am to 1 pm. I mentioned to them I would like to leave by 12.30 pm! The boss was fine with this, but he asked me, "Why"? So I can walk to the children's school in case there is a riot, I pointed out. The 1984 riots were still fresh in everyone's memory, so he was unfazed by this. "I look forward to seeing you on Monday", he said. "Fine, "I replied, but if my children are unwell, I will not come to work. "And what if you are unwell, Gitanjali?" he asked me. 'I know what you are trying to do. You are trying to get me to say it won't work because you don't want to leave your children even for a minute. Well, I won't say it. I think you can add tremendous value, so I hope to see you on Monday. But if you don't show up, I will understand.'

I did not report on Monday. Instead, I wrote long articles, passionate articles on how women who wanted to be working mothers had to struggle with such tough choices. The letters to the editor in response to these articles informed me, and society at large, of how many young women were coping with even more difficult situations. These articles were perhaps instrumental in my being offered the Press Fellowship at Wolfson College, the University of Cambridge in 1999.

Moreover, this later led to my book, "The Great Indian Family: New Roles, Old Responsibilities" which explores how work has influenced values, relationships, and lifestyles in middle-class urban India. The book also compellingly advocates better work-life balance. I am now a coach certified by the International Coaching Federation and coach and counsel women and men on both relationships and career issues. This is something I find very rewarding indeed.

CHAPTER SEVENTY-TWO
THE INDEPENDENT DIRECTOR

Her family named her Suhasini, from the lyrics of Vande Mataram. Suhasini Maniratnam was born on 15th August 1961, yes on India's Independence Day, in a small village called Paramakudi, in Tamil Nadu. Home to around 200 families, then. I was the third child, my brother passed away at birth and the second child was a girl. Instead of celebrating, the villagers came to sympathize with my mother. In the bygone days in Tamil Nadu, when a girl child was born, you either dropped three drops of cactus serum (poison) in the child's mouth or inserted two grains of paddy in the nostrils! 'I am grateful to my mother that she did none of that!' I was very ordinary to look at, however, I believed that someday, my looks would be an asset. This was further corroborated by my family, who would say, 'you are our family's lucky charm!

My grandfather was a straightforward man, a freedom fighter, a congressional representative, and an aesthete~ someone who deeply appreciated works of art. Interestingly, when he built the family home in the village, he first built the stage for the artists and then the home. He also built an outdoor kitchen, where the villagers could come and eat, while attending the performances of artists. The house did not have doors, he always said "if someone needs to steal from me, it means I have not been kind enough!" He did not want to keep anything for himself, and those are the values I grew up with. It was more like community living and I recollect my young cousin's sister, going from one room to another with a comb in her hand and telling my aunts, 'uncle is coming, comb your hair, look nice!' Just very simple living!

I come from a family of criminal lawyers, and we lived in a joint family. My home was full of geniuses and in those days, my father would listen to cricket commentary, my grandfather discussed politics, and my mother taught the poor children. I think everyone was a role model! I recall my grandfather teaching us to eat healthily. They also taught us to say ours, never mine or I. My memory goes back to when I was four years old. Those are my greenest recollections. My brain clearly remembers those foundation years, the values instilled in me when I was growing up in Paramakudi and for a reason, I keep going back to that time of my life. I don't think I aimed for anything. Things happened.

I studied in a Municipal Elementary School and most of my classmates came to school for the midday meals, which were free for the school children. The strength of the class would be thirty children in the morning and post-lunch it would be five. I used to see my schoolmates sell products on the footpath and hide when they saw me. I invariably ask my mother, 'why is he running away,' and she would say, 'he feels embarrassed.' I would then counsel the children and start guiding people at an early age!

My grandparents had grand ambitions for me. They wanted me to study in a top school in Madurai but my father wanted to keep me grounded and enrolled me at the Ramakrishna School. While the men of the house continued to stay in the village, since they were practicing lawyers, my mother, sister, and I moved from our village to Madurai. Can you imagine that my neighbour's daughter wanted to come with us as she too wanted to study in Madurai and she did! The four of us, my mother, sister, friend, and me, shared the household work and I remember traveling alone by bus to school those early years are of great importance and play a strategic role in my life.

We grew up in a religious family and Lord Murugan, our native deity, was of reverence and worshiped with great fervour. On the last day of the yearly festival, we had to worship the deity before immersing the idol in the river. As children, they gave us the task of collecting money from all the villagers. We would buy gingelly oil, shikakai, a sari, and dhoti and go to the huts and give it to the families and ask them to oil their hair with the gingelly oil, wash hair with shikakai and wear the sari or dhoti and worship the Lord. These slight gestures and values while we were growing up stayed with me!

From Madurai, I would visit my uncle in Trichy, with a one-way bus ticket. My uncle would buy the return as we believed and still do, that it depends on the host family, how long they want the guests to stay, therefore a one-way ticket! I can't imagine that happening today. When guests come home today, the hosts are keen to know when they are leaving! Even to this day, when I visit my sister-in-law's home in north Karnataka, they tell me, 'please travel light.' On arrival, the family place freshly starched towels, saris, petticoats, and nightwear for us and for every guest who visits. This is what I learned and I practice the same in my house to date. We just grew up with these principles and, in many ways, instilled them in us.

Post my studies, my grandfather encouraged me to become involved in films, like the rest of the family members. I had planned on becoming a banker and, of course, boss around, but all that changed when I moved to Madras to live with my grandmother and uncle. My uncle Kamal Hassan was a well-known actor and enrolled me in a Film Institute. The M.G.R. Government Film and Television Training Institute are where I studied cinematography. I began my career as a camera assistant and then became an actor, director, and writer. I have acted in Tamil, Telugu, Kannada, and Malayalam films. The exposure to Madras changed my life, and I truly blossomed. All the credit goes to my grandmother and uncle.

I learned about cinema from my uncle. At fourteen I would go alone to a theatre, buy a ticket and watch a film. 'Through cinema, I saw the world.' My uncle encouraged me and enrolled me as a member of different film associations and that, I think, was a turning point. In my second year, I was the assistant cinematographer for a film. The director of the film was making his next film and was casting an actress, which fell through as she was on contract with another filmmaker. I remember he looked at me and said, 'will you act' and I said no, as no girl from my family was an actor. But my father said, 'why not, go ahead and I did!

I was studying cinematography and acting. When I graduated in 1981, I had a line-up of producers and directors waiting to sign me, and that started my career as an actor. I had my set of rules clearly defined right from day one. Women were mere commodities in films-blink your eyes and attract the audience to watch films! I did not know of any woman who blinks eyes! So I said no to blinking eyes or showing skin and certainly no intimate scenes! This surprised the film directors and producers, but they agreed. I remember in one scene; I had to fall at my husband's feet! I was going to do nothing of that, so I requested the director to change it and he did. Right from the beginning, I knew change happens if you put your foot down. I wanted to bring decency to films. After all, people watch films with their families. I am the first actor in the film industry to have firmly refused to do things I did not believe in and it has always been like that. I say this to people "Let us earn respect from people who see our movies and shower us with so much love. Why should they disrespect us in the roles that we do?' I think in the 1980s and early 1990s we could speak our minds. There was no digital trolling like it is today!

My father would say,' the more progress for women, the more bitterness from others.' He said, 'Suhasini, you speak your mind so theydon't like you, but just be yourself I am not here for people to like me, but to make life better for others. I got married in 1988 to Mani Ratnam, a director, screenwriter, and producer. He encouraged me to do my thing and gave me space for my creative freedom. One fine day in 1989 whenI was 27 years old, he shut me in a room and said to write a script and make films-I wrote and directed 8 short films! I wrote of women from tradition to transition. 1989/1990 were important years for women. There was a slow transition happening and I think we had the best of both worlds. My first story is based on a strange relationship between a mother and daughter, both often fought with each other. This was basedon my mother's and my sister's relationship! Both are alike and yet they fight! The second story I wrote was that of a woman who, with her two children, moved back to her parents' home as her husband did not want her. Her parents, family, and friends insisted she go back to her husband, but little do they know he did not want her back and thus the dilemma. Another similar story, is the film director Satyajit Ray's movie, Apur Sansar-of a loving relationship between an arranged married couple. I acted in the movie and my husband directed some of the scenes since I could not do both at one time!

When my son was six months old, I got back to acting in films. I recollect going to Hyderabad for a shoot and being back in Chennai after every ten days. It was tough, but I did it. I would say if a woman working on a construction site with a baby on a swing can do it, it was no big deal for me.

In 1994, I directed the movie, Indra. My son was 4 years old and old enough for me to get back to both acting and directing. I showcased Indra in Japan, where other women directors were showcasing their movies, and, believe me, they were no different from us. We are better off as we have families looking after our young when we go to work. They don't have those conveniences or supports. While I was working in Indra, I worked with NGOs based out of the UK and Italy, who were funding the girl child in India, and that is the time I thought of starting my own NGO.

I remember a year that the panchayat election did not take place for 14 years in Tamil Nadu, and when the opposition won the elections, because of 33% reservations for women in the panchayat, most of the husbands and brothers of the women elected became Benami elected leaders. I made a film on this to encourage women to contest elections. We went to the villages to shoot the film, where we stayed in their huts and ate food cooked by the women. This way I was reaching out to the women, hearing their stories, and writing about them.

My husband and I started having these discussions about what and how we could support women. He said we have done whatever we wanted to do in our professional lives and now we should tell stories of women in the villages. We directed Ladies Junction. Every weekend I would go to a village and shoot the touristy part of the film in the morning and at noon, I would sit under a banyan tree, surrounded by the women from the village. These women would tell me their stories, the diaspora, and restrictions, and then we would share a meal. In the evening, we would create a pit again and we would speak to all the women. I told my husband that I was at ease in these surroundings, from the real world of the village to our exaggerated lives of parties and socializing, which in my mind is a superficial world. A world that is far from reality and made up! It's when you grow up in a village you can relate to villages and that is my foundation.

There were two things I wanted to do: one was to become a doctor, and the other was to start an NGO. I was keen to launch an NGO with a niche for one section of women. My son was going for his higher studies. The actor Ashish Vidyarthi spoke to me about the Landmark Forum, designed to bring a fundamental change to the way you think. He said to me, 'why don't you do a course there?' I did the course on self-expression and leadership. That course changed my life! I realized I could gather people to do things.

During the course, we came up with different ideas. The first was to create an area in Chennai called Pondy Bazaar and make it into a promenade. The second was to introduce Karnatic music in all corporation schools. The third was to create a train ambulance for emergencies from point A to point B. As well as to create an NGO which only worked with women. I am given to understand that the Pondy Bazaar promenade has progressed and during the pandemic; the government introduced train ambulances. I launched my NGO in 2010 and called it NAAM, focusing on single women from marginalized backgrounds, their health, entrepreneurship, and education for their children.

I believe women are the fabric that holds a family together and well-adjusted children are the future of a stable society. These single women have tough battles to fight in nurturing both themselves and their children. I must share a startling fact: only 35% of single women in the marginalized sections live a full life. 65% of the single women are not accounted for, they were either murdered or give up the will to live and hence stopped taking care of themselves.

We skill them and give educational aid to their children. There are many social issues we deal with. For instance, in the absence of their fathers, the children don't respect their mothers. Most of these single women with children blame themselves for their condition and our volunteers have to counsel these women. Strangely, there is resistance from other people towards our efforts to help these women become self-sufficient. But we continue with our mission to empower and educate women and make sure of their financial independence. The women make perfumes, paper bags, carpet weaving, etc. I have also learned how to make perfumes! When I ask these women 'how do you feel when you make the perfumes' they say, 'we smell good' and these are minor pleasures I get from my interactions with these women. When I go to functions to light the lamp, I take along a woman from my NGO and ask her to light a lamp. After one such function I asked one of the women, 'Ela how did you feel on lighting the lamp' and she replied, 'I did not know that I would get 60 kisses from women post lighting the lamp and that was the most significant thing that happened in my life, in my entire life I have not got 60 kisses!'

We watch films, sing, there are games we play, etc. The women work in different houses and then they spend time at the NGO. As trustees, we spend 2 days a week at NAAM and at least 6 days a month. The government needs to do much more for these women. They give freebies during the elections but post the results; they stop assisting these women. So when these women join us, they come into large groups but suddenly 30% leave. We now have 350 women beneficiaries. I aim to look after their health, through yoga, good for both the mind and body. We provide medical help. We asked the women what was most important to them and they said education for their children. Therefore, we pay for the children's education. We fund these activities through events that we organize. For instance, during 'the joy of giving week,' I collected saris from my friends and auctioned those saris, and collected the funds.

In 2015, during the Chennai floods, NAAM was the Centre for collecting clothing for women affected by the floods. A person by the name of Bhoomika was cooking meals for 10000 people affected by the floods. When I heard Bhoomika had taken an overdraft of 65 lacs to fund this, I wanted to help her. I suggested we collect jewellery from jewellers and auction them. We opened our lockers, collected 35 pieces of jewellery, and auctioned them. The mood was sombre, so we did not want models to show the jewellery. I suggested we recreate Ravi Verma's paintings and requested actors and Bharatnatyam dancers to take part. Mr. Amitabh Bachchan was gracious to not only take part, but he donated 65 lacs as well. We collected over 4 crores for building houses for the people affected by the floods.

In 2020, we asked 8 actors to pose as per the artist Ravi Verma's paintings and we printed calendars which were then sold and the proceeds handed over to NAAM. 25% of my earnings go to NAAM. We constructed the building on my son's plot of land. The building is green, made from shipping containers, and sustainable. If we ask the government for land to build institutions for the marginalized, they allocate land which is 40 km from the city. Women can't travel 40 km to attend classes, etc. They need these activities in the city where they work.

As the Honorary Council of Luxembourg for 5 years till 2020, I interacted with various chambers of commerce. We looked at ways to invite people to invest in Luxembourg. I showcased the country in the films that I made.

I could have ended up as a schoolteacher or a homemaker and there is nothing wrong with that, but I decided at a very young age to come out of the circle and move to the city-connect with more people and expand my horizon. My husband and I run our production company, Madras Talkies and I continue to direct movies.

Suhasini dons many hats with ease, and as a multifaceted woman, she knew right from a very young age she needed to blaze her trail! I took a break from writing to focus on my husband's career. The way I look at it, if you know a family member is deeply talented, then you have to make time and effort to help them achieve their goals. I have always been very supportive of his aspirations.

An award-winning actor, Suhasini, made her film début in 1980 with a Tamil movie, Nenjathai Killathe. In 1986, she won her first National Film Award for Best Actress for her role in the Tamil film Sindhu Bhairavi.

During the pandemic and lockdown, my husband and I wrote five short films and shot these on the iPhone! We got an offer from Amazon to make films for them, with two instructions: one to shoot with only seven people on a film set and the second to finish the shoot in three days! We called it Coffee Anyone, shot remotely with instructions over the phone.

When I am acting in a film, I am a woman~ graceful and feminine. When I am directing a film, I am an animal~ hunting, gathering, and wanting the best from the actors and production team. I deeply focus on the work-if I am acting then I don't care about anything else, it's only my acting. I don't need to know what is happening at my home. Whether the food is on the table or the home cleaned! I focus on my acting. The same holds when I am directing. I am centred only on my directing the film. I am part of a WhatsApp group called the '80s Club.' This group has people connected with the film industry from the 80s! It is said that many are in hibernation, lonely, and ignored. When we are in the prime of our careers, we have an enormous fan base and then suddenly we disappear because of age. Fewer movies and human memories are short-lived. In this group, we connect on issues. If someone needs help, we reach out, and it's our bonding club. We started this group in 2009 and today we are 40 of us!

A friend describes me as a 'Tsunami Stopper'. She says, 'Suhasini, you don't know how you will do it, but you will do it!'

CHAPTER SEVENTY-THREE
THE SUSTAINABLE ENTREPRENEUR

Anita Dongre the queen of prêt, from being a clothing supplier to owning her own very successful brand. Born in Mumbai, on 3 October 1963, she considers herself a rebel child in her growing-up years. At five, she fought with her mother, since she wanted to learn to dance. With great persuasion, her mother enrolled her in a dance class, but only for a few years. 'In my growing-up years, my wings were clipped and I always wanted to fly and do my thing.'

I studied in a convent school, with just too many rules! I remember right from the 10th standard, I wanted to become financially independent. There were subtle dynamics at home where the man had the power. Daddy will allow or he will not allow and in my mind, I started questioning, 'why do men have the power? 'And the answer to that was because he was the one earning! I realized then why India is a patriarchal society because men were the ones economically in charge. I found it demeaning that we had to ask my father for money. And that is the time. This deep wish for financial independence became my mission.

It was a given that I would not be allowed to study fashion design. 'Women in the family did not study fashion.' My eldest sister was a schoolteacher and my family was happy, as she was in a noble profession, which was teaching mentally challenged students. I had to challenge this social condition carefully and over time, I won over my parents, who agreed to my pursuing my ambition to study fashion. That was my moment of realization, 'it is not easy whenever you have to make a change, but you have to face it!

After passing out from SNDT Women's Institute for fashion in Mumbai, my younger sister and I started a design label, and we called it MASQUE. The inspiration to name the brand came from our initials and our family name (Meena, Anita, and Sawlani). With small funding which we borrowed from our father, we set up two sewing machines at home and started embroidering Indian wear. These garments we supplied to boutiques on Linking Road, Bandra. The stores were looking for new manufacturers. We also exhibited MASQUE directly to customers, which was good for us, otherwise, the boutiques sold out clothing under their name. The feedback from the customers was noted and worked upon. We built our database with direct interactions with the customers and our business expanded from 2 sewing machines to 40!

My sister Meena managed the store, while I designed the clothes. However, it shut down after a year. Post that, I interned with a company, belonging to Bapa Dhrangadhra, of the erstwhile royal family of Dhrangadhra, Gujarat. He was operating a small high-fashion business. I learned a lot from him and he was a wonderful mentor. We made high-end and bespoke couture pieces, dresses, and evening wear for the US market.

Initially, Dongre was assisting them and later she worked full time and learned the ropes of the business. After a year, Dongre worked with Melco, a buying agency, for a year. 'I learned how the ready-made garments industry works.' Melco was a leading exporter catering to large American brands.

I think every experience of mine taught me and still does. I then went back to my fashion design college, SNDT, to teach fashion. And for the next two years, I taught Fashion. 'I was born an entrepreneur.' When my sister completed her studies, we launched our company AND twenty years ago. I called it AND as I saw so many possibilities in the word 'And.' I thought of it as an abbreviation. Three months into launching the brand, a journalist asked me if the N in AND was something to do with my husband's name!

Anita Dongre has built an organization at the top of India's fashion houses. Headquartered on a green 120,000-square-foot space, nestled in the hills of Navi Mumbai, the House of Anita Dongre (HOAD) has five brands under its banner: AND (western wear,) Global Desi (boho-chic,) signature label ANITA DONGRE (couture,) Anita Dongre Grassroot, (sustainable and luxury pret) and Pink City (handcrafted jewellery.) There is a common thread running through all the brands: the designs are a matter of fact and the use of traditional craft.

With 257 outlets and 750 large-format stores across cities in India and abroad, the brand also has a firm presence across online platforms. Many celebrities and dignitaries have worn Dongre's brand, which has positioned her brand on top of the chain. On her visit to India, in 2016, the Duchess of Cambridge, Kate Middleton, wore a printed Jaipur-inspired tunic dress by Anita Dongre and a pair of earrings by Pinkcity. Photographs of the Duchess in the outfit were all over magazines in India and overseas. It was no surprise that the Canadian Prime Minister's wife, Sophie Grégoire Trudeau, also wore a Chanderi suit from Dongre's brand during the family visit to India in 2018. The queen of fashion Kim Kardashian was on the Vogue India cover wearing a handcrafted lehenga by Anita Dongre. As well as the former US Secretary of State Hillary Clinton, on her visit to India, wore a bandhini shrug from Grassroots. And the list is long. All of them showcased the Indian handicrafts through the ensembles they wore, making Dongre a very proud Indian.

'I wanted to launch with pret [or ready-to-wear] but instead started my career with bridal wear. I was the one who introduced pockets in the lehengas, the dress that the bride wears on her wedding day is extremely uncomfortable. 'So nine years ago I brought in this new era for bridal wear and everyone followed.' As an empathetic designer, Dongre understands clothes are a source of happiness and joy. 'One should feel happy to wear a particular outfit.' Fashion needs to revolve around what women want, 'therein lies the secret to my success, and 'my clothing is wearable.'

In addition to AND, Global Desi 'happened,' because we were in India, and I felt we must design Indian wear. Launched in 2007, the brand is now available at 146 exclusive brand outlets and 402 multi-brand stores across the country. Global Desi is a vibrant and free-spirited brand of boho-chic ensembles and affordable contemporary cool Indian wear. A fun brand of Kurtis, prints, and just casual clothing, it became a cult brand. Many brands copied Global Desi. 'In fact, I must share this incident. A designer bought 80 samples of my brand, she copied them and put them in her store. It has become tough to stay ahead of copycats. Though Global Desi is a hugely successful brand.'

Right in the beginning, in all our social media reach and advertisements, we showed the Indian bride dancing at her wedding. We projected a woman driving a jeep and in another advertisement, I showed a woman drinking a glass of wine while browsing an iPad. The statements were bold, and I wanted to project a woman, who is intelligent, strong, and well-travelled and that is very important to me when I design.

Dongre begins her day meeting with designers on their sketches, checking samples of their designs, and interacting with her social media team. 'I think on my feet and avoid wasting time. We have built speed and efficiency in the company. We have an all-India manager WhatsApp group which connects me with my team. I am an accessible boss. I speak to everyone, from the designer to the tailor to the peon.' Visiting most of the stores and meeting with the frontline staff, 'they give me first-hand feedback and inputs which matter and which I inculcate in a new collection.' I love doing surprise visits, just for maybe five minutes! I think it's important to stay in touch with the customer, listen to them as their opinion makes a big difference in the way I design.' Dongre has met every vendor, block printer, and artisan who works with her, and when she is in the office, she interacts with 300 to 400 persons a day, including her team!

Dongre launched her brand Grassroots in 2015. She started work with SEWA (Self-Employed Women's Association) for this brand. SEWA had an extensive network of women who knew how to stitch but did not have the design sense. Since Dongre had passed out with crafts as her major subject in fashion design, she wanted to launch a separate label focusing on crafts, and 'that's how Grassroots was born, a cruelty-free, sustainable brand, which uses crafts and natural fabrics.'

Our clothes are hand-crafted with a story and the person behind each craft helps you build a more thoughtful wardrobe. Through Grassroots, we want to make sure the crafts continued existence, along with supporting the artisans, their skills, and nurturing of craftsmanship. We intend to keep traditions, by employing conscious processes and becoming a part of the solution. I was looking at expanding AND, and launched it along with Grassroots in New York in 2017, it's an interesting story! When I went to New York, I wanted to launch my brand, Anita Dongre. I started with a pop-up of Grassroots and it was crazy. Everyday people would pop in and they loved the concept. But wanted bridal wear as well. Running two different stores would have been costly, so I took a last-minute decision and launched Anita Dongre along with Grassroots as part of Anita Dongre.

I met Poonam Mahajan from the BJP. A couple of years ago, she had adopted a village in Charoti and asked me if I could have embroidery work done in her village. 'You can't teach embroidery overnight,' so we set up a tailoring unit. First, we needed to enable women and for this, we partnered with 35 local women, today I am happy to say we manage five such villages.

Dongre believes that women will become game-changers in their communities and it is imperative for India to make sure that rural women become financially independent. 'Dynamics change when women realize that money is empowerment.' I think more companies should set up spaces in villages and give women work, it keeps families together. The solution is not in setting up factories in cities but in villages, entrust the women where they live and where they can work. As an organization, we are committed to working with the women artisans.'

The Queen of Pret and a sustainable trailblazer!

CHAPTER SEVENTY-FOUR
THE PRODUCTION DESIGNER

Elahe Hiptoola was born in Bombay in August 1969. 'My father was a maverick and an enormous influence.' A chartered accountant he made a career move midway while designing clothes for film stars. He did whatever interested him. 'My father wanted to retire early in life and one fine day in the 80s he just gave up working! After that, his everyday routine was to drop my brother and me at school and then come back to pick us up. He was one of those very 'cool' parents. I am not sure if he knew how much we appreciated the things he did for us.' He passed away very young at fifty-eight. My mother was a Montessori teacher at Casa Montessori in Bombay. She ensured she was home when my brother and I came home from school. Commitment to family and work, I learned from her. The nicest person ever and I never wanted to disappoint her.

I recollect many funny instances at home. One time in a heated argument my father said, 'Don't Yale, I am not Harvard of hearing!' A thorough gentleman, well-spoken, and the good part was that he believed in living a good life. The one important thing I learned from him was, 'never to be embarrassed, if I was to change my mind mid-way, I could.'

At our home, we could air our thoughts freely! We could say anything that we wished. There was never any fear that it may not sound right. My parents would say to my brother and me that there was no one like the two of us. We were created from a cast, post which they broke the cast and we believed we were! That helped build our self-confidence in life as well. Disciplined but never pushed to do things! Go to school every day, but not to score or to come first in class.

I studied at NASR School in Hyderabad and remember; we called our teacher Aunty. Restricted to twenty children per class, therefore very focused and intimate. I truly came from a secular place and was proud of my religion. The school's principal, Mrs. Anees Khan, had converted a large house into a school. When we went back to school from our holidays, there would be something new we went back to. Everything was free, our books, pencils, erasers, etc. thus uniformity without making it a big thing. Presumably criticized for putting us in that school, my mother knew what she wanted for us.

During the time I was growing up, we had conversations about Sun signs! And Linda Goodman played an important part in our lives. As per her, Leos were outstanding leaders and I may have unconsciously worked around it! Interacting with strangers and people was never an issue and came naturally to me since school. A friend remembers attending a school play and just before the second act, there was an unscheduled break. I happily went on stage and entertained the audience! I believe if you put out an image of yourself; you see yourself like that image.

I was popular at school and was the House Captain. I am only 5 feet tall and recollect one year when I was in class 10. During the school annual parade, I was marching as the House Captain. Right in front of the class, signaling to class 3 students to march a little away from me, as I did not want to look short in front of them! Maybe I was 'designing' myself as a leader. Preordained or futuristic planning, projecting myself in a way that I wanted to see myself.

I think everyone needs that one person in their lives who shows you the mirror! That one person in my life is my best friend Varsha, a strong woman and an enormous influence. If you see us together, you would wonder why we are the best of friends-we are different. Quite the opposite she is very calm, controlled, and deals with issues logically and by the book! I look for her reactions to gauge how differently we think. She is my emotional and moral compass. We make it a point to spend every New Year together.

In 1991, after schooling in Hyderabad, I landed in Mumbai to study Law. I was attached to Hyderabad. It was home. I belonged there. It was an enormous influence and an identifiable character in my life. While in Mumbai, I met a wonderful person, Anuradha Bose, who took me under her wings. She genuinely shaped me into the person I am today, confident with a mission. The Mumbai school gang was these very cool friends I hung out with. College would get over at 9:30 am, post which I was free for the entire day. I needed to earn my pocket money, so filled in for a friend at Ravissant, the fashion store. I continued to work there for a while, till my exams started, and then I resigned. Later I joined the designers Abu Jani & Sandeep Khosla. This is where I learned responsibility and was hobnobbing with the society women for whom we designed outfits.

In 1993, I graduated with a law degree and returned home to Hyderabad, where I belonged. I did not have an understandable ambition or what I wanted to do. I think God had other plans for me and Law was not one of them! Experienced with my stint at Abu Jani and Sandeep Khosla, 'I thought to myself, why don't I open my store and I launched the city's first designer boutique and called it Elahe.' The store experience was wonderful. I was honest in dealing with my clients' choice of designer wear, in terms of what looked good on them and what did not. It was not about the money, but the ethics that always mattered to me.

The following year, in 1994, I got married to my childhood friend Vidyut, who was a cricketer and played cricket for Hyderabad. We separated two years later, in 1996. I always joke, that my wedding lasted longer than my marriage did! We were two good people, just not for each other! I have a cordial relationship with Vidyut's family, just that both of us are not in touch anymore. I remember a time when asked to act in a play and Vidyut turned around and said, 'No wife of mine will be on stage!' Marriage was important to me, as my parents' marriage was perfect, and wanted mine to work, so I declined the offer.

Nagesh Kukoonoor, the film director, who I work with presently, had just returned from the USA and was directing his first movie and asked if I could suggest someone for a part in his film and I did. He went back to the USA and when he returned in 1998, my marriage was over. He asked me to audition for a movie that he was directing, called Hyderabad Blues, and of course, I said yes, the rest is history. 'I don't say no to opportunities!'

Hyderabad Blues is written, directed, and produced by Nagesh. A film from an Indian American's perspective, vacationing back home in Hyderabad. In the film, he finds himself as a foreigner in his city. The film heralded a new age in Bollywood cinema. For this film, Nagesh invested the money he earned from his engineering career in the US. Made on a shoestring budget of $ 40,000 and shot entirely in Hyderabad in 17 days! While we were rehearsing for the film, Nagesh said 'be my assistant director.' There was no pressure. Since he wanted me to help him with the production, my calling fell into my lap. I learned on the job and was happy to execute the production bit. While on the film set, no one took me seriously. As I mentioned, I am 5 feet tall and, of course, the bias of being a woman! Nagesh started telling people 'go ask ma'am', creating a situation where people had no choice but to report and take orders from me!

Producers in India don't get the attention that directors do. I would tell Nagesh, 'you are not giving me my due in the articles that the media would write and he would say, 'I do, but nobody writes about that.' Well, that got sorted as time went by. 'In life, you have to speak your mind, be assertive sometimes even bordering on aggression and, of course, drive with conviction.' We have two Verticals in our company. One is the direction that Nagesh heads and the other is production, headed by me. There is nothing I would not do on a film set. My motto is 'if you can't do it then I will do it.' I arrive on the sets with Nagesh and leave the set when he does. We run a tight ship and walk the talk. If it is my film, as a producer, I am responsible. I must do everything relevant and do whatever it takes for the film to be complete!

No matter what, I leave with something real from every meeting, never empty-handed. In our film industry, perceptions and optics play a significant role! People give money to people with money. I live in Hyderabad and in the early days of my career, when I would call people in Mumbai, say at 7 pm. They would invariably say, see you tomorrow at 11 am. I would take a bus that night and reach in the morning with an airline tag on my bag, so they thought I took the morning flight! What does one do? Everything is about 'impression' and I am conscious of that fact, even today! My grandmother always said that even if you were giving alms to a person, you should 'offer' it, makes you a better person! Well!

My work is not 9 to 5 but more like a 24 x 7. For better time management, I keep my phone in the next room,   just so that I can focus on things that are important and I am not constantly replying to messages which can wait! Before the pandemic I joined an Urdu poetry club that was offline, however, now it is online. It is quite interesting to listen to poems and exchange notes on zoom! My other interest is practicing and teaching yoga. Some of the yoga asanas teach you how to land back with grace! If you apply the techniques of yoga to life, it just makes you stronger and more focused. Every one of us gets into situations. During which times I apply the rules of yoga, it's my way of accepting things.

For years, we had discussed converting a bungalow into a unique centre of creativity, where we could celebrate freedom of expression in all forms. We wanted to have everything under one roof. The idea came from the feeling that in the last decade or so; we have taken away open spaces from people and communities. These spaces like the Alliance Française centres are imperative for people and there weren't many spaces where one could get together and meet similar thinking people we thought of launching 'The C Club' where everything with C would be available in this space, chai, coffee, carom, cartoon, chess, cinema, comics and so on! And in 2010, along with three of my friends, we launched a social club called 'Lamakaan' in Hyderabad. Lamakaan means 'house without boundaries.' Emulating our living rooms and drawing rooms, Lamakaan is a democratic and progressive cultural venue in the city. A space created for people to read at one end and play the guitar, a hub for culture-a place truly without boundaries.

This cultural space is always open to everyone and is free. We have a team of people who run the kitchen, and a team that curates events and operations. Over the years, I am so proud of how it has grown. In the bygone days, when people visited, they stayed at our home and not at a hotel. Life was always about community and that's what we have tried to create, 'the face of Lamakaan is people!'

We have always made films for entertainment. I make films I would like to watch, ensuring all my films have a happy ending. It's a make-believe world, therefore we need to create a world that is better and at least strives for. If you can take something from the films that I make, that's good and if you can learn from it, even better, however, I have nothing new to teach you.' When we shoot, it is my world. I can't think of spending an entire day at a shoot and then going to a party the same evening. I'm focused on the shoot, so no distractions. Every actor's performance should be perfect as both Nagesh and I are passionate about our work and what we do on a film set. When we shoot films outside of Hyderabad, we make sure we shoot from start to finish. We shoot in remote locations, many places, and towns, with no television connectivity. I remember the time we were shooting in Rajasthan. We stayed there for one full month. I was happily disconnected from reality for that entire time. It is a mission. When we shot a film called Iqbal, in a small town in Andhra Pradesh, the highest class of hotel was a small hotel called Gautham! I wanted an intimate place for the entire team. I got my team to place family photos of the actors in their rooms. These may be slight gestures but of value to an actor who would spend a month away from the family. Nobody cares where we shoot. The actors are the face of our hard work. When actors put their craft in front of 150 people, they need to be treated with kids' gloves! I look after them as I would look after my guests at home. I can't control the place or where we are shooting, but what I can control is my production.

I believe film production is all about being involved and creating the right environment for the teams. Since I work with a small team, I want people who are effective for those 35 days when we shoot. Every job is important and one missing link can de-link a chain! Nagesh as a director is a taskmaster, he goes by strict rules and straight lines since he is an engineer! So I make sure we have fun at locations we shoot, celebrating birthdays and eating meals together is a given. 'I think the reason our films are successful!'

Film Production is the last resort in India, as people still think that a producer's role is of a financier or is to bring in the money to produce a film. Typically, a man's job. But over the years, a producer's role has changed. It is like being a designer. You learn the design, and the cut, and then become a designer. Nobody teaches you production. I don't think there is a course for it and to think of it, it's a thankless job. In the west producers raise the money, in India, you need a movie star to raise capital. To be a film producer, you need passion and how best you make everything come together within a budget. 'Balancing the budget and your returns!'

I became a producer by chance, but it was my people skills that has taken me forward. It's a very responsible thing to make a film and make sure you are proud of the result. Being a film producer is not the only identity I have. Everything is important to me. I am not only known as a producer, I run Lamakaan, and had launched Elahe which was the first designer store in Hyderabad. That was an important time in my life. These are different hats that I wear. I have worked on 'designing' my life. People look at me in a larger role than just movies.

I go by this line, 'If I don't recognize failure, then there is no failure!' A line from our movie, Rockford.

CHAPTER SEVENTY-FIVE
THE CANDLE

Dr Hena Singh was born at Begusarai, Bihar, on 5 July 1972. The youngest of six siblings. Her father Ganesh Lal Das was an officer of the coveted Bihar Administrative Service (BAS) and mother Punya Prabha Das was a conscious, upright, and doting homemaker.

My father's job was transferable which meant that every three years our family had to be on the move, accommodating ourselves in subdivisions and district headquarters in Bihar, as per his posting. By the time I entered high school, three of my eldest siblings had already moved to Delhi for their higher education. During one of those frequent posting of my father from Patna to Purnia, the family decision was that while my dad and mom would move to Purnia, the three younger siblings would continue to live in Patna in rented accommodation with our grandmother. The decision was taken to ensure continuity in our school education. It was a tough decision for me, as being very close to my mother; I always wanted to be with her. But then, my dad was a diabetic who needed more care than us, and who could have been better to be with him, than my mother. On her part, my grandmother took good care of us but she would also often travel to my uncles living in Hazaribagh and Ranchi respectively. Though most often she lived with us at Patna. Our bonds with her were meaningfully significant and we gained tremendously on counts of her mythological knowledge and conventional wisdom. On her part, my mother would visit us quite frequently just to ensure that we were under proper care and guidance.

My mother was an intelligent woman. Daughter of a popular doctor at Supaula sleepy little town in North Bihar, she was married at the tender age of sixteen. She may have ideally wanted to continue her education even post-marriage, but being the eldest of the daughters-in-law to our grandparents she had her domestic constraints and she understood them well. Possibly those constraints hindered accomplishing her aspirations, but she never complained about them. Rather she completely immersed herself in mothering and caring not just for her six children but also in looking after the familial needs of my paternal grandfather's family.

I think that might have been a plausible factor behind her major advice to us that it was crucial to have an alternative backup plan a Plan B in life. Although she would often say this in the context of our aspirations to be civil servants, I now realize that her utterances could well have been inveigled by her latent desires to pursue her education post marriage. Her advice however was intensely ingraining for me at least, and at a later stage in my life, it certainly worked for me. I knew well, that if I were not to get through to civil services, then academics would be my alternative career and so I needed to do exceptionally well in my subject, Political Science at the university level.

My parents were doting, optimistic, and quite inspiring. They never scolded us for our failures. Rather they continuously encouraged us to work harder to achieve our goals and targets. My father would often motivate us to be prepared and willing to face challenges in life, while my mother always wanted us to be economically independent. It is said that parents often expect their children to achieve those very milestones which they may have aspired for in their adolescence. My parents surely wanted all of us (brothers and sisters to get into the civil services). They never differentiated amongst their kids. Honestly, while gender discrimination has continued to be an important marker of our social existence, I must admit that I was not even aware of it at least during my growing-up years. Spending most of my time at home with my two immediate elder brothers I never realized that there could ever be inequality based on anatomy. Our grooming was different. I was indeed fortunate to grow up in a family that accorded its women utmost respect and dignity and treated them with equality.

Managing the household chores kept my mother engaged and yet, she was particular that we finish our homework timely and that our study schedules at home (early morning and evening) were time-bound and regular. She had a schedule for everything. In those years, power outages were quite common in Bihar. The outages were not only very frequent but many times would last for hours. In such situations, she would ensure that all the siblings had enough candles to enable us to complete our study schedules. I now realize that her acts must have been determined by her passion for not just ensuring that exigencies of power outages do not hinder our study schedules but also the understanding that her younger kids imbibe a sense of responsibility. Unflinching faith in the dictum that if the elderly study and learn, the younger would naturally follow by learning from them was indeed the raison d'etre of her thought processes.

After completing my secondary schooling at the Mount Carmel School at Patna, I joined Patna Women's College for my senior secondary education. Located in the heart of Patna, the women's college in our days, used to be (I think it still is) a dream destination for a young girl in Bihar. I was privileged enough to not only secure a seat in the college but get hostel accommodation as well. Must say that staying in a hostel run by missionaries is a different experience altogether. Convent culture is well known for its strictest rules and sense of discipline and the hostel at the college was no exception either. We were a group of five friends, nicknamed the Pandavas (imitating the five brothers from the Mahabharata tales). We were known for making excuses, often flimsy ones though, to go out of the hostel, to nearby markets, and even for running to nearby cinema halls. I was interested in reading and practicing astrology. Many of my friends would often approach me to know what was in store for them. Acting as a true professional, I would read the lines on their palms and as luck would have it, a few of my predictions did turn out to be true, making me instantly the go-to person for palm reading. The newfound fame was both enjoyable indeed.

It is a coincidence that we are discussing my early years on a day when the results of the Civil services examinations have been declared. I can certainly feel and relate to the enthusiasm and jubilation of Bihari families whose sons and daughters have succeeded in the examination, for we had our share of it as well when my elder sister cracked the civil services examination and became an officer of the Indian Police Service. Appearing in the civil service examination and cracking it is still a major aspiration of the youth of our country and we were no different. My father was very keen that all of us (brothers and sisters) become IAS officers. They had groomed us for it as well. We had already heard several stories of how women civil servants were shaping the country, and they sounded inspirational indeed.

My eldest sister had cleared her civil services in 1989. During the 1990s, University Academic sessions were not regular in Bihar. A university degree there would take more than the stipulated three years. Consequently, many students from Bihar would go to the University of Delhi where the academic sessions were regular. Additionally, DU also provided a culture that allowed students to prepare well for the Civils examination. Either way, my two elder sisters by this time had already been there and I followed them. The nervousness of moving to a completely new city was palpable yet I was convinced that Delhi would open up an ocean of opportunities and provide me the freedom to explore my potential. And girl! It eventually did.

Things started falling in line. Even though I had thought of pursuing Honours in sociology, I eventually settled for Political Science, at Miranda House. I was lucky again to get hostel accommodation. The association with Miranda House has continued since then. It has given me everything I could have dreamt of. A decade later, I was not only to be appointed as an assistant professor in the same department but it was near the gates of the hostel that I was to meet someone who has continued to be the strength of my life.

My husband-to-be would visit Miranda Hostel to meet some of my hostel mates from his hometown, Munger. The gates of the hostel stand to witness our first-ever meeting. There was instant chemistry and bonding. That relationship has continued to blossom albeit under conjugal bonds since 2002. We both wanted a job before getting married. Chandrachur got a professorship at Hindu College in 2000, though a few months later, he lost his mother who by that time had known me and I guess had not only started liking me she may have had an inkling of our relationship as well. Chandrachur and I were to get married the following year on 7 July 2002. My husband was in a job but having been disheartened by the UPSC I was still struggling to get one for myself. Plan A had failed, so Plan B had to be worked upon. I had earned an MPhil degree in Political science, and by this time and having cleared the necessary UGC NET examinations for an assistant professor's job I was qualified to join academia. A year post-marriage, I was expecting my first child. We had a daughter in 2003. The arrival of my daughter also coincided broadly with the professional opportunity I was looking for. Just a year later I was recruited as an Assistant Professor at Miranda House.

My husband is my best friend of 28 years. A wonderful partner and an infallible friend. The first day I began my teaching career at Miranda House, I had to address around 120 students. I was very apprehensive. Would I be able to get through to them? My father-in-law was in the hospital at that time undergoing heart bypass surgery, and here I was, standing in front of students in the very room where I once sat as a student with my friends. My husband had however sketched out in detail how I would engage with the students. Leaving a 10-month-old at home, I had to go for a lecture. Voila, my lecture went well, and the reviews received were phenomenally encouraging. In my approximately 20 years as a lecturer at Miranda House College since then, I have tried my best to touch the hearts and minds of the students that I have taught and currently teach. I am passionate about imparting knowledge, about both the theoretical concepts of freedom and liberty and the practicality of realizing them.

In 2012, I was awarded a fellowship from the School of Global Ethics at the prestigious University of Birmingham (UoB), for pursuing an MSc in Global Ethics. I preferred to forgo it as my husband had by that time received a Universitas 21 doctoral fellowship and the position of India outreach coordinator at UoB. Given that the fellowship contained a clause of serving three years compulsorily at Miranda House, after availing one year's leave, it meant that while I could have joined him for a year, I would have to come back after that. Moreover, I would have only gotten a year's master's degree at the university. So, taking a calculated risk, I let that opportunity go. Fortunately, after one year, I joined him as the University of Birmingham offered me the opportunity to pursue a Ph.D. there because of the constant efforts of my husband.

Life in Birmingham was wonderful but equally tiresome as we had to manage studies with household chores and two school-going children. Life for my daughters was particularly difficult as they had to adjust to a completely different system. Suddenly life became tough for them. They have had to relocate twice in the brief span of five years. Settling in first in Birmingham and then in Delhi within a short period was not an easy thing for kids who were yet to move into their teens, but to my utter delight, both had done it so well. I was aware of the hardships they had to face, given that both my husband and I were doctoral students in the UK and did not have the resources required to support a family. Yet, I can proudly say that they never complained or felt deprived within themselves. My daughters are the blessings and miracles of our life.

During our stay of five years in the UK, I lost my mother and father-in-law—the two engines of my life. Finally, after successfully defending my doctoral research, we came back to India in 2018. After returning from Birmingham, I was determined to do more with what I had learned in the five years of my stay there. I observed that they teach the research methodologies lessons at the undergraduate level, unlike many Indian universities where this is done at post-graduation levels. After consulting with my senior colleagues and friends, I set up a policy centre and gender lab (PCGL) at Miranda House. PCGL is a research platform to engage young minds in gender-related issues and dig deep by conducting research on gender issues as well as policy decisions. I also started organizing awareness workshops and sessions for the benefit of the larger communities. For my contributions to education, I was felicitated with the Dr. S. Radhakrishnan Memorial Award in 2021 for extraordinary service in teaching and learning.

I firmly believe that 'it is never too late to overcome your fears. Coming from a small town, I did not have exposure to speaking in front of large gatherings. As a lecturer, I did get the opportunity of overcoming this fear. I started speaking at conferences and delivering lectures to students across the colleges under the aegis of the University of Delhi. Overcoming my stage fright encouraged me to speak more confidently and connect with the students. I believed in what my parents would say, never give up. My life lessons revolve around this. My mother believed that a teacher is like a candle, who helps light others with knowledge and willpower, and I am passionately trying my best to be an exemplar of that, though the results would come only after I have traveled to the other world.

Sometime back, I came across a distressed woman running a toy shop in Sadar Bazar, Delhi. Unfortunately, during the first wave of the pandemic, the family lost everything. With the support of the Principal at Miranda House and some colleagues, we took the lead to help herset up a small eatery inside our college premises. The smile on her face the day she started the eatery was amazing.

I have also set up two skill hubs under the Pradhan Mantri Kaushal Vikas Yojana (PMKVY) in collaboration with the National Skill Development Corporation (NSDC) at Miranda House for school dropouts belonging to the age group of 15 - 40. These centres, impart training on green jobs and artificial intelligence. The basic purpose is to equip the students with skills that they can utilize for their career advancement and successful entrepreneurship.

As the Joint Dean of Students Welfare at the University of Delhi, I ensure that all queries and problems of the stakeholders are taken up immediately and resolved. I hope I have touched the lives of students. I feel happy and elated whenever I receive messages of gratitude from them. I think that only by bringing smiles to the faces of students who approach me for their issues and grievances I can justify the purpose of my position at the students' welfare office. As a young girl, I wanted to be part of the civil services to help those in need. Today, I truly believe that one doesn't necessarily need to be a bureaucrat to serve communities. Avenues get created; alternative pathways get charted, as long as, the zeal and will as well as passion to enlighten the 'other' is alive in oneself. The need is to lighten the candles by one's flame whatever and howsoever it might be. The moral distance between the self and the other must be bridged.

As I conclude my book, I have to admit, I learnt a lot from the remarkable women in history. Their courage, dare, and spirit to carry on in spite of adversities at every step. Their dedication to building and equipping the lives of others was most critical during the freedom struggle. And most importantly how they established and reinforced the identity of Indian women in reimagining their position in India.

To be free is to be you!

Jai Hind

www.ingramcontent.com/pod-product-compliance
Lightning Source LLC
Chambersburg PA
CBHW031246160726
47993CB00001B/44